ARRIBADA

Samantha Kochharr is the Managing Director of a leading cosmetic company in India. She is also the Chief Expert for hairdressing for IndiaSkills, and the Deputy Chief Expert-Hairdressing for World Skills International. She has been mentoring young talent for many years now. She started her journey in the hair and beauty industry at the age of 11 and has worked in the movie and fashion industry internationally and nationally for many years. She is also an avid painter and potter. Born into a business family, she is the daughter of the legendary aromatherapist—Dr Blossom Kochhar.

She has been a practising shaman since 2013 and has extensively studied energy healing. Over the years, she has worked with people from all walks of life as a grief whisperer. *Arribada: The Arrival* is her first book and it is an extension of her spiritual journey.

Samantha lives in Delhi and loves to cook and bake for her family and friends. Following her passion, she runs a popular delicatessen in Delhi, The Tea Room, where the menu is based on her old family recipes.

A story that helps us realize that when we surrender to the universal energy, and trust in miracles, we will be healed because we all deserve to be happy. A story that transports us to several places, but more importantly helps us to travel within ourselves, and emerge dancing, towards light.
        —**Dr Hansaji Yogendra**, Yoga Guru and the Director of The Yoga Institute

Samantha Kochharr, already known for her distinguished business career, has now turned her talents to fiction. *Arribada*, a work of what she calls spiritual fiction, tackles questions of meaning, belonging, and inner peace, while telling a moving and entertaining story. An intriguing and unusual read.
        —**Dr Shashi Tharoor,** Member of the Parliament, Lok Sabha

As a mother, and a book lover, I am so happy that *Arribada* is in your hands. The book was conceived during my walks in the park with Samantha. It began with the doctor advising me to walk regularly and me loathing the idea. Samantha coaxed me to go for walks and to make it interesting, she began telling me a story about a man named Joy and his friend, Ollie. Every day, I would be so engrossed in the different episodes of the story that I would complete 3-4 rounds of the park, which I could never do otherwise. I even did some extra rounds because I wanted to hear more of the story. My daughter has a wonderful way of expressing herself, and I'm immensely delighted that Joy and Ollie's story will live forever through this book.

  Samantha is deeply spiritual and her spiritual growth in the past few years has been much more pronounced and has changed her completely. One of the best practitioners of healing, Samantha's grief healing methods are exceptional. Even though her healing work for people often draws out every ounce of her energy, she doesn't stop.

This book is about life, all its emotions and how to live it joyfully.

—**Dr Blossom Kochhar**, Chairperson of
Blossom Kochhar Group of Companies

A powerful storytelling in the form of a fable that is simultaneously thought-provoking and entertaining, reflective of Samantha's search for truth and life purpose.

Here is a fascinating new Indian voice that is remarkably reminiscent of Richard Bach's *Jonathan Livingston Seagull.*

—**Vinita Dawra Nangia,** Executive Editor, *Times of India*

Love unlocks the abundance within us. When we love another, we learn to love ourselves too. Samantha's touching and poignant story reminds us of the amazing power of love and compassion, a power that can surmount any obstacle.

—**Dr Alka Pande**, art historian and author

This book is Samantha's gift of love, awakening and healing. Wrap it around yourself like your favourite shawl, soak in its warmth and feel whole once again. I urge you to read this. Today.

—**Rajshri Deshpande**, actor, social worker and filmmaker

A heartwarming tale, told in simple language, of a sad and bitter man who reconnects with his childhood friend. Together they embark on an inner and outer journey across the ocean of life. A charming example of Joseph Campbell's *The Hero's Journey*, leading to wisdom and a fulfilling destiny as Joy traverses a dreamscape of England, Goa and Africa.

—**Sharon Lowen**, classical Indian dancer, author, founder of
Manasa-Art Without Frontiers

ARRIBADA
—THE ARRIVAL—

Samantha Kochharr

Published by
Rupa Publications India Pvt. Ltd 2023
7/16, Ansari Road, Daryaganj
New Delhi 110002

Sales centres:
Allahabad Bengaluru Chennai
Hyderabad Jaipur Kathmandu
Kolkata Mumbai

Copyright © Samantha Kochharr 2023

All rights reserved.
No part of this publication may be reproduced, transmitted,
or stored in a retrieval system, in any form or by any means,
electronic, mechanical, photocopying, recording or otherwise,
without the prior permission of the publisher.

This is a work of fiction. Names, characters, places and incidents are
either the product of the author's imagination or are used fictitiously
and any resemblance to any actual person, living or dead, events or
locales is entirely coincidental.

While every effort has been made to trace copyright holders and
obtain permission, this has not been possible in all cases; any
omissions brought to our attention will be remedied in future editions.

P-ISBN: 978-93-5520-763-0
E-ISBN: 978-93-5520-764-7

First impression 2023

10 9 8 7 6 5 4 3 2 1

The moral right of the author has been asserted.

Printed in India

This book is sold subject to the condition that it shall not,
by way of trade or otherwise, be lent, resold, hired out, or otherwise
circulated, without the publisher's prior consent, in any form of
binding or cover other than that in which it is published.

Sometimes it takes a mountain
Sometimes a troubled sea
Sometimes it takes a desert
To get a hold of me...

—'Sometimes It Takes a Mountain',
the Gaither Vocal Band

CONTENTS

Prologue   *xi*

1. This Thing Called Life   1
2. Dream A Dream   15
3. Being Present   33
4. Perfect Imperfections   55
5. A Friend Indeed!   67
6. A Vision   94
7. Alignment   116
8. The Wise One   128
9. Flipper to Flipper   147
10. Time to Let Go   155
11. Second Time Lucky   167
12. Spirit Animal   189
13. The Promise   208
14. Passing On   229
15. Unity   250
16. Initiation   273
17. Home   293

18. The Arrival	307
19. Master Plan	322
20. Four Years Later	343
21. The Reveal	348
Glossary	351
Acknowledgements	353

PROLOGUE

He was a storyteller like no other, and this was a story like no other.

It all started four years ago, with his evening storytelling at the annual village fair. To his surprise, it became a highlight and both locals and tourists from far and wide flocked to listen to him every year, and the numbers kept growing. This year, he had been assigned a larger space.

It was time. He had to get to the stage now. As he stood on the podium, the buzz of the audience subsided. He put on his collar mike, tied back his salt and pepper hair, rolled up his sleeves, took a few sips of water and smiled at his audience. There were children, young people and adults there.

The stage was set for our storyteller.

'I am sorry to have kept you waiting. The story I am going to tell over the next few evenings is a special one. I hope you will be here for a couple of evenings, because stories take time to unfold,' he said.

He paused to take a look at the audience—some of them were smiling, while some shook their heads in agreement. Soon, they all settled down. It was as if they knew that they were all in for a treat for the next couple of hours. The room fell silent and he knew it was time to begin. He smiled and sent up a small prayer of gratitude. This was a special story and he hoped to do it justice.

'Before I start, I'll lay down some rules. As I narrate

this story, I will keep moving in and out of the story. I will interrupt the story to share my thoughts and comments. Occasionally, I will reflect on the story as well. I talk, you listen. I may even address you directly. If you want to leave early, please do so quietly. May I start now?' he asked.

'Yes, please!' they replied in unison.

1

THIS THING CALLED LIFE

Joy walked down the sandy, partly rocky path. Even though it was dark and late in the evening, he knew each rock and turn that led to the beach. Even as a young boy, he had used this short cut to escape his life—to hide, think and make peace with the way things were turning out!

Joy did not look like the average Goan man. He was tall and lanky; his skin was fair but it had tanned to a warm amber under the sun. His hazel-coloured eyes, which often spoke volumes, were set in a face with an exceptional bone structure, framed by a curly mop of hair. His mother was of Portugese descent—fair, pretty and petite—while his father was also a good-looking man in a dark, rugged Goan way. But today, Joy looked as if he had lost a war. The lines creased on his forehead; the wind had ruffled his hair into an unruly mess. His eyes seemed confused, and his shoulders had a droop to them.

He had a special spot to himself behind a patch of Suri trees where it was breezy and cool. There was a large, lava rock on which he could sit, quite comfortably, and watch the sea, the sky and the birds. A fish would occasionally flip out of the sea and dive right back in, and the sea creatures would crawl out of the sea when there were no humans around.

As the colour and mood of the sky and sea changed, so did his own. After a few hours of contemplation, he would walk back to the life he had left behind. Nothing about his life ever changed unlike the sea, the sky and the animals—these were somehow always new. He learnt by just watching them. Nature was so dynamic, but his life had been stagnant for a while now.

Tonight was no different. Only that he was now thirty-four years old. In his youth he would escape from fights with his father, or violence at home, or his failures and heartbreak by running away to his safe spot. A couple of hours later, when he had made peace with himself, he would walk back home to his little room and turn on his transistor. As he grew older, he felt that the only way to escape this life he was stuck in, was to get far away from his father, his home and Goa. So, he studied hard and made sure he topped his class, which made it easier for him to get better opportunities abroad for higher education.

Whenever he talked about studying abroad, he would often end up arguing with his father. His old man point-blank refused to support him if he left India. However, that did not deter Joy. After borrowing some money from his mother, he managed to get admission into a good college in England. While attending college, Joy worked two jobs—one in the day and another at night—to support himself. He got by, barely managing on four hours of sleep that took a toll on his health. But he persevered. Finally, he graduated with honours and landed his first job in England.

His dream was slowly becoming a reality.

The job required his complete commitment. He worked till late in the night and would rush to the office in the early morning hours. He remembered working all the time, being called a workaholic by most, a perfectionist by some and a genius by others. His colleagues wondered what drove him, but he alone knew that he had created a mental checklist, a sequence of life plans—leave Goa, foreign education, job, car, house, wife, children and lots of money—all of which would guarantee a happy life. He went about systematically, ticking off the boxes. All he needed now was a companion in life.

> 'I bet all of us in this room have also made a mental checklist. We call it goals or dreams. We fail to realize that at some point we have to stop and take stock of what our mind desires. We need to ask ourselves if these wants, needs and dreams are genuinely ours or just a by-product of our conditioning. Does our wish list nourish our soul and make us better human beings? Does it help make the world a better place? We, humans, are masters at manifesting all we want, just like Joy and his checklist, but will it help us awaken to our true light and potential? Are we born to fulfil a wish list or is there more to this thing called life?'

So on one of Joy's trips back to India to meet his mother, he bumped into Maria—his childhood crush. She was as beautiful as he remembered. They ended up dating. Interestingly, they had a lot in common and shared the same beliefs. She reminded him of his mother and she had no qualms about living in a foreign country, which suited him perfectly. She was the best candidate for the role of a wife in his life. They were married without much fanfare. He picked up a better job and they both settled into a beautiful, new house in the bustling city of London.

The few moments Joy got to introspect, he realized that his life was on a fast lane. It was difficult to slow down, even if he wanted to. At such moments, he wondered if he really liked the life he had so carefully crafted. Each day was just like the previous one. But he could not even complain because it gave him the money, the lifestyle, the security and control that he had always wanted from life.

> 'We, as a society, as a collective whole, constantly feed each other with messages of what a perfect life should look like, what perfect relationships should feel like and how our spouse should be and behave. We are told what we should eat, drink, buy and become. We are given timelines to follow; we even have a yardstick to measure our success. We are encouraged to work at a pace that overwhelms us, makes us feel insecure and worn out, and at every stage the feeling of insecurity sets in.
>
> 'We are programmed into slumber. Our inner light dims and we are left wondering why we don't feel good about ourselves anymore. That's what was slowly happening to Joy.
>
> 'But awakening always takes place at some point in a human's life.
>
> 'At some point in my life, when I realized that the journey was not about becoming anything but, in fact, about unbecoming all that was not really me, that was the day I became a storyteller.'

Joy's life moved forward as planned and a couple of years later, he and Maria were blessed with a son. They named him Julian, in memory of his maternal grandfather, a kind and happy soul. From the moment he held his son in his arms, Joy realized the miracle that had taken place in his life. Every day was a happy day. Spending time with his son infused him with energy and vitality. Joy realized that he felt alive. This was to be the happiest phase of his life.

But then, Joy was always scared about being too happy. The old grandmother's tale had always haunted him—too much laughter and happiness always leads to tears and sadness. And his worst fears came true.

> 'And then, one day, the universe steps in, to affirm your beliefs and worst fears. Our perfectly laid out life starts to crumble around us.'

Joy's life, unexpectedly, took a turn for the worse. His son was around eight months old when he suddenly passed away. Instead of condolence calls, Joy and Maria were taken for questioning by the local authorities. After the tragedy, everything lost its sheen. England, which had felt like home to them, was no more safe and secure. It was alien, cold and heartless.

Something broke in both of them and they no longer knew how to fix it. To make matters worse, grief had worked its way and they had started to drift apart. Silence was the only language they now shared.

For a long time, Julian's death felt like a nightmare that Joy was caught in and he felt he would wake up, see his son smiling and gurgling, stretching out his chubby hands to be picked up and cuddled. He just could not comprehend life without his son anymore.

Life carried on around him, but everything within him had come to a halt. At some point, Maria and Joy started to have terrible fights. When he got back from work, the house was always in a mess—the kitchen sink was full of dirty dishes and Maria would invariably be asleep. He wondered if she was on sleeping pills since she would pass out for hours on end. He, on the other hand, was unable to sleep for days. Fatigue was setting in and his performance had started to suffer at work. He had received two official warnings for incompetence. Everything was suddenly falling apart.

> 'What I have come to realize is that grief is messy and unpredictable; and it often spins out of control. There is no sequence to grief and there is no right way to grieve. Every one grieves in their own unique way.
>
> 'There are hours when you feel you are okay and then, there are days when you feel completely paralysed and disoriented. No one and nothing can replace the loss of a loved one. We start to hurt so much that we build armour around us, and within that armour, we quietly start to mourn. We form habits, patterns, addictions that isolate us even more. Grief sometimes creates a dark place within ourselves, where our life force starts to dim.
>
> 'But we carry on, because that's what the world tells us to do: bad things happen but we will heal with time; we need to be strong and pick up from where we had stepped off the grid. Joy believed what the world told him, because till then, the world had been absolutely right about everything.'

One day, Joy's mother called. She sounded so lost and vulnerable when she told him about his father's illness. She needed him to be with her to choose the right course of treatment. He agreed immediately. He too needed to get away from everything that reminded him of his son.

Post diagnosis, it was confirmed that his old man had stage four liver cancer. There were endless hospital trips and heaps of paper work to sort out family assets and finances with his dying father. Meanwhile, time kept passing by. He extended his stay. Days turned into months. Joy missed his life in London but he felt guilty for wanting to leave when his parents needed him the most. He kept pushing the dates, requesting an extended leave from his employer, until he was asked to quit. His worst fears had come true—India had managed to keep a tight hold on him.

His phones calls with Maria were very short and brusque. He could feel her simmering with anger. He finally told her about losing his job. He would have to stay a bit longer in India before returning to England to look for another job. Maria screamed at him and mocked him for being too attached to his mother, destroying the last bit of happiness that the two of them had been holding on to.

Maybe it was true—what people said about Indian men being mama's boys. He just loved and cared about his mother.

> 'Now back to the beach, to the present day. You remember that Joy liked to visit his special spot...'

The wind was picking up and Joy could see from a distance that the last of the fishing boats were making their way back home. He remembered how his father loved the wind in his face, especially while sitting out in the rain. He remembered how his father sang and danced on the boat. He was a fisherman, and he had taught Joy how to sail on a boat and be out at the sea. However, Joy did not want anything to do with his father or fishing. He hated his father.

Joy settled down in his favourite spot, closed his eyes and a tear escaped the corner of his eyes. He was surprised. Was he *finally* going to cry again? The last time he had cried was when he buried his son. Since then, he had felt numb to all the pain and happiness in his life.

He lay down on the sand and his mind wandered to

the day when his mother woke him up in the middle of the night. She informed him that his father was breathless and was suffering from an intense pain in the chest. One look at his father's ashen face and Joy knew that the old man was not going make it.

He mechanically went through all the right actions expected of him as a son. He calmed his mother, called a doctor, called his uncles and patiently waited around the old man's bed till he breathed his last. Then, in a very calm and collected manner, Joy looked into the funeral arrangements and wondered if he had become heartless.

> 'Haven't we all, at some point, felt heartless and numb? Please put your hand up, if you have.' The words of the storyteller struck the right chord with the audience and a number of hands went up, while some others just nodded.
>
> The storyteller smiled gently and said, 'Thank you for your authenticity. You see, emotional numbness is our reaction to the fear of feeling pain again. But we forget that when we block out pain, we block out life itself! We block out happiness and the possibility of transformation. We forget that the pain is not permanent. So, you should have the courage to be as human as you can! On the beach now...'

As Joy walked towards the water, he started to whistle softly. Last month, he had found an unlikely friend, or maybe, the friend had found him. It looked like he was the chosen one and the thought warmed his heart and made him smile. His friend was an Olive Ridley turtle, a young male. The tail of male Olive Ridley turtles are always longer than that of the females. His kind were found in and around Goa, especially in the rocky part of the beaches, eating algae, sunbathing, romping around, warming up to the female turtles who came ashore to lay their eggs. The turtles rarely mingled with humans, especially male turtles. Once out in the deep sea, they were solitary roamers.

Within a week of knowing the turtle, they had developed a strong bond and Joy took the liberty of naming him Ollie. Joy was a practical man and he knew that the turtle belonged to the wild and a day would come when they would have to part. He hated partings and endings, as they always brought pain and grief. But sometimes, some relationships were destined to end in separation and this felt like such a relationship.

He soon realized that his turtle was special. Ollie's shell was scarred and one of his flippers was smaller than the other three. He was not the prettiest to behold, but he did have the gentlest and kindest of eyes. Joy often poured his heart out to the turtle, spoke to him about his frustrations, addictions, sorrows and his anger. Joy even confessed that he would often say and do things that he was ashamed of later. Joy felt that Ollie understood and accepted him, unlike humans.

Joy had always belonged to this little, sleepy, old fishing village called Galgibaga. It was known as the last few hidden treasures of south Goa. The place had a unique charm that the locals were very proud of. The beach itself was a delight, a pristine stretch of golden-brown sand, fringed with coconut palms and Suri trees, with crystal-clear water on the other side. During the monsoon months, the village landscape turned lusciously green—like a tropical jungle.

What Joy loved the most was the river that meandered at a slow space through his village to meet the sea. He had many happy memories of playing near it as a young boy. The northern portion of the beach was often visited by these Olive Ridley turtles—they religiously came every year and laid their eggs. Unfortunately, the number of visiting turtles had declined considerably over the past few years, and now the villagers were worried. Many felt that it was a sign from above—a bad omen that something was going wrong in and around Galgibaga.

> 'When the wild ones choose a place to give birth to their young ones, like the turtles chose Galgibaga, we need to take note and make an effort to preserve the land, water and air of the place to make sure they have special, nurturing energies. The turtle is believed to be one of the four ancient ones of the ocean.'

Joy did not understand much about the dwindling turtle population and felt that the smallest of events had been blown out of proportion by the villagers. He did not care; he was neither a conservationist nor an environmentalist. But he was worried about the safety of his friend Ollie, and so he kept an eye out for him. Sadly, many turtles were washing up—all scratched, cut up and bloodless—on the beach of Galgibaga. It may have been due to the presence of those large illegal fishing trawlers that he saw late at night in and around his village.

Joy's stream of thoughts was cut short when Ollie emerged from the rocks at the far end of the beach and waddled up to Joy's hideaway. Both man and turtle sat down on the sand, side by side. Joy stroked the cool, scaly head of Ollie. It gave him a feeling of comfort and calmed the emotional storm raging within.

His heart was heavy because his wife wanted to leave him for another man. He had known for a while now that their relationship was ending, but then one day he happened to see her in the arms of another man. He saw true love and longing in their embrace and eyes. He had forgotten how love felt and looked like, and this was a rude awakening for him. It jolted him out of the daze he had been caught in since his father had passed away.

> 'When a series of incidents and setbacks in our life start to break us, it's actually a time of grace and transformation. Transformation is not easy, it's painful and confusing. We need to look at patterns, and see how to break them. Instead, we get busy playing the victim!'

Joy felt a mixed bag of emotions when he saw his wife and her new love. He first felt a wave of relief wash over him because now he had an excuse to end something that had ended many years ago. She too had finally cheated on him like he had, not once, but many times with other women. The only difference was that he was never in love with the women he slept with.

But that night, he had seen Maria smile, giggle and laugh in her lover's embrace. He had seen her happy after such a long time and that, oddly, made him feel happy for her, but he also felt let down by life.

So much had come to an end for him in the past few years, but he had not found the courage to end things with Maria. She was the only constant left in his life and being with her was more of a habit, like it is in most loveless marriages.

The truth was that theirs was a marriage of convenience. He was needed to keep the money coming, provide for all the comforts, support her dreams, like every good husband should, and he did. She was needed to run the house and keep things functional for them, which she did. Both husband and wife deserved the credit, they did a good job and were a great team.

They were so good at this little pretend game that everyone believed that they had a good, strong marriage. Their spasmodic, half-hearted efforts to make it work over the past few years had even made Joy believe, albeit occasionally, that they had something good going. They would often have bitter fights and not talk for days, and then there would be few weeks of peace between them. The slightest touch, even a casual caress exchanged between them was rare these days and proximity felt awkward. They slept in the same bed, lived in the same house, but were each lost in their own world.

For Joy, his one-night stands were more real. He had often wondered if marriages really made people happy. Did love really last beyond the initial, feverish romance? Why did people stop loving or wanting each other again? Did married people stay loyal to each other all their lives? Or did they cheat at times and keep it under wraps? Were he and Maria the unlucky ones? Was it worth investing so much time and effort in a relationship when it had to come to an end?

There was something fundamentally wrong, something amiss in his marriage for sure, but he was too much of a coward to point it out and talk about it. As an afterthought, there were so many little things that they should and could have done to save their relationship, but anger and unprocessed, suppressed grief did them in.

He slowly got up and made his way back home and waited for her. He sat in the living room with the lights switched off. He heard her come in after an hour or so. In a very calm and collected voice, he asked her to switch on the lights and sit with him.

She took a seat opposite him and when they locked eyes, she knew that he knew. For many months, she had been trying to find the correct time and space to let him know that she had made up her mind to leave him; it did not feel right to be in love with another man while being married to this one. She had fallen madly in love with Anthony and it felt so right with him.

She had seen that Joy was facing many hurdles while running the beach shack because the village association was breathing down his neck. So she kept putting off the inevitable, but the look in his eyes tonight gave her the courage to speak up. Hearing her words brought everything inside of him to a standstill but still, he silently listened to her.

She expected him to lash out but he did not. That made her feel terrible and guilty, almost like she was the villain. He got up, paused and then told her that she was free to walk out of their marriage; he had no reason to hold her back. Even though she could feel that he was angry and upset, he did not show it. She felt cheated of an explanation, and a feeling of worthlessness washed over her. 'Am I not good and precious enough for him to even consider putting up a fight, instead of letting go so easily?' This provoked her to hurt him more. As her parting shot, she said that she would always care about his well-being but she was no longer in love with him. Her words had the desired effect and she saw him tear up. But such victories were bitter victories.

Joy, at that point, just wanted to walk away as fast as possible, and get to his safe place on the beach and cry. He was so confused and lost. He had nothing left in life.

> 'You know, what I have realized over time is that the creator, sometimes, has a weird sense of humour.'

All the people Joy loved were slowly disappearing from his life and he felt truly alone. He had started to believe that he was not meant for good things, that he was supposed to be unhappy. Maybe he was being punished for all the bad things that he had, knowingly and unknowingly, done to people. He was quite sure that he had run out of luck. The thing Joy did not know is that when a greater force and energy, one that had created this world, decides to step into our lives, everything turns upside down. We are not being punished. We are actually the chosen ones.

2

DREAM A DREAM

Exhausted by the happenings of the evening and all the reminiscing, Joy finally drifted off to sleep. He woke up with a start a few hours later. It was cold and wet and the tide was high. The water rarely reached so far, but the sea around Goa had been acting up for a while now. He was drenched to the bone and the ocean had turned rougher than he had ever remembered it to be.

The waves were crashing on to the beach with a vengeance. He saw lightning streak across the night sky and heard the thunder rumble in the distance. There was no sight of Ollie. He must have gone away while he was sleeping. Joy slowly picked his way back to whatever portion of the beach was left untouched by the waves; and the walk proved to be quite difficult! The waves crashed against the shore, a slight drizzle had started and he kept slipping and sliding on the lava rocks.

He saw some of the fishermen's boats bobbing up and down in the distance—one of them, he could tell, was Anthony's. Joy had often seen Anthony pushing that same boat out to the sea. It had an image of St. Francis painted on the front and two colourful stripped flags on either end of the boat. He remembered Anthony taking this particular boat out more often than the others he owned.

Joy felt a huge wave of jealousy swell up inside him. He hated Anthony for being all that he was not. He stood still for a while and then something snapped inside him that set him into motion. He half-swam, half-walked his way to the boat and untied it. Had it been any other day, it would have taken at least two people to roll and push the boat into the water. But because the tide was so high it was bobbing around in the water, ready to sail. He wanted Anthony to feel crippled and helpless, like how he felt most of the time these days.

Fishermen were superstitious about their special boat. As a young boy, Joy had seen his father take one of the smaller boats, his special boat, out into the ocean, come rain or sunshine. Even when his father was told by the doctor that he only had a few months to live and he needed to rest, he would untie his little boat, get some of the younger fishermen to help him push it into the sea and climb into it and row himself slowly to the middle of the ocean and sit there for a long time. The middle of the ocean may have been his father's safe spot.

As Joy pushed Anthony's boat out into the ocean, he felt alive. Joy finally felt he was doing something pro-active; he was standing up for the wrong done to him by his wife, Anthony and the world. He felt justified in taking revenge. He felt like a different man. A stronger, more powerful man who did not take things lying down.

Ollie was watching his friend from the crevice in the rock. He was confused. Normally, humans did not take their boats out in this weather. His friend needed to be cautious. When the tide started to rise, he had tried to snap Joy out of it, but failed. And now looking at Joy's antics, Ollie was worried.

Joy was so taken up with the task of pushing Anthony's boat way into the ocean that he did not realize that he was dangerously close to the rocky part of the beach. This was the worst patch and all the fishermen avoided it. The waves were higher and rougher by now, and suddenly, Joy lost his balance and slipped. He tried hanging on to the boat, but it began capsizing and he hit his head on the edge of the boat.

> 'No action, whether done consciously or unconsciously, is a coincidence. At some point, it all ties up with what was meant to happen, for us to learn or unlearn things.'

The blinding pain made him lose his bearings, and he went down, into the ocean. He ended up gulping large amounts of water. The pain was tremendous and slowly, he began to lose consciousness. He felt himself sink deeper into the waters. Everything slowed down around him. Oddly, he remembered his son's eyes and his smile. He remembered the way his baby smelt after a bath, all fresh and clean, and somehow, he knew he would be okay. If he was going to die now, he would cross over and be with his son and his mother again. He missed them both so very much. He stopped struggling and just let go.

The moment he consciously decided to die, he started to sink very rapidly to the bottom of the ocean. He had wished many times, during the past few months, to just drop dead and now it was finally happening. This was what he wanted and his wish was being granted by the universe. There was complete darkness around him.

Ollie saw Joy disappear into the sea and moved out of his resting place and dived deep into the ocean. He saw Joy drifting further into the ocean, far from the shoreline, caught in the strong current. He swam towards Joy with a speed that turtles are known for, slowest on the land and fastest in the sea. He reached Joy and nudged his fingers with his snout. The fingers he had come to know so well were lifeless and limp. He tried with all his might to push Joy back towards the beach but it was a difficult task. He was only forty kilograms and Joy was a much taller and bigger man. Joy was drowning and Ollie could not get him to safety. He could taste Joy's blood in the water around them. Ollie had found someone like Joy after so many years, and he could not lose him so soon. He needed to find help and soon.

Ollie swam up to the surface of the ocean and saw nothing for miles in the choppy water. And then, in the far distance, he could faintly make out the outline of fins. They were large fins, and Ollie was now nervous, as Joy was bleeding. Sharks were a common sight in that area. Joy could be in danger and Ollie knew he too was in danger. He was much lower in the food chain than these sharks! But he also knew that he had to find bigger sea creatures to save Joy tonight and time was running out.

As he swam towards the fins, he knew that these fish were larger and faster than the regular ones. He could feel it in the water; there was a higher frequency and vibration to the water. As Ollie got closer to the fins, he realized they were humpback dolphins! He was so relieved and elated that he did three turtle somersaults in the water. Dolphins were the protectors of the sea, they brought harmony and peace, and they were known to ease conflict among sea creatures. The ancient ones of the sea often said that the Great One created each species, unique with special qualities and abilities. Each had a job to do to keep the ocean alive, well and healthy, and they all fit together to paint and create the most beautiful world under the water.

The dolphins played their part with fun, ease and gentleness. Ollie swam to the centre of dolphin's pod and the three dolphins slowed down and turned their attention to the turtle flapping his flippers to draw their attention. They all exchanged smiles and started to giggle because Ollie looked quite cute with his three flippers and disfigured shell, swirling and twirling, telling them a story of how he had a human friend who was sinking to the bottom of the ocean and would die if they didn't help him.

Ollie knew they were listening to him intently now because they immediately stopped giggling. They were big fish with bigger hearts and they would help him as humans and dolphins had a special bond. Sometimes, we just need a much larger force to protect our loved ones and right now, these dolphins were way bigger than him.

The dolphins followed Ollie. When they found Joy, he was floating, lifeless, face down in the deep waters. The dolphins got to work immediately. They flipped and turned Joy around, they swirled him up towards the surface as Ollie swam to the surface and tried to find the boat. It was bobbing up and down in the rough seas. He guided the dolphins to the boat and then they tossed Joy into the boat.

Ollie's turtle heart hurt as he wondered whether Joy was alive and if he had been too late to save his friend. After a long time, he cried tears of despair as he realized he had come to love Joy in such a short time. Once touched by the feeling, it always remains, sometimes buried deep. He remembered crying like this when the raven had dropped him in the middle of the ocean. He had been so scared then and had not known how to live or how to find food for himself as there was nothing familiar about the ocean. Even though the grand crab lady took him into the ocean to teach him basic survival techniques, he still felt that it was a very dark and dangerous place to be.

He loved Joy for so many little things he had learnt about him. Joy had no clue that Ollie actually understood what Joy was feeling when he talked to him about his innermost thoughts. Joy would end his monologues by saying, 'I know you don't understand anything at all Ollie, but it helps me a great deal just to be able to say this out aloud.'

Ollie knew that humans thought that the wild don't understand their language. But he had heard some of the old, wise sea folks say that all species in the universe can actually understand each other. The birds understand the fish, the fish understand the elephants, the leopards understand the breeze, the sea understands each grain of sand. But humans had stopped believing in the magic of the universe and in their own power of communicating effortlessly with everything on this planet.

'I hope you are not nodding off to sleep. We will soon take a break, I promise. But before that, I would like to tell you what a wise man once told me about how the world came to be created.

'There have been stories, told by many ancient tribes, that the whole universe was created by a sound uttered by the Great One. The sound vibrated through the darkness and, suddenly, there was a creative explosion of light and energy that brought life on earth. The sound had different tones and dimensions to it, which then created water, air, fire and earth, and then different species came to be in each of these elements, each having a unique soul signature. Together, they created the web of life.

'He often said that the sounds in the universe are understood, deep down, by each and every species. There exists a universal language, as everything has been created and comes from the same source. All that is needed to understand each other...is to get past our limiting beliefs, our fears, our misunderstanding of separation and the constant need to alienate ourselves from the other. We need to reduce our internal conversations and consistently train ourselves to hear the whisper of the universe in everything, especially within us. Slowly, the whole world will open up for us, and we will know things even before they happen and this is how ancient wisdom will become a part of us.'

When he had no friends of his own, a young boy made Ollie feel loved and wanted. Joy was his friend even when he felt so disfigured, small and worthless. As a new born turtle, he played on the beach with the smaller crabs who often left him behind because he was slow and clumsy. Ollie was fed by the raven and the grand old crab lady taught him lessons about the sea and life, but his human friend brought him true happiness. Joy played with Ollie and did not mind his slow ways. He carried him around the rough patches of the beach and kept him safe from other animals. Ollie's happiest memory was when Joy allowed him to walk all over him, making Joy laugh and giggle as Ollie's small flippers tickled him. Being able to make Joy laugh filled Ollie's heart with so much pride and love.

One night, a few years ago, Ollie dreamt of the boy. The boy was sitting all alone on a desolate beach, building a sandcastle. Suddenly, a big bird swooped down and destroyed what he had built. The little boy cried and looked out to the ocean, calling out to Ollie to help him. The dream made no sense to Ollie, but he was suddenly filled with the urge to find his human friend again.

Ollie had faint memories of the beach where he was born. As he grew bigger and stronger, he made efforts to find the beach. He visited many beaches but none felt like home. And then one day, he swam towards a beach that was known for its soft white sand and crystal blue waters. As he came within a hundred metres of Galgibaga, he knew instantly this was where he had been born. The smell and feel of the water and sand was part of the energy that he felt in himself. He went looking through every crevice for the crab lady. He never found her, but then she was old and must have passed on. The raven too had been long gone apparently, and he could not see his human friend anywhere around.

Then one evening, Joy stumbled back into Ollie's life, but this time all grown up, angry and sad. The child was gone and a bitter, drunk man had replaced his childhood friend. As the weeks went by, Ollie could see glimpses of the little boy in Joy, and it convinced him to stick around a little longer.

Ollie had realized in the first week of meeting Joy, that Joy did not remember him. He could not blame Joy. Twenty long years had passed since they had last seen each other. But he knew Joy's soul had recognized him, because there was an instant ease and acceptance between the two of them.

As the night progressed, the sea slowly calmed down. Ollie did not leave the side of the boat, waiting to hear a sound or a movement of life from the boat. Joy, in the meantime, was alive but was in a deep, restless slumber. His body would jerk and shiver violently and then go still for a long spell. He was moving in and out of a conscious dream-like state. He tried opening his eyes but was not able to. It felt like they were stapled together.

At some point, he drifted into a dream where he found himself inside a huge bubble, deep under the sea. He saw how life slowly moved around him. The sea angels with their vibrant heads flapped their wings, darting around the bubble elegantly, schools of fish came around his bubble to check him out, but the moment he raised his hand to them, they would all shy away. He saw big fish, small colourful fish, the sea floor alive with sea urchins, glowing corals, and even colourful starfish. He saw so much beauty around his bubble that he felt his eyes mist up with sheer wonder. 'Was this how the sea was designed to look like?' he thought.

When he watched the sea from the shore, it looked inviting, always shimmering with different shades of blue. As a young boy, he would often find the smallest and simplest of excuses to dive in and it made him feel clean, healthy and alive. But recently, the sea had turned murky and muddy. The water had started to taste different, as if riddled with chemicals and oils. The deeper he would swim, he would find stray fishing nets, plastic bags and bottles floating around with unsuspecting fish caught in it and more often now, he would come across larger fish entangled in discarded fishing nets, bleeding, scared and struggling to get free. But the sea he was seeing around his bubble now was alive, colourful and abuzz. All the sea creatures knew what was expected from them, every one of them was so different, but they all still worked so well with each other. They emitted a slow, assured vibe of peace and freedom.

Joy realized he was someone different in this bubble. He was feeling at a much deeper level. He felt he was a wiser man here, calmer, more centred. He also felt small, yet so expansive and whole, and he was very sure he was connected to something far more pure and greater in the universe. Joy wondered if this was how the fish felt and whether he was picking up their thoughts. Joy remembered he had once heard that the outer world is a reflection of what happens within us. Looking at all the beauty around him, Joy concluded that he too must be equally awesome.

Joy silently watched the sea around him and then, at some point, his analytical brain went into overdrive and he wondered how he had found himself inside this bubble. He remembered hitting his head. He touched his head and it did not feel sore, even though he had received a hard whack. Maybe this was a part of the process of dying—no pain, no sound. 'Is this heaven? Or the sea heaven? Or is this just a dream? Am I still alive?' Despite being in a semi-conscious state, he could still feel the breeze and hear the sound of the waves.

He felt something tugging at his hand. He looked down and saw a boy standing next to him. The eyes looked very familiar and, suddenly, he recognized them. He felt a little confused because his son had been eight months old when he had died and there he was, standing next to him, a little man in the making. All this was happening deep down in the ocean inside the bubble. 'Is this even real?' His logical mind kept nagging him into questioning the reality of things. He had heard of near and dear ones coming to meet the soul once they pass on.

So yes, he was dead.

His son asked him in a clear, steady, grown-up voice, 'I have been waiting to see you for a while now. If you decide to stay we can be together, but grandma and grandpa have said it's not your time to be with us yet.'

Joy went down on his knees and hugged his son, tears rolling down his cheeks. He had heard his son's voice for the first time! He had heard him gurgle and giggle when he was tickled before. But this was his son talking! Joy had often wondered how his son's voice would sound. So death granted many wishes, after all. Joy did not want this moment to pass; he wanted to stay with his son.

'I have nothing to go back to, darling. Nothing! All I want is to be here with you. I love you,' Joy said.

'Dad, you are not alone. You have Ollie and he is waiting for you to wake up. He also needs you, just like you need him. I want you to know that I am okay, Dad,' his son said.

Joy remembered Ollie and wondered why he and a turtle needed each other. He could hear the sound of the waves clearly now. It seemed like the world had shifted. His bubble started to fill with light and his son started to glow, and slowly, he became a faint apparition. Joy tried to reach out and hold him but the young one faded away.

Ollie saw the sun rise and he was still not sure what had happened to Joy. He saw the birds fly across the morning sky, the sky turn from dark orange to a light pink to a pale morning blue. He saw the water glistening because of the sun's rays, as if a million stars had settled on it. With every minute, the sky and sea changed. Ollie was getting increasingly anxious. He saw a number of seagulls fly past him, high up in the sky. He tried calling out to them, he waved, he flapped, but they just kept flying away.

Ollie noticed one of the seagulls slowing down. It flew back and perched on the rim of the boat. The bird saw Joy inside the boat and Ollie beside the boat. In a very shrill, high pitched voice she asked Ollie why he had called for help. She said that she could hear the distress in his tone. Ollie was taken aback. How the sea gulls could hear him from there was something he simply could not understand. 'She must have excellent hearing!' he thought. But seagulls, after all, were known as scavengers with keen eyesight, the opportunists of the sky.

Ollie told her about what had happened. He had heard that the seagulls were known to be resourceful and kind-hearted.

After hearing him out, the seagull flew down to the deck and walked up close to Joy to see if he was breathing. Joy's breath was shallow but steady; he was alive!

She told Ollie that the human was alive but looked parched. A splash of water across his face would do the trick.

Ollie splashed some water with his flippers, but it did not reach Joy. The seagull had a small beak and a few droplets was all she could manage. It was not sufficient to wake him. The seagull, by nature, was a survivor. She quickly thought it over and then suggested that they needed a pelican since pelicans have a deep beak. So after sharing her great idea with Ollie, she flew off to find a pelican.

Ollie swam, and ate a little; but even the jellyfish that he so relished eating did not give him much happiness today. He kept looking up at the sky, waiting for the seagull to return. After a few hours, he saw a speck above and it grew larger as it flew towards the boat. The seagull had returned, as promised, with a pelican that could sprinkle lots and lots of water on Joy.

The seagull and the pelican flew in circles, assessing the situation. The pelican swooped down into the ocean and filled his beak. He then flew closer to Joy and splashed water on to his face. The combination of water splashing on his face, along with some wiggling fish, and the seagull trying to peck him, woke Joy up. He sat up with a start!

That was the first time that Ollie saw Joy awake since the accident. Ollie splashed around in glee and swam around in circles because Joy was alive and upright.

Joy felt dizzy. His head hurt, his skin was on fire, his tongue felt like sand paper and he was terribly nauseous. He leaned over the side of the boat and threw up and that's when he spotted Ollie, right next to the boat. He remembered his son telling him that Ollie and Joy needed each other. Joy was confused. 'Am I alive or dead? Or is this a continuation of the dream? Is this the second part of the dream?'

He looked around. It seemed as if the seagull wanted to have a conversation with him and there was a pelican sitting on the edge of the boat.

Joy and the seagull were keenly watching each other while the fish flipped between them. The seagull knew in her heart that Joy was going to be okay. 'He is lucky to have found a friend like you,' the seagull told Ollie before flying away to join her flock. The pelican, on the other hand, walked up and gulped down the fish on the floor of the boat. He was not going to waste good, fresh food. He then flew away.

Ollie and Joy were left alone. Joy gingerly rubbed his head. It was so bright that his eyes hurt. He was now certain that this was no dream, this was the real world. His body hurt, he smelled of fish, seaweed and puke. He was not sure how long it had been since he passed out. He was far at sea and there was no sight of land, not even a ship or a boat. He stood up, but he felt unsteady on his feet. He then realized that the turtle must have stayed with him through the ordeal.

Meanwhile, Ollie was suddenly overcome with tiredness. He could feel his body go limp. He needed to rest and he dived deep down into the ocean to find a spot.

From the corner of his eye, Joy saw Ollie disappear into the water. He needed to feed perhaps. Then Joy considered his situation. He knew he had to find what the boat could offer him. He got busy sorting out the little treasures he had found on the boat, which included a net, some hooks, knife, rain cover, a flare gun with two cartridges, some rope and some empty alcohol bottles. So Anthony did drink and was not a saint after all!

A few hours passed and Joy realized that Ollie had not surfaced. Joy tapped the surface of the sea with his hand and whistled, but Ollie did not appear. Joy started getting a little desperate now. Ollie represented the safe world he came from. He did not realize it, but out of sheer desperation, he was repeatedly slapping the surface of the sea with all his force. The salt water and tears drenched his face. For the first time since he had woken up, the magnanimity of the whole situation hit him. He realized he was lost at sea. He was scared and did not know if he could survive this ordeal. The ocean stretched endlessly in all directions around him, she could swallow the best of fishermen and destroy the biggest of ships when angry, and he was alone, sitting in a small boat.

Ollie was sleeping, slowly drifting in the water, the gentle currents lulling him into a deep sleep. He drifted into a dream. He saw a giant sea turtle swimming towards him. His first instinct was to scuttle away, but he was no match for this large leatherback sea turtle. It was dark and monstrous in size, with sea moss and barnacles growing all over him; his shell was battle-scarred and thick, and seaweed was entangled around his large flippers and webbed feet. To Ollie, he looked like a warlock in a black cape, ready to cast a spell on him.

Ollie wondered what he had done wrong! He turned around and swam at a speed that he had mastered over years, and after a while, he turned back and realized that he was still being followed by the large, old turtle. His worst nightmare had just come true. Male turtle fights could get nasty. He had always survived by not being confrontational. Ever since he was young, he was the jolly turtle; he looked funny, did funny tricks and twirls to make everyone laugh.

Ollie swam for his life, but the grand old turtle caught up with him and opened its mouth.

His voice was deep. It rumbled and echoed in Ollie's ears. At first, Ollie did not understand what the old turtle was saying. However, once he realized that there would be no fight, he calmed down. In a very calm, deep voice, the old turtle told Ollie that he should not take Joy back home. Instead, he would have to take him across the ocean to the eastern coast of a continent called Africa.

Ollie was confused and doubtful as he knew Joy had to go back home to Goa. Additionally, Ollie knew nothing about the route to Africa and he was scared. The old turtle looked at Ollie and in a very firm voice, he told him to deal with his fear, right then and there.

'Just know that we all want him to go on this journey and you have been chosen to take him,' the old turtle said grimly.

'But he will die, or maybe I'll die! The human does not know how to survive a day on the sea nor can he understand me. Can't you see? I am not capable of performing this task,' protested Ollie.

'You will just have to do what you are told. That's the message from the divine ocean. You will look after him, keep him alive and the ocean will support you and keep you alive. The human has to cross the ocean and that's your responsibility now.' The grand old turtle's piercing eyes looked straight into Ollie's. 'You have to do this,' he said, and then he slowly disappeared into the inky darkness.

Ollie woke up with a start. He realized that it was a dream, but everything felt so real and alive in that dream. There was a crazy amount of seaweed floating around him, like the ones that were entangled around the grand old leatherback. He rubbed his turtle head with his flipper; he was confused but he knew that the time had come to travel to Africa.

After all, he had been taught that dreams would guide him to do the right thing and that he should never doubt the wisdom of dreams. He belonged to the ancient species and his kind were one of the most important pillars of the oceans. They kept the sea creatures grounded and they knew the importance of understanding and following their dreams. When he was young, his dreams were about food, about playing with his own kind, about having four strong flippers. But as he got older, he had fewer dreams, till one day he dreamt of Joy crying on the beach. Acting on that dream was instinctive, and he was lucky to have reconnected with his old friend and to be able to save him when the time came. Now this dream had told him to take Joy all the way to Africa. But he was still worried and wondered whether he was doing the right thing.

'...*So how many of you dream?*' A few hands rose.

The storyteller smiled.

'And the rest of you?'

Someone from the front row got up, shuffled his feet, smiled shyly and mumbled. 'I dream but rarely do I remember my dreams. Is that bad or good?'

'It's neither bad, nor good,' said the storyteller, 'but know that dreams are important. Before you go to bed, ask the universe to gift you a dream. The ancient civilizations and tribes used to say that dreams are important because our ancestors, guardian spirits and the universe speak to us through them.

'Sometimes, these dreams can overwhelm us, especially our nightmares. But even nightmares are not to be feared. Our dreams are a source of sacred knowledge and carry messages from the divine. Our dreams help us expand our consciousness, besides enabling us to open up to the powers and energies that can guide us to do the right thing in life. They have a creative potential, which when tapped and understood can bring about miracles in our life. Dreams can alter our course, and the day we stop dreaming, we should know that something has gone missing in us.'

Someone from the audience spoke. 'And once we are gifted a dream what do we do? Ollie has such a clear and precise dream. He knew immediately what he has to do! Mine are often jumbled, randomly sequenced. I cannot make head or tail of them.'

The storyteller laughed out loud. 'The wild ones know

what is expected of them. We, humans, are not taught to live intuitively but instead, we move logically. You need to slowly train yourself to become a wise dreamer. Write down your dreams, ask the universe to help you understand them. Someone will come along; something may happen that will give you clarity but until you ask, you will not receive help.'

3

BEING PRESENT

It was quite late in the evening when Joy saw Ollie emerge some distance away from the boat. He was so overjoyed that he jumped into the water to greet his friend and gave him a hug. Man and turtle swam around and played in the water. Joy felt as if the warm, salty water had cleansed and absorbed all those unwanted, negative thoughts that had been weighing him down, like it would do when he was younger. He felt like a young boy and was happy that he had a friend who had decided to be with him on this journey. After a long time, he felt truly blessed.

Joy got back on the boat and he felt hungry, but the urge to have a drink was growing by the minute. Drink and drugs won this round against food again! He needed it now! His hands were trembling. He felt feverish, his stomach started to hurt and he felt a dull ache spreading throughout his body. It felt as if he had the flu. He was aware that these were withdrawal symptoms. He needed something to calm his nerves, even a cigarette would do at this point. Perhaps the boat had a cigarette. He would not even mind the last dregs of alcohol from those bottles he had found earlier. He started ransacking the boat and he even looked below the floorboards.

All he did find though were the oars, nicely secured at the bottom.

Joy was desperate for a slight high. He started throwing things around the boat, cursing loudly and by the end of the hour, he was crying, rocking himself back and forth, like a child throwing a tantrum.

Ollie heard the commotion and was confused. Just a while ago, they were enjoying themselves and Joy was laughing and happy. Now he sounded like a wounded, crazed animal. He could hear Joy sobbing and wondered what had gone wrong. Simple Ollie with his simple wants, like food, sleep and freedom did not understand this major mood swing.

Maybe his friend was hungry! Ollie felt guilty for not thinking of feeding Joy earlier. He dived into the sea and caught a fish that he thought was good enough for Joy. He surfaced and tried throwing it into the boat; the fish hit the edge of the boat and fell back into the sea. Ollie was now a turtle with an agenda. He dove down again and went in search of another fish. He kept trying to get a fish across into the boat but kept missing.

The thudding sounds caught Joy's attention and he got up to check it out. That's when he saw Ollie's antics. He was in no mood to play with the turtle! Joy shooed Ollie off, but Ollie was determined to feed Joy. He did not let Joy's bad mood stop him.

Joy angrily shouted at Ollie's attempt to give him a fish; he even tried whacking Ollie on the head with the oar. Ollie ducked in time and swam away from the boat. He watched Joy from a distance. In the moonlight, Joy looked like a mad man. He was trembling, his face was glistening with tears, his hair was wind-swept and flying in all directions, and after a while, he saw Joy collapse into the depths of the boat.

Joy watched the turtle swim away. Maybe Ollie had decided to leave him after all! He thought of looking for Ollie but everything appeared dark and gloomy around him. He felt a little nervous when he thought about what was lurking in the dark, around and below the boat. Soon, Joy felt bad that he had lashed out at Ollie, who had just wanted to play.

Joy knew that the fault always lay with him. He had loved his wife, but at some point, he had started to take her for granted. His father had always made an effort to be his friend, but even as a young boy, he spurned it, never allowing the connection to develop. He was even hurtful, telling his father how ashamed he was to be his son. He could never make it up to his father or ask for his forgiveness. The funny thing was that as a young man, he had always assumed that time was on his side, but now he knew that time was the one thing that would always run out. Joy wondered if he had lost Ollie forever too. Loneliness, withdrawal symptoms and hunger got the better of him and he finally curled up at the bottom of the boat, crying himself to sleep.

Ollie came back to the side of the boat once he heard silence. Night turned to day and Ollie felt it was best to swim away from the boat. His self-preservation had kicked in, and so he disappeared deep into the ocean. He felt the need to spend time with his kind. He did not understand why Joy was acting the way he was. He decided to still keep an eye on Joy, but he would do so from a distance. He needed to figure what his next move should be. 'Is it time to leave Joy to his destiny?' he thought. 'The ocean was determined to make sure Joy travelled across to Africa. It could rope in someone else to take this human on his journey,' Ollie thought.

Ollie knew that it was tough to survive within or upon the ocean. He had learnt his way around with great difficulty. He never belonged to a group, nor did he have a mentor to guide him. He learnt everything by himself; he was the loner, the solitary one, the deformed one, and if he could figure out a way, so could Joy.

Ollie knew that many sea creatures were not very fond of humans now. The sea creatures felt that humans were reckless and had no regard for the ocean and the sea life. They dumped their garbage in the ocean—tonnes of plastic floated in the ocean everywhere, choking and killing unsuspecting fish that were consuming it. The sea creatures were losing their habitat rapidly. As fishing activities kept increasing, so did their fear of being hunted. Many species were extinct. But humans just did not seem to care.

He had heard of cases where bigger fish had started to attack humans and Joy was in danger if he fell prey to them. However, Ollie was fond of his friend and he felt guilty that he was allowing Joy's boat to float towards Africa because of a dream. What if it was just a dream and he was taking it too literally? Ollie loved fairy tales and all things magical since he had been a young turtle. It helped him live his solitary life in peace, but he had noticed that the other male turtles were not like him.

How could he, a small turtle, keep Joy safe? The ocean was a dangerous place, merciless at times. How would Joy survive the long journey on a small boat? There was the rain and strong currents, which could smash his boat to pieces. Maybe he needed to find a way to turn the boat and let Joy float back home.

Joy woke up with a start. The sun was shining brightly and he lay on his back and felt the gentle rocking of the boat. Bile rose in his throat and he could taste it. He felt nauseous. 'Is it hunger or am I feeling sick because I am thirsty?' he wondered. He leaned over and splashed some sea water on his face. He was sun burnt. His skin had started to peel and the salt water made his skin itch.

'Where could I get water to drink in the middle of the ocean?'

He sat silently, remembering a story his dad had often narrated to his friends and family about being caught in a patch of bad weather and being lost at sea. He was proud of how he had survived for three days without water or food. Whenever the old man recalled one of his adventures, Joy would poke fun or insult his father with hurtful words. How he hated his father for being an alcoholic! He remembered his dad saying that fish bones and eyes had water that a human could survive on, but just the thought of chewing on the bones and eyes made him want to throw up.

'How am I going to survive this ordeal?' While he gingerly made his way across, from one end of the boat to the other, he noticed that the plastic tarp that was lying in a messy heap looked damp. In its fold a little water had collected. He dipped his finger in the water and tasted it. 'It isn't salty! Yippee!' It seemed like morning dew. The water tasted like sweet nectar to Joy, but it was such a small amount. He needed to collect a large quantity, but he could only do that tomorrow.

He dragged the fishing net from the corner of the boat and started to detangle and sort it out, all the while looking out for Ollie. Joy's fingers were trembling and he was losing patience. His mind was all over the place and this simple task seemed impossible. His body was itching and he felt as if ants were crawling all over him. His brain felt foggy and thick. He could detangle only a small part and decided to cast that part of net over the side of the boat, hoping to catch some fish.

He waited for a while with the net in the water, then checked it, but the nets were empty. He just did not have the energy to pull it up again.

He lay down and wondered: how had he landed on a boat that he never climbed into in the first place? He remembered that he had drowned while pushing the boat. His head hurt when he tried to remember, so he dropped the idea. He was so confused. He did not know whether he was floating away or towards Galgibaga. He missed home, he missed his shack and he missed Ollie.

Ollie slowly swam towards the boat and saw Joy's efforts to fish. It was likely that what some of the sea creatures felt was true: humans were an extremely foolish species! Joy had tried to hit him when he was offering him fish and now, here he was, making futile attempts to catch one.

Ollie was still wondering whether he should help Joy or turn around and swim far away from him when he felt a playful nudge from the back. He could feel a soft, spongy snout, with whiskers that tickled him. He turned around and came face to face with a dugong. Dugongs were also called sea cows because they were the grass grazers of the ocean. Ollie was relieved that he had not come across a big fish that could just swallow him up.

Ollie felt so small next to the dugong. This dugong had a large, cylindrical body that tapered at both ends and a dolphin-like tail, but it still moved around gracefully and gently.

The dugongs were in danger, like everything else in the ocean. Ollie knew that the oceanic council always wanted to hear the dugong's views when an issue cropped up because they gave sound and fair advice, like no other. They were peaceful aquatic mammals who always spoke of friendship and harmony. Ollie wondered why the dugong had come so far since they were normally found only in clear, shallow waters.

The dugong gave Ollie another playful nudge and spoke in a very sweet, child-like, soft voice. It was surprising to hear it from an old, wise sea soul with such a huge, awkward body.

'Little turtle, you need to be with your friend. Go to him,' she advised.

'Dugong, you don't know how unthoughtful and unkind Joy is! I think that we animals are kinder and smarter than the human race.' Ollie was clearly in a mood to vent.

The dugong gently patted him on his shell.

'I know you are hurt and upset and are considering abandoning the human. I could feel it from miles away, and knew that I had to come to you. I have come to know that this friendship is important—not just for you and Joy, but also for the ocean. We all come into each other's lives for a reason, there are no chance meetings. None of us are perfect, and we need to learn from each other's shortcomings. It's easy to be judgemental. When the one we love hurts us, we have the choice to hurt them back or be compassionate. With compassion comes understanding and growth. When we feel hurt by someone's action, we need to ask ourselves what needs to be healed inside of us and what can we do differently,' the dugong said.

Ollie was quiet. He swam circles around the dugong, processing all that had been said to him.

'How can a turtle with three flippers and an emotionally stunted human being be of any use to the ocean?' he asked earnestly. 'I have followed all the messages from the ocean. I dreamt of Joy crying and I followed the thread of the dream and crossed oceans to find him. In the first few days of being with him, I realized that he was not the Joy I knew. I liked the young Joy more. This Joy and I can't be together,' Ollie ranted.

The dugong smiled gently, 'Joy had to grow up. But the little boy is still hidden in him. He's just a little hurt and lost. No one is perfect, we are all broken in some way. But that does not mean we deserve to be abandoned. It is difficult to see beyond the obvious, but it can be done if this relationship is important to you.'

'I have been told to take him to the east coast of Africa, but he has no clue where he is going. But I know. I feel guilty and confused about taking this man away from his hometown. And what if we are not able to make it to Africa? Have you seen the size of his boat?' Ollie asked.

'Everything does not have to make sense right away, little turtle. From chaos comes clarity. You are upset about what Joy did to you in the past and you are worrying about what may happen to both of you in the future. That is not going to help. You just be in the present moment. Sometimes it is best to just focus on the now,' advised the dugong.

'What do I do next dugong? How will I keep him safe? And what after we reach Africa? How will I figure out all this by myself?' Ollie was determined to find all the answers.

The dugong laughed. It sounded like a low rumble around Ollie. 'Right now, you are all about doing! What to do next? Where should we go next? How much time will it take? You don't have to have all the answers before setting out. I promise you, along the way, you will find them. The ocean spirit told you to go to Africa, so just go. Trust and flow. Humans and sea creatures feel and think alike. I know it does not feel like that at the moment, but trust me on this,' the dugong said.

Ollie hung his head and felt a little ashamed. 'Why do I have so many doubts?'

'It's okay to question and have doubts; the biggest and the smallest of creatures, and I bet, even the wisest ones, have doubts. Be kind to yourself. The Great One has a bigger plan for all of us. Trust in it,' said the dugong.

'Dugong, I am a simple turtle and all your talking is making sense, but it's way too much for me to digest right now.' Ollie held his head with both his flippers.

The dugong wanted to hug him at that moment. 'Stop saying that you are a simple turtle! You are an extraordinary turtle! If you don't believe in your own magic, how will you teach the world how wonderful you are? Know your own worth and the worth of others, Ollie. You have chosen your path even before you were born. Now is the time to follow it, otherwise your destiny will again come knocking in a way that could be worse,' warned the dugong.

'I don't remember making this choice,' protested Ollie.

'None of us remember what we have chosen to accomplish in this lifetime. But it's our duty to find out and to do that we have to live, cry, laugh and struggle and let go, and of course, we have to help each other. Your destiny is now tied to a human, for how long or why, we do not know! It's a mystery right now, but that's the beauty of life. It will unravel when it has to, so learn to live this life one day at a time. Follow the signs that the Great One is sending you. Count your blessings, little turtle. At least, you are able to see the signs. Some are so blind that they don't see any sign. We all have the free will and choice to follow a sign or to give up on it. I heard your thoughts across the ocean and I had the choice to ignore them. But I chose to find you. I am in danger too, as this is not my habitat. But I was told that I am supposed to guide you and here I am. Sometimes we just have to be courageous enough to find the hero in ourselves. It has been buried under self-doubt, limiting beliefs and fears for too long.'

'So Joy has a grand destiny awaiting him?' Ollie asked the dugong earnestly.

The dugong smiled. 'I don't know, Ollie, but I do know that the destinies of the smallest and the largest creatures tie up collectively into the grand plan of things. If you love this human, then find it in your heart to help him become the grandest version of himself. That will happen only if he aligns to his life purpose, and the east coast of Africa is where his destiny awaits him. Right now, you have to trust that what is happening is for the good of all.'

'Be grateful, little turtle,' the dugong continued, 'for the good, for the bad, for things that you don't understand and for things that you are receiving. Gratitude is the key.' The dugong then patted Ollie on his head and slowly turned around and swam away.

Ollie slowly swam up to the surface and saw the boat from a distance, he saw Joy get up and slap the water and call out his name. Ollie knew, in his heart, that there was no turning back any more. So he swam towards Joy.

Joy saw Ollie swimming towards him. It made him smile and he felt tears of love and pure gratitude mist up his eyes. Ollie dived down into the water and then surfaced closer to the boat. He immediately got tangled up in the net that was trailing on the side of the boat. Joy immediately pulled the net up and gently freed Ollie from it.

He took the turtle's head in both his hands and stroked it; then looking into his eyes, he brought his own head down to touch Ollie's snout. Joy could feel the life ticking through Ollie's body. The turtle was alive and so was he! Joy was so humbled by the thought of this wild animal choosing to be with him. He knew now, for certain, that their connection was special, far unlike anything he had shared with any other living thing. He took a deep breath, tilted his head back to look at the blue sky, and thanked God for still keeping him alive and for Ollie. He hugged Ollie and then released him back into the water.

He felt strong after a long time and was filled with hope and possibility. He started to detangle the net, and he hummed a happy song as he worked. After a while, he began to whistle a song he used to sing as a young boy. He had heard it on the radio. He stopped and smiled as he acknowledged that something had shifted inside him. He worked on the net; his hands were still shaky, he still felt woozy and sick, but he did not feel gloomy any longer.

Joy managed to detangle the net. He folded it and kept it in the corner in a neat pile. He was too tired to fish. His lips were chapped, his skin was peeling, his fingers were raw and he had stopped peeing since yesterday afternoon.

He again heard a thud against the boat and saw Ollie with a small fish in his mouth. Ollie would throw the fish towards the boat and then dive down again and surface with another fish in his mouth. That's when Joy realized that Ollie had been trying to feed him all along. Joy felt terrible for lashing out at him.

He reached out and took the fish from Ollie's mouth.

Ollie was glad that the human was not so daft after all, and he dived down and got another fish. Soon, Joy had a small, wiggling heap of fish at his feet. He took out a knife and he skinned and cleaned the insides of all the fish he thought he could eat. He released the others back into the ocean. He gouged out the eyes and kept them in a heap and they, lifelessly, stared back at him. It really creeped him out. But he needed water, and if this was a source of water then he was going to do his best to eat and swallow them to survive.

It was difficult to eat the raw fish, but he did so. It was getting hotter by the hour, so he decided to create a shelter with the oar, rope and plastic tarp. He was busy most of the afternoon, creating this shelter on one side of the boat. It took him longer than usual, but he was proud of himself for finishing the task. From under his shelter, he saw the fish drying on the other end of the boat and knew that he was doing okay. He finally settled down, and after a while, fell into a dreamless sleep.

Ollie watched Joy throughout. He could see that Joy was in a more positive mood about his situation and this made Ollie feel relieved and happy. Both man and turtle slept peacefully, one in the sea and the other on his boat, knowing that they were there for each other.

After a few hours, Joy woke up feeling sick—a mouthful of vomit nearly choking him. He half-walked, half-dragged himself to the edge of the boat and emptied the contents of his stomach into the sea. His throat was burning, his eyes were watering. He lay back, shivering.

Joy realized by now that his urge for alcohol and drugs was strong enough to trigger mad, frenzied, desperate episodes, which left him in tears, scratching himself. Over the past day or so, several times, he had even considered killing himself. But today, he was certain he wanted to live. As he lay on his back, his mind was blank. He saw the evening sky turn from deep pink to orange to dark grey. The night sky was lit with stars and the moon glowed gently. His tummy felt slightly settled. *He was not going to die; he had survived this too.* He crawled across to the shelter he had built, and took the oar down, and got the plastic tarp ready to collect the morning dew. He washed the bottles in which he had decided to collect whatever water he could. He crawled under the tarp and slept. He found comfort in the hardness of the floorboards.

Joy woke up earlier than usual the next morning. He woke to the caress of the cool morning breeze. It reminded him of his mother who always woke him up gently, with a cup of coffee. They used to talk about the weather, the birds and then, he would find a spot to sit peacefully by himself, listening to the sound of the waves and the music streaming in from the radio in the kitchen. As a child, the radio was his best friend and he loved listening to it. The radio knob fascinated him; he could turn it and tune into different countries across the seas. His mother often sang along with the radio while he sat on the tall, blue trunk in the kitchen. The radio was his most precious belonging, and it went everywhere with him. He realized that he missed his mother's voice, her laughter and her off-key singing. This morning, he closed his eyes and could hear her voice in his head and heart.

Soon after his father had died, his mother had

contracted tuberculosis. She had refused to travel back with him to England and his heart would not allow him to abandon her.

He requested Maria to pack their life in England and return to Goa. He could feel that his decision was met with a deep, simmering resentment, but he was past caring. His mother needed her son. And that was that.

He also realized that he had to keep himself occupied. After a lot of thought, he decided that he would open a beach shack in Galgibaga. The only issue was that he lacked experience in the hospitality business. And so, he decided to acquire some work experience. He found a job in Agonda as a restaurant manager, and every day, he learnt a little more about the business.

One night, while he was sitting and chatting with a group of foreign tourists after work, he smoked his first joint. He loved the high it gave him. For a few hours life was so good that confusion and grief took a back seat. After that, smoking hash slowly became a daily habit and gradually he felt the urge for stronger drugs. Goa had a notorious reputation for sex, drugs and trance parties, and Joy was getting more and more entrenched in the scene.

His mother's treatment was moving at a steady pace. During the days he was home, he would religiously keep a tab on her progress and organize her medicine cabinet for the week and go through his father's paper work for an hour. His interaction with his wife or mother was minimal—nothing beyond basic pleasantries. He noticed that his wife had settled back into the Goan way of life and looked happy. She had since reconnected with all her old friends and family.

But what Joy did love was the house he lived in. It was

a quaint, old, white and blue house with red terracotta tiles lining the roof. The old, Portuguese architecture gave it a picture-perfect charm. It was surrounded by lush green trees, tropical flowers and fruit trees, and had a well. The house was near the sea, so Joy grew up hearing the hum of the waves every waking moment. The spaces were sunny at just the right spots and it was always breezy and cool, even on the hottest days.

The house echoed with memories. For Joy, it was his mother who had turned the house into a home. She sang when she cooked on the old wood stove, and the burning wood and coal lent a musty warm aroma to the kitchen. They both loved to cook together and she had taught him the basics. Joy could rustle up a good meal, if he put his heart into it. Joy's mother also loved listening to the radio as she had her morning coffee. The smell of coffee greeted him when he walked into the kitchen. The house creaked and leaked, but it was filled with memories.

His wife, on the other hand, never really made it feel like home, not since his mother had fallen sick. When his mother had been well, his wife rarely entered the kitchen. Now, she was in-charge and she did things efficiently, but mechanically.

One night, he could feel someone standing beside him, gently nudging him to wake up. It was his mother. She took his hand in hers, like she used to when he was a young boy, and walked with him to the porch. The night air was cool and the sky was clear. The moonlight lit up everything, including his mother's face and she looked like a beautiful, ethereal elf. In her gentle, steady voice she told Joy that she knew her time was coming, but would always be by his side and still believed that there was good in him. She was confused about the distance that had crept in between them, and it was breaking her heart because she did not know whether it was her fault. But she would like it if they made peace now, since she loved him so much.

She reached out and took him into a gentle embrace and he remained there for a while. She whispered that he had made a tough choice when he had decided to create a new life for himself in Goa. She was so thankful that he decided to stay back to look after her. She had feared that she would die alone, but his action had given her strength. She told him that once her time came, he should do what he wanted to do. She prayed every day that he never stopped dreaming, creating and aligning with his dreams.

Joy decided to mend his ways and move back to Galgibaga. The move back home was easy in an odd sort of way. After a week or so of spreading the word around, he managed to buy a popular shack in Galgibaga. The owner was a German man who had decided to move back to his country. A deal was struck between the two of them and Joy became the owner of a shack within two weeks of moving back home.

After a few weeks of taking over his new business, Joy realized why the German was so desperate to move out of Galgibaga and get rid of the shack. Many locals, with the backing of an environment and marine conservation non-profit, had started to harass him. Their major complaint was that the shack was way too close to the beach.

He fought and resisted all their efforts to shut him down. He enrolled his wife and his cousin to help him with the food and to decorate the shack. He started using the internet to promote his business, and soon tourists started visiting his shack. He was making Galgibaga famous, but no one around him wanted that to happen.

> 'Don't we all, at some point, feel the world does not understand us? We start to develop a few core beliefs that become our reality. Joy believed that he was all alone and slowly, he was growing more and more alienated from the world around him. But this loneliness is an important step because it's only in moments like these that we are pushed to know our true selves.'

One overcast, windy morning, his mother did not wake up. He should have known that she had left him because he woke up with a terrible feeling in the pit of his stomach.

He sat in her chair on the porch for quite a while, and not a tear rolled down his cheek. His mind was blank. He felt as if a he had lost a part of himself. He was distressed, fearful and wanted to scream. Joy felt that the hole within him had widened. He wondered how he would get through life without her.

A big wave rocked his boat and Joy was instantly transported to his current situation. He was still out at the sea and had to collect potable water.

Joy got busy collecting the dew. He found small pockets of water on the tarp and he collected a few sips, but that was not enough. He needed more water to survive. He felt like taking a swim and washing his clothes. He stripped and jumped into the ocean, but he was weak and could not swim for too long. His head still hurt and felt heavy. His skin was very sensitive to the salt water, and he felt as if he was on fire. He quickly got back into the boat.

Ollie surfaced and Joy leaned over and petted him. Ollie could sense that Joy was not well. Joy probably wanted water. He saw that Joy's skin was raw, red and spotted. How was he going to get water for his friend? *What could heal his wounds?* The raven had told him that land dwellers drank water without salt in it. When Joy got on to the boat, Ollie dived down into the sea. As he swam deeper towards the ocean floor, he saw a large patch of weeds swaying gently in the current. He was slowly gliding along the patch, lost in thought, wondering what he could find for Joy. He did not realize that one of his front flippers had gotten entangled in the weeds. As he tried freeing himself, he saw a fluttering, yellow, reddish and brown cloud emerging from the weeds. The cloud was suspended over the weeds, like an apparition.

Ollie soon realized that the apparition was actually a bunch of leafy, sea dragons who fluttered and swayed gracefully in the water. The grand old crab lady had often told him the story of a beautiful, small seahorse who wanted to dance gracefully with the currents. She often got so engrossed while dancing to the song of the ocean and its currents that she forgot about being careful. Her friends warned her about the danger. But the only way she could feel happy was through her dance. So she danced where no one saw her. Hiding in the reefs, or the weeds, she would sway with them, even sleep in them. One day, her faithful friends, the kelp and seaweed, decided to give her a part of their spirit essence. They believed that the sea world needed to see her dance in all her glory. So one morning, when she woke up, she found that she had grown leaf-like appendages and had fin-shaped wings. She twirled, swayed and swirled with glee, and as she danced, she became more beautiful and colourful. She earned purple stripes and red dots that were sprinkled like stardust across her weedy wings and body. Now she was called the leafy sea dragon.

Ollie had seen many leafy sea dragons during his trips and normally, they were found in pairs. Here he could easily count more than fifteen 'leafies'—as they were known in the sea world.

One of them turned towards Ollie and asked in a very playful voice, 'Are you the turtle with the human?'

Ollie nodded.

There was instant jubilation among the leafies.

'Finally, you have arrived!' said a smaller leafie. 'We have been waiting for you. We specially curated this cloud act to catch your attention. It was as if everyone but you had seen our performance. And we had given up all hope of ever meeting you. In fact, Bee had told us to move on by tomorrow if we did not bump into you. But you came and you found us...or did we find you?'

Ollie was a little surprised to hear this. 'Who is Bee?' he asked. The first row of leafy sea dragons moved aside to reveal a leafy sea dragon who was resplendent in her red and purple strips. Her wings were larger, more vibrant and translucent than the others, and the orange dots on her weedy wings glimmered and glowed.

'She is our Queen,' said all the leafies, chorusing.

Ollie wondered if this was the same dancing seahorse the crab lady had spoken of.

The Queen spoke. 'I know that look. You are wondering if I am her!'

Ollie was surprised that Bee was able to read his mind.

'That legend is ancient. Do I look ancient?' she asked.

'No, you don't. You look beautiful,' he said, awkwardly.

She fluttered her eyelashes at Ollie. 'Thank you. I have

been asked by the ocean to help you, as you still have not learnt how to hear the whispers of the ocean spirit.'

'Whispers? I would not hear her even if she screamed at me,' thought Ollie, feeling half-amused and half-confused by what was happening.

'You are made of the ocean, and one day you will hear the ocean spirit. Calm your mind. You always have a choice. You can swim away from the mind or lean back into the confusion that it creates. The moment you distance yourself from the mind, you allow all those upsetting emotions to pass by and you become the observer, not the participant. You watch fear swim by, you watch sadness or anger float by and after that, everything comes from a good, pure space,' Bee said.

Ollie shook his head in wonder. The ocean really had an agenda for him and Joy!

'I need help now, Queen. The human is not well. His skin is red and raw and he is thirsty! Humans don't drink salt water. I am worried. How long can he survive without water? I don't know what to do,' Ollie said.

'Have you tried feeding him sea weed? It's the healthiest source of nutrients that a human can digest and it is a great source of water. It will ease his thirst. But remember, he must have the flat, long, leafy ones that grow between rocks. The thicker, rubbery ones are harder to chew, but he can use those for his wounds. They will heal his skin,' advised Bee.

Ollie wondered how he could get Joy to eat seaweed, let alone wrap it around his wounds. Bee could feel Ollie's worry and confusion.

'You have been chosen to look after this human and help him cross the ocean,' she reminded him.

'The dugong said the same thing to me too! But why me?' asked Ollie.

'Your journey with the human is being watched with great interest by the sea creatures. There must be something special about you...or maybe, you have been chosen because you are an absolute idiot and need to learn a few important lessons in life. So instead of saying "why me" you can say "why not me". Trust the wisdom of the Great One,' she said.

'I like the thought of being slightly special. It may be because I come from the same clutch of eggs that the wise one was born from. Maybe all of my brothers and sisters are special in some way, and some sheen and wisdom of the wise one rubbed off on all of us,' Ollie said in jest and laughed gleefully, with a twinkle in his eye.

Bee smiled gently. The ocean had whispered to her that Ollie was a cute, little lost turtle, but she had not been told that he had such a pure and simple heart that radiated such child-like innocence.

'At the moment, you are like a father figure to the human,' Bee said.

Ollie was amused. He simply could not hold back anymore. Bursting into peals of laughter, he said, 'I can't see myself as a father to anyone, and definitely not to a human. I feel like a child myself most of the time. I still pee myself when I have a nightmare.'

'I could never see myself as a father figure either, but I am one. I know that I am the best father that my babies could ever have,' said a smaller, leafy sea dragon with a spongy tail.

'Bee just lays the eggs. I pocket them and deliver the babies. I am the one who goes through all the discomfort and heartaches once the babies hatch and leave. Then the very next day, I am ready to take the next set of eggs and keep them safe in my tail. Who says a male can't nurture?' the leafy said.

'I can't be a father figure,' Ollie continued to protest.

'Well, Ollie. Right now, in the middle of the ocean, the human is all alone. When I see you worried about his food and wounds, I see genuine concern. So take care of him like you would your own,' Bee said, twirling away.

And as she turned to leave, Ollie asked her cheekily. 'So Bee, are you five hundred years old or just five?'

'That depends on you. Whether you want to believe in magic and old fairy tales or just cold facts.' She winked at Ollie. 'Maybe the weeds and kelp have kept me ageless, who knows?' She laughed as she fluttered away with her tribe of leafies.

4

PERFECT IMPERFECTIONS

The sun was high in the sky. Joy adjusted the oar to raise the plastic tarp that sheltered him from the harsh sun. He tried eating some of the fish he had skinned and dried. After a few bites, he felt sick again, but he forced himself to eat a few morsels of the semi-dried fish.

As he sat under the shelter, his thoughts wandered back to his son. For once, there was not a soul around to see him mourn. He remembered crying when his son had passed away. He had cried for days on end. With every passing month, he had learnt to hold back his tears, he had trained himself to hide his emotions and feelings. Grown men were not meant to cry or show their vulnerability. And then, one day, his tears had dried up. He never shed another tear after that. Now, here out on the sea, the floodgates within opened without any warning. Even the smallest memory was like a trigger. He was crying like a little child. He knew he was a weak man, just like he thought his father had been!

> 'We humans forget to be kind to ourselves. We need to understand that there is a sacredness to our tears. It's a way to honour our fragility as humans and our powerlessness over death. Being human often means we hurt, we break, we feel

lost and sometimes, we feel forsaken by the universe. When we cry over a loved one's death, we are not crying for them. We are shedding tears for ourselves because we don't know how to be without them. We all are beings of light who have decided to wear a human spacesuit to live on earth, and as beings of light we understand death, but as humans, we will cry. So next time when you cry, just let it flow and honour your vulnerability and the love you feel for another. Know that it's okay to not be okay.'

Joy remembered Julian's favourite game, which involved Joy lying next to him on the bed and flipping the sheets over their heads, like a flying carpet. Julian would laugh and giggle, pointing at the cherries printed on the sheet. As the sheet moved in the breeze, it seemed as if it were raining cherries. Then Joy would flip it, again and again and again, just to hear his son laugh.

The day Julian died, Joy was getting late for work. He got into an argument with his wife. He remembered little Julian sitting on his high feeding stool, his wife standing by and feeding him, and all the while, they had fought. The little boy had looked so confused by the loud noises around him.

Just the memory of that morning filled him with pain. 'Will this pain ever cease?' He held his chest and cried. He could not breathe, but the memories continued unabated. When they had all come back home after burying Julian, he had quietly taken out their cherry-dotted play sheet and a tiny shirt belonging to Julian with small boats printed on it. He put them away in the chest that held his own childhood knick-knacks. The trunk held a large part of his childhood and now, it stored a part of his sadness too. Joy was a broken man after his son's death. His life was a haze. He stumbled along every day, wishing he would not wake up the next morning.

Joy decided to shake off the haunting memories and slipped into the water without a thought. The water was warm. The salt stung his wounds, but he was beyond caring. Being in the sea was more healing than lying on the boat. As he went deeper into the ocean, he realized he could hold his breath for longer spells. He then spotted Ollie headed towards him, a string of seaweed trailing around his face, like an old man's moustache. Ollie tried nudging the string of seaweed into Joy's hand. Ollie communicated in strange ways, and the best way to figure things out, Joy now knew, was to wait and watch.

Joy had to swim back to the surface for a gulp of air. He felt a slight tug on his arm. When he tried lifting it, he realized Ollie had managed to wrap the seaweed around his left forearm. The turtle dived back into the ocean, and after a few minutes, emerged with a leaf-like seaweed in his mouth. Ollie swam towards Joy and once he was face to face with this man whom he was supposed to take to Africa, he tried stuffing the seaweed into his mouth. Joy realized that Ollie was trying to feed him. He hesitated a bit, but then he took the seaweed and chewed on it. It tasted like grass. It was not too bad actually, better than eating fish eyes any day. He took another leaf and started to chew on it and, surprisingly, he enjoyed it. There was a mild sweetness to it. Ollie brought some more seaweed up and Joy ate it all hungrily. He soon realized that chewing on the weed had quenched his thirst slightly.

He collected the remaining leaves and swam back towards the boat to munch on later. He was impressed with Ollie's ability to look after him. As he got back on the boat, he looked at his forearm. It was covered with seaweed. He tried chewing on this weed as well, but it was extremely rubbery and tasteless. He spat it out, but he let the cold seaweed remain on his arm.

Ollie was overjoyed when he realized that Joy was ready to follow his lead. He no longer had to struggle to feed him. Joy had surrendered to what was happening. It was a long way across to Africa, but the way things were shaping up, he felt positive about their journey.

Joy decided to settle down for the night. It was slightly chilly that night. The wind was picking up. He took down the oar and ensured that he had created crevices in the tarp to collect morning dew. Joy tapped the surface of the water, calling out to Ollie. When Ollie swam towards him, Joy stroked his head with immense love.

A few hours into the night, Ollie heard the slow rumble of thunder. He swam up towards the surface and he could feel that the currents had become stronger.

Joy woke up with a start as he felt the boat lurching in the currents. He could hear the raindrops pattering on the plastic tarp, and the wind had picked up. He hurriedly got up to secure the tarp. The ocean had started to toss the boat around, and he toppled to the side. As he had seen in movies, it was time to cover the boat with the tarp and tie himself and his belongings down so that they would not be tossed off the boat. He was not going to let life push him around anymore. He was going to take control and do whatever was necessary to live. Under normal circumstances, he would use this situation as an excuse to have a drink. He shook his head to ignore the thought. He would not allow himself to go down that path again. Being alone had helped him become more aware of his patterns.

If he survived this spate of bad weather, he would have clean water to drink. Rain and thunder did not scare him anymore. A shift had taken place within him. He welcomed this gift from the sky gods. He readied himself for the worst. He pulled down the plastic tarp, knotted and strung the ropes, tied things down and secured all that he could. Joy propped the empty bottles, secured them with a piece of rope against the inner edge of the boat, and went under the tarp to wait it out.

The rain was growing more intense with every passing minute. He was also worried for Ollie and remembered his father saying that oceanic creatures swam deeper into the ocean during storms, where it was calmer.

Joy could feel the ocean heave and swell. The boat was swaying and he was swinging along with it. He had to hold on to the side of the boat to prevent himself from rolling around, and his arms were growing tired. He saw the rubbery seaweed lying in a tangled heap. He reached out for it, and then, untangled the string of seaweed and wrapped it under an elevated floorboard and around himself. Then he laid back. It was pouring now and his calves had started to cramp.

He was not surprised that his body was reacting in this manner since he knew he was low on salt. He started to take long, deep breaths, and with every new breath, his tense muscles started to unwind and relax. He felt strangely calm and started to let go of the fear of impending doom. Again, Joy saw himself surrendering and praying.

Ollie was worried about Joy's survival. Normally, when storms started to rumble, sea creatures would swim into deeper waters, but he could not leave Joy.

The undercurrents were strong and Ollie too was

finding it difficult to swim in choppy waters. He needed more information about the weather. The current was pushing him away from Joy. 'Why, Great One! Why was this happening just when everything was beginning to look up?' he thought, feeling frustrated.

> 'Don't we feel that something or the other keeps happening to us all the time? Life feels like a never-ending, broken roller-coaster. We are left to wonder whether we are plain unlucky or if the universe is actually throwing challenges our way? But here is what really happens. When we are on a path of self-discovery, we unlock the door to learning. So the challenges will keep coming, testing your limits, but through them we can polish our emotions and responses. Every incident will give us insight into what needs to be shed, what needs to be unlearnt, which wounds need healing and more. We have a choice to break or recreate ourselves and our lives, so we must choose wisely!'

Ollie descended deeper into the sea. The water was darker here. He could not see clearly, and suddenly, he slammed into a solid, smooth surface. He flipped backwards on impact. He felt disoriented for a few seconds. Then he could faintly see the outline of the huge creature he had crashed into. The last thing he needed was a shark in his life! The shark was fourteen feet long and had a flattened head that extended sideways. Oh, it was a hammerhead shark! The currents were still too strong and Ollie wished he could just roll up into a ball like land tortoises, but sea turtles cannot retreat into their shells.

The hammerheads were known as the gods of the sea. He had heard that humans believed that their ancestors were reincarnated as hammerheads and when they spotted one, they believed that the gods were watching over them.

He was sure to be food for the hammerhead. *He needed to escape!* He quickly turned around and tried to swim away but soon found himself eye to eye with the hammerhead.

The hammerhead watched him intently. Then it spoke. 'You are very quick for someone with three and a half flippers. You know my eyes are such that I have a fantastic view of everything. I can see below and above and miss nothing. But you are good at running away.'

This hammerhead did not seem to be the kind of creature that indulged in small talk. Their voice was deep and strong.

'Swim with me, turtle. I am not a shark that can stay still. I need to keep moving, otherwise I'll die.'

The great hammerhead was talking about his weakness. 'Is this their way of toying with the prey? First, make them feel comfortable and then gobble them up?' Ollie saw two more sharks around. There was a strong possibility that he would end up as food for one these sharks if he wasn't careful and sharp.

'Swim!' The hammerhead commanded.

Ollie obeyed and started swimming next to the shark.

'So you are the one who is crossing the ocean with the human?' asked the hammerhead.

Ollie let out a deep sigh of relief. 'Is this another friend sent by the ocean spirit to help me?' The sharks kept swimming around him in circles. Just looking at them made him feel dizzy.

'Are you here to help me or kill me?' Ollie asked in a shaky voice.

'Turtles don't make for good food, but if I am hungry and there is nothing around, I may eat one. But today I have been told to get you through this storm. But if you are going to act like a wimp, I may just kill you. You have been chosen for a task and you better have the turtle-balls to face the challenge and move ahead without any fear or doubt,' the hammerhead said.

'I have never been on this route before, the sea is different and feels more dangerous and I don't know if Joy's boat will hold up,' said Ollie.

'It's going to pour and rain for a while—as per father sky—and the sea is going to toss the boat around. If Joy falls off the boat, we will help and keep him safe. What are you scared of? It's just a storm,' the hammerhead said.

'I am worried about Joy and also about dying and not being able to get Joy across to Africa because I have been chosen to do that and I'm afraid of failing and disappointing the Great One.' Ollie hung his head. 'Nor am I whole!'

He looked so dejected and small that the hammerhead's heart filled with compassion.

'You need to stop feeling scared about death. You are not a failure! You are a turtle with a big heart, you are receptive and open to learning, that's what I have been told by many sea creatures who have guided you,' the hammerhead said, nudging Ollie gently. 'You know, by now, that you are the chosen one for this journey, so act strong even when you feel fearful, and in time, you will become fearless! You have the ability to turn any weakness of yours into your strength. Your fear of dying makes you cautious, and being cautious is good! Fear of failure makes you more real; it makes you humble, but it also makes you resilient. You have only three and a half flippers, but no one is perfect. Look at me, I have a weird head, a small mouth and humans and sea folk believe that I am the god of the sea. I am what I am, and I swim the oceans with pride. I look different, I feel different because I am different, and that's the beauty of life,' the hammerhead said.

Ollie looked at him, surprised. 'But you are the great hammerhead! You are big and strong and perfect the way you are.'

'Yes, little one, I am! And so are *you*. But the greatest also have weaknesses and imperfections. These we must take in our stride. I cannot rest, but other sharks can rest and breathe on the ocean floor. But I have amazing sensory pores on my head. I can detect and see everything around me. You have your own strengths, even though you have only three and a half good flippers. Have faith, little turtle! Have faith that all will be good, have faith that you are perfect and good. Come, let's go and check on the human.' The hammerhead said as he headed to the surface. The other two sharks and Ollie followed suit.

Ollie saw that Joy had covered the boat well. He too was now impressed by Joy's survival abilities. He had, by now, also realized that he had to really work on his faith. The hammerhead picked up his thoughts.

'Not only faith, you need to work on trust too! Trust in all things around you—in the Great One and also in yourself. You are unique and there is no other like you in this world.' The great hammerhead smiled at Ollie. 'Know that not all big sea creatures want to eat or harm you. You be cautious, but not overtly so. And don't be afraid to take risks. Facing the unexpected builds courage in you.'

'Hammerhead, how can you read my thoughts?' Ollie was inquisitive.

'Well, if you allow yourself, you too can hear all sea creatures and their thoughts. You have to just believe that you can do it and intend to do it. Build a strong muscle of intention in you, and one day, you too will hear the ocean spirit and all creatures.'

The hammerheads then positioned themselves close to the boat and when the boat rocked too much, the sharks steadied it. Ollie stayed close to them.

The night passed, the rain stopped, and at some point, Ollie saw the hammerheads swimming away. He was filled with so much gratitude and knew that the ocean spirit was not going to let him down. They were going to make it across! He had now learnt another thing about himself that made him happy. He didn't mind that he only had three and a half good flippers!

The ocean returned to its gentle rhythm and Joy slipped into a deep sleep. When he woke up, he could feel the peace around him. He realized that he was still encased in seaweed. The weeds had not snapped. They had kept him secured to the floorboards.

When he got out from under the tarp, he saw clear blue skies. He noticed that his skin was less blotchy and angry, especially around the areas that the seaweed had touched his skin. The ocean was calm and his empty bottles were filled to the brim with water.

Finally, he had water!

He drank a few sips and his eyes misted with tears. He could feel water trickle all the way, down his parched throat and into the pit of his stomach. It tasted like sweet nectar! He wanted to gulp down the whole bottle, but it had to last him till the next rains.

He saw Ollie at a distance and he took off his clothes

and jumped into the sea to swim with him.

Ollie was happy to see Joy. He swam around him and nudged him playfully. When he decided to dive to get some more seaweed, he saw Joy following him. Ollie smiled. It was a good sign. The human was getting stronger.

Joy swam back to the surface and floated on his back. It was cool. The sun was out and it looked like a good day!

Then, he felt the all-familiar nudge and he flipped over and saw that Ollie had gotten him more seaweed. He happily took it and chewed on it. After having his fill, he got back into the boat and set about cleaning it. *It was to be his home for god knows how long!*

By mid-afternoon, he had finished cleaning the boat and was hungry. He unfolded the net and threw it over, just as his father had taught him, and after a while, he felt the familiar tug that told him that he had gotten lucky. When he pulled it up, he whooped with happiness. He had caught some fish. He sorted out what he thought he could eat and released the rest of his catch into the sea.

After eating some fish, chewing on seaweed and drinking a few sips of rain water, Joy lay down and a feeling of contentment washed over him. This simple, saltless meal made him happy. Thank god he was not a foodie. He ate because he had to, but remembered that when he was younger, he had relished eating his mother's home-cooked food.

In hindsight, he realized that his childhood was actually not as bad as he had made it out to be. Yes, there were many moments where he thought he had been given a raw deal, but then there were also moments that filled him with warm, happy feelings. He laughed when he remembered how, during his childhood, his mother used to run after him around the dining table, trying to feed him. It was a happy little game between them. At bedtime, she told him stories of his ancestors and of the bird that fell in love with a fish, stories that came alive in his little mind and stayed with him during the day while his father taught him to fish and swim in the sea. When he was young the world was a magical place to live in!

Then one day, when he was five years old, he woke up to some noise and saw his father beating his mother in his drunken state. All that was solid, secure and happy in his life came crumbling down. He started to fear his father and avoided him, and slowly, the fear turned to discontent, and as he grew up, it turned to hate.

The past few days had brought back all his sad memories, all that he thought he had dealt with or buried and forgotten. Sometimes as these memories surfaced, Joy would have a breakthrough, or a breakdown.

> 'Unpleasant memories often take precedence over happy memories. Strangely, the bad ones are easier to remember and hold on to, and we get stuck in a loop. A number of bad memories mesh together and that becomes the theme of our life, our go-to story, one we love to constantly bring up. It becomes our excuse to not do and be what we desire. I realized, after hearing and telling so many stories, that the only way to escape the loop is to use these memories to constructively alter the course of our lives. After all, even in the bad and broken memories, are our biggest life lessons. In them, we are given the clue to the purpose of our lives on earth. Know that their occurrence is not a coincidence. Events like these are meant to propel us towards the greatest and grandest version of ourselves.'

5

A FRIEND INDEED!

As the days rolled by, Joy slept, woke, swam, ate and cried. He had lost count of the days. He had no clue where he was headed and he was clearly lost at sea alone. Well, not exactly alone. He had Ollie with him on this journey. He wondered if it was safe for the turtle to be so far out in the sea? He remembered an activist, Chandrakant, mentioning to him that the turtles were known to be the best navigators of the sea, how they always swam back to the beach where they were born! Maybe Ollie was born in Galgibaga, that's why he must have come to that beach in the first place. That very instant, he decided that he was going to follow Ollie and he was quite sure his turtle would take them back home.

He smiled when he thought of Chandrakant Satoskar and his buddies. He called them the Green Tribune of Galgibaga. They would often contend that Joy was partly responsible for destroying the turtle nesting sites in Galgibaga. They would have such a laugh, if only they knew that it was a turtle that was helping him stay alive now!

Joy and Ollie had gotten into a simple, clean rhythm of living with each other. They would swim twice a day, and Joy could now go deeper into the ocean. His lungs were growing stronger with each dive. He saw the world underwater with clarity. He loved the play of sunlight as it filtered through the layers of water. As he picked up courage and went deeper, it was darker, but the fish were more vibrant and colourful. Sometimes, he bumped into schools of fish and they gleefully played around him. Everything under the water had an intelligent and wise energy and he felt that it was healing him.

He often saw the fish nibble and swallow stray bits of plastic that had travelled far into the ocean and he felt anger well up inside of him. He knew these bits of plastic would not disintegrate or dissolve. They would just bob around, destroying the pristine beautiful ocean and the life in it. He had gotten into the habit of collecting these bits and bobs of man-made garbage and stringing them on the side of the boat, as there was nowhere else he could dump them.

Together, Joy and Ollie braved another spate of bad weather that came within a week of the first one. This time, the storm was mild. Joy had enough seaweed to tie himself to the boat and like the last time, the sky gods gifted him with some more rain water to keep himself hydrated.

Joy had heard people talk about the misery of loneliness and the pleasure of aloneness. It always confused him, as to him, the two were the same. But here, out on the boat, he was coming to understand the difference. He missed people, but he was actually getting to know himself a little better.

He was sure he was on the way to being healthy again. The staple diet of fish and seaweed was doing him good. It felt as if it had cleansed his body of all the toxins and the withdrawal symptoms had tapered off. His long swims in the ocean helped him feel fit. Besides this, he had been detoxifying emotionally too. The painful memories kept surfacing. His tears had not dried but sometimes he also caught himself smiling over some funny incident that happened in the past. He did not feel guilty about cheating on his grief by being happy. It felt slightly okay.

'Some of you must have lost a loved one...' As he scanned the crowd, expecting a reaction, he saw that many of them were nodding in agreement.

'And also, some of you must have felt lonely after losing a loved one and struggled through the nuances of being alone.'

A hand rose at the back of the room. The first thing the storyteller noticed was the woman's sad eyes. She was a petite lady in her early thirties. Even though it was time for a break, he knew he had to give her a chance to speak. 'Is there something you want to share with us?' he asked.

'I must confess, I cannot be happy without feeling guilty after my husband's death. I feel as if I am cheating even if I smile at something mundane. To make matters worse, I feel so lonely and lost without him. At this point, being lonely and being alone feels like one and the same thing, I guess,' she said.

The storyteller nodded. 'I know and understand what you have just said. Many of us experience the loss of love or a loved one. We all grieve. But, you see, grief flows. You can't stop it, you can't remain stagnant in it ever...that is not how it is designed. Grief and loss are meant to wake us from a deep slumber and we are given a chance to recreate our life. Grief peels off layers that need to be shed, layers that are not needed by us anymore as a soul. In this phase, we experience life-altering moments of fear, rage, anxiety, pain, denial, and these feelings come and go. The irony is that we will sometimes feel all these conflicting emotions all at once.

'Ride the wave, allow the emotions and then, a time will come to let them go, to allow your true self to thrive again. For that, we need to laugh and smile, because as humans, we are designed to ascend every day to higher, life-enhancing frequencies. So it's normal and okay to feel sad, but it's not okay to be stagnant in that state.

'Coming to loneliness, know that it is a part and parcel of the grieving process. Loneliness is the beginning of our journey towards aloneness, which is a state of being. It's a space we claim as our own in the universe. Aloneness grounds and centres us; it brings us closer to our mind, body and soul. We will still cry and hurt, but we start to understand the whys! When we live and love from a space of aloneness, we love unconditionally and authentically, and we live with gusto and then, happiness just flows naturally, from the simple act of being a alive. So, don't be scared to feel lonely, to grieve or to be angry. Our loved ones would be so sad if we stopped being happy just because we miss them!'

One morning, Ollie did not join Joy for their early morning swim. Joy wondered if he had gone wandering around to forage for food, since he knew that Ollie would feed during the day and sleep at night. A few hours into the morning, Joy kept tapping against the water, like he always did when he wanted to get the turtle's attention. He called his name many times, he dived into the sea but he saw no sign of Ollie. By mid-afternoon, he started to get worried. Something was definitely wrong.

Joy swam in all directions around the boat and went quite far out into the sea. His arms had started to ache with all the swimming. He swam back to his boat. Finally, early in the evening, he spotted a very large ship at a distance! This was the answer to all his prayers. All these days he had been asking to be rescued and for some human contact. He waved and screamed and then, with the help of the oars, he tried paddling across. As he came closer to the mammoth ship, he saw large fishing nets sunk deep into the ocean. That's when he realized that this was an oversized, commercial fishing trawler. 'What if this was the reason Ollie had disappeared today? He must have sensed danger and headed somewhere deep into the ocean to keep himself safe. Or maybe, he had gotten caught in these nets!' Just the thought of Ollie being in danger galvanized Joy into action. He slowly manoeuvred his boat away from the ship. Then he slipped into the water and swam across to the nets.

His heart broke when he saw thousands of fish, all of different colours and sizes, trapped in the net. Over the past few weeks, he had started to feel an affinity with all sea forms.

He went from net to net, but he could not see Ollie anywhere in the large heaving mass of fish. His lungs were on fire. He had stayed too long under water. He swam to the surface, gulped in air and then, he dived back in and relentlessly kept searching for Ollie.

He knew he had to cut the net to find his friend.

He swam back to his boat, found the knife and secured it tightly around his waist with a rope and swam back to the net. Even though the knife was sharp, cutting the net proved to be quite a task. His fingers started to hurt, but slowly and steadily, his efforts paid off and he managed to cut a small hole. The net unravelled as he pulled it apart and the hole grew wider and wider as the sea creatures burst forth.

Joy was pushed back by their force.

He swam back up to the surface and dived back into the water to find Ollie, but in vain. He made his way back to the boat. By now he was completely out of breath. His heart was heavy as he remembered that his father often mentioned how unsuspecting turtles would get caught in fishing nets and be dragged through the water with no access to the surface air. It caused them to drown. He checked around again. That's when he spotted Ollie in the water.

Joy swam towards Ollie. He immediately saw that Ollie was bleeding profusely. He was cut in several places and his body was unusually cold. Joy rushed to the boat and created a double sling with the rope. He gently put that around Ollie and hauled him up into the boat. He took off his shirt and tried to stop Ollie from bleeding, but the cuts ran too deep. His shirt was soaked in the turtle's blood. He could see Ollie's eyelids had begun to cover his large expressive eyes. Joy's heart started to beat faster as he wondered if this was a sign that Ollie was dying.

He needed to stitch up Ollie's wounds and the only place where he could get that kind of help was on the fishing trawler. He took up his oars and started to paddle furiously towards the trawler. When he reached the mammoth trawler, he tapped the sides with his oar and screamed at the top his lungs. No one came forward, but he kept screaming and shouting. Soon, his throat started to hurt. 'How am I going to get their attention?' he thought. That's when he remembered that his boat had a flare gun with two cartridges. He backed up his boat away from the trawler and took out the flare gun. He fired into the air! The flare burnt a bright red, high up in the sky.

And sure enough, the sailors came out on to the deck and spotted the boat. Joy put down the oar and waved his hands frantically above his head.

'Please help me, I am begging you, please help me,' he shouted.

He paddled his boat closer to the trawler. Suddenly, a rope ladder appeared on the side of the trawler and he saw a man climbing down. He could see the man had slung a gun across one of his shoulders. The man stopped half way down the ladder and asked Joy who he was.

'My name is Joy and I have been lost at sea for the past few weeks along with my pet turtle. My turtle is hurt and may die. We need your help,' pleaded Joy.

'Show me some ID,' the man said.

'I have no ID,' Joy said.

'I need to go back and check with the captain. Show me your turtle,' asked the man. Joy pointed to Ollie. And then, he bent down to check if he was breathing. Ollie opened his eyes when he felt Joy's touch on his head, but Joy knew from the look in Ollie's eyes that time was running out.

He saw that the man had climbed back up and was hauling himself across the ship's railing. The man leaned over and shouted at Joy to wait. Joy waited somewhat patiently. After ten minutes, he saw three men climbing down the ladder. All three were armed. Two of the men slowly dropped into Joy's boat and they started to rummage through the boat's things. Joy was too worried about Ollie to be really bothered by the men who were searching his boat.

One of them saw Ollie bleeding on the floor of the boat. He said, 'The turtle looks quite bad.' Joy could not contain his tears anymore.

He folded his hands and pleaded to the sailor. 'Time is running out for him. Please help me help him. I need to stitch up his wounds, he will bleed to death otherwise. He is the only friend I have in this world. Please don't leave us to die.'

Hearing the desperation in Joy's voice, one of the men walked up to Joy and patted him on the back.

'Don't worry, my friend. This is regular protocol we have to follow. The seas are a war zone at times.' The man seemed to be European; he was short and stocky, with a terrible scar running across his face and an unruly mop of auburn hair that made him look dangerous. But his eyes were kind.

The other two men nodded an affirmative. 'Nothing on the boat looks suspicious, let's just do a body search.' He asked Joy to empty his pockets, which Joy promptly did.

They saw Joy's shirt, now soaked in Ollie's blood lying on the floor of the boat. One of them said, 'You need to get a new one, I guess,' while another flipped out a walkie-talkie and spoke into it. 'This seems like a genuine situation.'

He looked at Joy, smiled and reassured him. 'We will haul up your boat, along with you and your turtle.'

They barked a few instructions into their handsets and then, hooks and ropes were thrown over the side of trawler. The boat was secured and then, one by one, they climbed back up the ladder. Joy could feel his boat swinging and jerking as they slowly made their way up the fishing trawler. When Joy stepped out of his boat and onto the trawler, he felt oddly lost. The floor under his feet felt so solid.

There were a number of people on the deck, watching him. One of them came forward. He seemed to be someone important as he wore a uniform and also because everyone made room for him as he walked.

He smiled at Joy. 'Young man, where are you from?'

'I am from India, Goa. I got lost in a storm.' Joy could see the surprise on the man's face.

'Goa? You have come a long way! You are in the middle of the Indian Ocean now. How many days have you been lost at sea?'

'Many weeks now, I have lost count.' Joy felt disoriented. He would have asked them what day or date it was, but at that moment he did not feel like saying anything; he just wanted them to help Ollie.

'You are lucky to be alive,' said the man.

Joy did not know this, but he looked quite the mess! His skin was peeling, his hair was matted, his shorts were torn and ragged and hanging on his thin frame.

Joy shrugged. 'I really don't know where I am. I lost consciousness when I hit my head. This turtle has been my companion for a while now. He followed me all the way from Galgibaga.'

One of the men who had searched the boat informed the uniformed man that the turtle was badly hurt.

Another distinguished-looking man standing in the crowd, again in uniform, spoke with a French accent. 'That can be looked into.'

Joy was asked to get his turtle down to the infirmary as soon as possible. The man with the auburn mop of hair came forward and helped carry Ollie out of Joy's boat. Then Ollie was taken through a maze of corridors until they all arrived at a door. On the first knock, the door was opened by a man who looked a lot like a mad scientist. He wore round glasses, which made his eyes look larger than they were; he had a face that was all wrinkled and weather-beaten. He wore a doctor's coat.

'Doc, we have an emergency. This is Joy. We found him lost at sea along with his turtle. His turtle needs help, it's almost dying,' the auburn-haired man said.

The doctor looked surprised and indignant. 'Scott, you forget I am a doctor who treats humans!'

'I know, doc! But this sea turtle is quite badly cut up. I guess he needs stitches,' pleaded Scott.

The doctor looked a little doubtful as he took Ollie to the table. 'His cuts are deep. I'll clean out the wounds with clean saline water and then stitch him up. Let's hope for the best.' The doctor's movements were deft and quick. It seemed like he was doing the needful.

'He seems to have lost a lot of blood. I can't remedy that but, if he can survive the next two days, he will live!' he declared in a matter-of-fact voice after he was done.

He asked Scott to fill up a small inflatable dinghy with salt water and put it on the deck and instructed him to place Ollie in it. 'I guess that's the best I can do. Later on, you can try feeding him the stuff turtles like.'

Scott did what the doctor asked. When Ollie was well settled, Scott took Joy to the upper deck and he was introduced to Captain Alain Berger.

'So young man, I guess you are not a pirate after all,' said the captain.

Joy looked at him, puzzled. 'Pirate?' he asked.

'Yes, that's how they operate. The first man pretends to be lost at sea and then the rest follow. Then they try to take over our ship,' explained the captain.

'No, I am not a pirate! I was genuinely lost at sea,' Joy said.

He told the captain his story: how he lost his balance and hurt his head, how he survived the incidents of bad weather, and how one day he found Ollie injured next to his boat. He skipped the part about cutting through their net.

'Okay, young man! We are going all the way up to Madagascar. We can drop you off there, but if you are to stay on the trawler along with your turtle, you will need to earn your board,' the captain said.

Joy smiled with relief and said that he was ready to do anything. Instructions were passed and within half an hour, he was assigned a role in the kitchen. Scott was instructed to escort him and make him comfortable. After an hour or so, Joy was handed two changes of clothes, some basic body care products and bedding. Then, he was shown the cabin that he was to share with two other men from the Philippines. Both the men just grunted an acknowledgement when he was introduced to them.

For the first time in weeks, Joy had access to a mirror. With shock, horror and disbelief he saw himself in the mirror. He could not recognize himself. He set about having a bath and just could not get himself to turn off the shower knob, even after a good twenty minutes. A bath in fresh water felt so good! He finally turned off the shower and slathered body lotion all over his parched skin and when he brushed his teeth, he felt as if he had scraped off layers of plaque. He felt like a new man by the time he wore his new clothes. He looked at himself in the mirror and sighed. He had a long way to go before he would look normal, but this was the best he had felt in weeks.

He made his way to the kitchen for a meal. When they served him soup and some pieces of bread, he was nervous. He was eating cooked food after such a long time. He carefully added a little salt to the soup and hoped his stomach would not revolt. When he took his first sip of soup, the flavours exploded in his mouth. He could taste every spice and vegetable. He feasted on the food.

He asked for a soda instead of the customary wine. His body had detoxed and he was not going down that path again.

He went to the deck to check on Ollie. He saw the turtle lying still at the bottom of the dinghy. Joy gently touched his head and Ollie slowly opened his eyes. Joy sat next to the dinghy, stroked Ollie's head and spoke encouragingly to him. At some point, exhausted, the turtle and man fell asleep. When the first officer was making his last round of the day, he saw Joy fast asleep next to his turtle, his one hand still in the water. The scene warmed his heart. He gently took Joy's hand out of the water, checked on the turtle and arranged for some food for the turtle. He wondered if he should wake Joy, but he decided to let him be next to his turtle. He looked so peaceful.

Over the next few days, Joy was working in the kitchen—washing dishes, peeling garlic and chopping vegetables. During his breaks, he would hurry to check on Ollie, who had started to eat a little by now. He was still not moving around much though.

One day, after a few weeks, Joy saw that the nets he had destroyed to save Ollie were being repaired on a higher deck. He felt terribly guilty as it was going to take the sailors many days to get them mended. Their fishing operations had not stopped, as they had many nets in the hold. He would watch as the nets would be drawn up and the catch of the day would be mercilessly splayed on the deck to be sorted and ice-boxed immediately. He was told by the crew that many countries paid a high price to eat the delicacies of the ocean. He also saw many turtles and other sea creatures trapped in the nets. Many died of suffocation and were thrown overboard because their meat was not in demand. He was happy that he had made a difference at least when he had cut the nets while looking for Ollie.

By now, Ollie was swimming again and was visibly restless. The small dinghy was confining for a turtle who had lived most of his life in the open sea. Joy could see that most of the stitches had naturally dissolved. The doctor would often come by to check on Ollie and, one day, he finally gave him the all-clear sign.

Joy still wanted to go all the way with the ship to their last stop, but he also knew that at some point he would need to release Ollie back into the ocean by himself. Just the thought of being separated from Ollie was extremely painful and sad for him. Joy had permanently taken to sleeping next to the dinghy since the past month. It was difficult to get down and sleep in the lower decks—in a closed room—as he felt extremely claustrophobic. He had received special permission from the captain who was extremely amused by Ollie and Joy's friendship. One such night, when Joy was fast asleep, he dreamt of his father.

Joy's father looked young and happy. He was sitting in his favourite boat and Joy was sitting next to him. Joy felt peace in his father's company and it felt perfectly natural. His father bent down and stroked Ollie who was quietly sitting next to his feet.

'Joy, this turtle needs to be back in the ocean. In it lies salvation,' he said.

Joy looked at his father and nodded. 'I understand, father.'

He was drawn to his father's eyes, they were brimming with love and pure bliss.

Then, Joy woke up! The dream had felt so real. It was still very dark. He checked on Ollie who was circling the dinghy like always. Recently, Ollie's appetite had also taken a slight dip. Perhaps it was a sign that Ollie needed to be back in the waters.

Joy lay on his back, going over his dream. For the first time in his life, he had experienced complete peace with his father. Maybe his father was right, he needed to release the turtle back into the ocean. Madagascar, where the trawler was headed, was way out. Ollie would suffer if he had to live in the dinghy for that long. It would be heartless on his part to keep Ollie trapped like this. But he could not bear the thought of being separated from Ollie. So if Ollie was to be released into the ocean, he would have to go with him.

Joy waited till the first light and went about his job. In the evening, he saw the captain out on the deck and walked up to him.

'Captain Berger, may I please have a word with you?' he asked.

'Yes, Joy, what can I do for you?' asked the captain.

'I think my turtle needs to be let back into the ocean,' Joy informed him.

'Yes, I have been wondering about that too. When will you release him? A wild animal always belongs in its natural habitat.'

'Until they are caught in fishing nets and land up on someone's table.'

The captain smiled. 'What we do may seem like a heartless job, but it does feed our families. There is a worldwide demand for such exotic food. But I have seen that over the years, the balance has been wrecked. We, sailors who love the sea, keep trying our best to maintain the circle of life wherever and whenever possible. We catch some fish, we leave some! We don't fish during breeding season and we know where and when to throw our nets, but many fishing trawlers don't pay attention to the rules,' explained the captain.

Joy nodded. 'I have lived in the ocean with my turtle for a while now, and I have watched his world from close quarters and it is beautiful. It would be a pity to see some of it disappear! Coming back to the point, Captain, I have this urge to leave…along with Ollie. I'll try to make it across to wherever he takes me…or you can guide me to the closest land mass.'

'That's quite brave of you, Joy! But there is a risk. You may get lost again,' the captain said.

'I know that it's a scary idea, but I want to give it a shot. It just feels right,' insisted Joy.

The captain was quiet for a while and said, 'I will not stop you if that's what you want! I'll get your boat equipped and get someone to teach you how to read a map and use a compass.'

'Thank you so much, Captain! I will be indebted to you forever for all that you have done for me.' Joy beamed. Then, he turned around to leave.

'By the way, Joy, I would like to know something before you leave. If you don't want to answer, it's fine. The night you came up on the trawler, we also had a major tear in our nets. I have always felt that Ollie got stuck in one of them and you cut the nets to free him…'

Joy's face turned from red to white.

'You know that your fingers were bleeding that night. They were not just covered with Ollie's blood. You did not realize you were hurt too!' the captain continued.

Joy remembered it. For days his fingers had felt raw and sore. He wore gloves while he worked in the kitchen. Joy looked down at his feet, shuffled them around, and weighed his choices. He could just deny the matter. He was not sure of the consequences of admitting to the truth. But then, Joy decided against it. He decided that it was best to tell the truth to the captain, who was a kind-hearted, good man.

He looked at Captain Berger straight in the eye and said, 'Yes, Captain! I was the one who cut the nets to save Ollie! You see, he is the reason I am alive. I would do anything to save him.'

Captain Berger's face broke into a smile. 'Thank you, Joy, for being honest with me. Not many people have the strength to own up what they have done! I have seen your love for the turtle and I completely understand why you did it. It's okay. Come, let's meet the first officer and put in your request. It will take us a few days to get your boat ready. We would have to repair and equip it first, and then it would be sea-worthy again.'

The next few days were spent fitting Joy's boat out with oars, canned food, a self-sustaining water apparatus that could turn sea water into drinking water, solar charging lights, a diving kit, plenty of clothes, a solar food-plate, air horn, flares, a first-aid and medicine kit, a temporary sail and more. He was also taught to navigate his boat. They threw a party for him on the last night. It felt as if they had all needed an excuse to party. That night, even though Joy was offered alcohol, he kept away from it. It was not an option for him anymore. He had finally cleaned up his act.

The next morning, they lowered Joy's boat into the water, with Ollie and Joy in it. The entire crew leaned over the railings, singing seafaring songs along with a chorus. 'He was a jolly good fellow!' Joy had not expected such a farewell and he was truly grateful to the captain and all the other friends he had made during his short stay on the trawler.

Joy slowly made his way away from the trawler. It was a scary feeling to be out in the ocean all by himself again. He looked back after a while and saw that the trawler was just a small speck in the horizon. He gently picked up Ollie and placed him back into the sea.

Ollie excitedly swam away from the boat. This was absolute heaven for him. Finally, he could swim deep into the ocean, not around in circles, which had made him so dizzy. The other thing that had been driving him completely nuts on the trawler was the smell of death. He knew his sea friends died every time the net was pulled up.

Ollie dived deep into the ocean, floated and swam around, then dozed off for a while. When he woke up, he would swim back to the surface to check on Joy and get his bearings right. He had to take Joy to the east coast of Africa, as soon as possible. As the sun set, he saw Joy settle down to sleep. Ollie floated around the boat and like always he got a few larger fish to help him steer the boat in the correct direction.

For the next few weeks, Ollie could see that Joy was upbeat. Joy, on the other hand, would check the map and the compass. He came to the conclusion that Ollie really knew where he was going, because the direction he was swimming in was on track to the nearest landmass. As the weeks passed, Ollie had started to feel more confident about fulfilling his promise to the ocean. Ollie and Joy had developed a better understanding of each other's ways. Joy did little things that made Ollie realize that Joy had started loving the ocean too.

One day, while they were swimming around, Ollie could feel the wind change and the tug of a strong undercurrent. It made him slightly worried. *'Are we to brave another patch of bad weather?'* He looked at Joy who was happy frolicking around in the water. Lately, Joy had taken to diving deeper into the water. Ollie had to keep an eye on him, as deeper into the sea the water was colder and the fish were bigger. The leafies were right when they told him that he was like a father figure for Joy. Looking after him was a full-time parenting job.

Ollie decided to ask around about the weather. Many of the large schools of fish were oblivious to the change in currents; they were too busy flitting around, making odd shapes in the water. As he went deeper, he came across other fish and sea creatures. When he asked them, they all agreed that there were chances of a massive storm. Some even spoke of an earthquake on the ocean bed. That really worried Ollie. An underwater quake would unleash havoc. *How was Ollie going to keep Joy safe?* He swam to the surface and saw Joy busy cleaning the boat, whistling a happy tune, the breeze was ruffling his hair and he looked younger, healthier and happier since they left the shores of Galgibaga. The human really had no idea of the impending dangers.

He needed to get some help! Over the next two days, Ollie swam around, trying to find a way to save Joy. He bumped into a large school of tuna fish and got caught in their midst. They swirled and whirled around him; he tossed and turned and felt dizzy and nauseous, and at some point, he really needed the joyride to stop. Before he knew it, he was pushed out of the school and it took him a few seconds to get his balance back. By then, the school of tuna fish had queued up to form a shimmering wall in front of him.

'Thank you for the ride, guys. Would you all be kind enough to help me with some information?' Ollie asked.

'Sure!' They all spoke in a chorus. 'What can we do for you?'

'I just want to know if it is true that there is going to be a big storm soon.'

From the shimmering wall, out popped the smallest fish, and when he spoke, Ollie knew that the little one was wiser than his size.

'This storm is going to be one of its kind!'

The little squiggling tuna had just confirmed his worst fears.

Ollie was now rattled. 'I have a human friend on the boat, and I need to keep him safe. He is not the best seafarer,' he said.

The wise, little tuna spoke. 'We can't help you save your friend. But there is an ancient one who lives deep down in the ocean. We see him when he emerges to breathe, he is called the Great White. He has lived for eons in these waters and has been hunted for years by the humans for his colour, but he has outwitted them all because of his sheer size, wisdom and speed. He is gifted with the sight and always has a solution for us sea creatures who live in and around this area. Find him and maybe, he can help. But hurry, the storm is approaching.'

'How will I know who he is?' asked Ollie.

'He has seven deep slashes across his body. They have been made by harpoons and nets, and like I said, he is the largest and grandest of his species. You will know it when you meet him,' the little tuna assured Ollie.

He thanked the school of tuna and quickly swam up to the surface. He wanted to check on Joy.

'Ollie! Where do you keep disappearing to? You have been acting strange!' Joy said as he patted Ollie's head. 'Now please stay with me.'

Ollie understood Joy's words and stayed close to the boat. Joy settled down for the night and that's when Ollie dived deep into the sea to find the legendary Great White.

As he swam deeper, the waters were quite dark and murky. There were fewer fish around, but the ones he asked pointed him further down, deeper into the belly of the ocean. The pressure of the water on his shell was getting to him now. Turtles rarely ventured so deep into the waters. He was slightly breathless and was not sure if he could go down any deeper. He kept stopping, trying to recover. Everything looked eerie. That's when he saw a shimmering light that glowed in the dark like a beacon.

'Light? So deep down in the ocean?' As he swam closer, he realized that it was a lantern fish, a deep-sea fish that glowed. Ollie enquired about the Great White and the lantern fish signalled for Ollie to follow him. They swam for a kilometre or so. Ollie was really not feeling well, but his determination to save Joy was motivating him onward.

A Friend Indeed! ▪ 87

Pointing towards a spot at some distance, the lantern fish said, 'He is resting at the back of those weeds. Please don't startle him, he has not been in the best of moods these days.'

Ollie was now a bit worried for himself. All the big creatures ate small ones when they were hungry. As he swam towards the Great White, he said a little prayer. When he turned around the seaweeds, he saw, right there in front of him, the biggest sperm whale that he had ever laid eyes on. He was, like his name, stark white!

Ollie swam closer. He spoke in a shaky voice. 'Sir! Excuse me, sir! Can I please talk to you?'

There was no response or movement. Ollie's survival instincts kicked in. He wanted to run. He could feel his heart beating. He felt like such an idiot, putting himself in such grave danger. If the Great White did not kill him, the water pressure on his shell would!

He swam closer and tried his luck again. 'Excuse me, sir! I need your help,' he said loudly.

This time, the Great White opened his eyes, stared at Ollie and in a voice that sounded like it came from somewhere deep in the ocean, enquired. 'What do you want? Can't you see I am sleeping?'

Ollie now gathered his courage. 'Sir, sorry to disturb you, but I need your help! There is a great storm brewing and I have a human friend on a small boat who has no clue about the storm. I have also learnt that there are chances of an undersea earthquake, which can lead to a tsunami.'

Ollie had partially managed to get the attention of the Great White.

'Hmm! How did you and a human get to be friends in the first place?' he asked. 'I understand that you are a part of the sea, but humans are designed to love and also give grief to the ones they befriend. They are a confused species, I hope you know that.'

'Yes, I agree, but being with this human I have also realized that they are not as daft or bad as we think they are. They hurt, they cry, they are quite lost and clueless. They think they know everything and they believe they are the intelligent species. They can be selfish at times, but I also see possibilities. I see love,' Ollie said.

Ollie then told him their story, but he had to keep it brief. He was short of breath, and he felt like his heart was skipping a beat. Or was it slowing down? Perhaps it was out of sheer fright of being so close to the Great White.

'Are you okay, little fellow?' enquired the Great White.

'No, I am not. Actually, I am feeling really sick. But you see, I made a promise to the ocean spirit to take the human across to the east coast of Africa. We have come this far and have been doing quite well. I had hoped that we would reach our destination in a few days but with this unexpected weather situation cropping up, I now am not sure.' Ollie suddenly realized that everything was slowly becoming hazy around him.

'You need to go up and take a gulp of air!' said the Great White.

'I'll go if you assure me of your help!' insisted Ollie.

'I really don't know how I can help you! We cannot stow him anywhere on the surface of the ocean, nor can he live underwater! Why is it so important for you to save him?' asked the Great White.

Ollie now spoke with complete clarity and conviction. 'He is my friend! I have really understood the meaning and essence of friendship over the past few days. We can live in isolation, but it's not required. Loving another is a wonderful experience. The other does not have to be perfect. They can be whoever they are supposed to be. With them in our lives, we get to become wonderful. I have learnt about the emotion called love. It's so powerful that it can make you do anything to keep your loved ones safe, even if it means giving up on your own life. I will be ever so grateful to you, if you can help me.'

The Great White now took a good look at the little turtle in front of him. The sea creatures had made many requests before but this one had to be the rarest and the most touching.

'I can't promise you much, neither am I going to refuse your request! Let me think, maybe I'll come up with something!' said the Great White.

'I am so grateful to you for even considering my request.' By now Ollie was slurring. Slowly, everything started to darken around him and then, everything went blank.

The Great White saw Ollie pass out and he shook his head. The human must be important to the little chap for him to swim all the way down and put his life at stake! Slowly, he lumbered out of his resting space and very gently picked Ollie up in his mouth and swam upwards. When he broke through the surface, he released Ollie's unconscious body. He saw a boat swaying gently in the water at some distance. *'This must be the turtle's friend!'*

He saw the size of the boat and knew that there was no way the human would be able to survive the storm that was approaching. He had to do something! All the sea creatures approached him when they were in trouble and he was responsible for all of them; he maintained the equilibrium. All his kind were the ancient ones, the keepers of the secrets of the ocean, the stars and the universe. This little chap really needed his help. He had heard the love, sincerity and hope in the turtle's voice. Over time, the Great White had lost touch with the purity and intensity of this emotion. The ocean spirit had most likely sent this turtle to remind him of it.

A sudden burst of air rushed through Ollie's nostrils and it brought him back to life. He greedily took deep breaths and realized that he was alive and not below the ocean any longer. As his eyes were able to focus, he saw the Great White dive back in and swim away. He did not get a chance to thank him, and in any case, all he wanted to do was rest and conserve his energy. Tough times were ahead. And he needed to be fit.

The next day, he could feel that the currents were becoming stronger and the wind was slowly picking up. By mid-afternoon, he saw the sky darken to a steel grey. He swam closer to the boat; he could see that Joy was worried and busy preparing the boat and himself for the storm like he had done earlier but this time he had more stuff to keep secure.

Lightning streaked across the sky and it started drizzling. Ollie wondered whether the Great White had come up with a plan to save Joy, but there was no sign of him! Ollie just needed to stay close to the boat throughout the storm. But this would be a daunting task because the ocean would definitely toss him around. In any case, this was the best idea he had. As the hours went by, the rain came lashing down. It poured and poured, and the ocean became dangerously rough, like he had never seen before.

Ollie knew this was only the beginning, it was going to get worse. The water was rippling in a different manner.

The waves were mammoth-like in size and then, he heard the ocean rumble and growl. Ollie trembled with fear. The plates of the earth under the ocean had begun to move. And then, he saw the Great White emerge out of the water. Ollie was relieved. The Great White had kept his promise. He had come to save Joy!

He wondered if he should swim to the Great White to discuss their plan of action.

He saw that the Great White had come dangerously close to the boat. The whale flipped and twirled in the air. He knew then that the plans did not involve saving Joy! The waves were already high, and the splash that the whale created was just too large for the boat to remain steady. The boat flipped over. The whale flipped again, and this time the sheer force of the wave split the boat into two!

Ollie's heart sank. Joy was going to die! Ollie tried to rush forward. His mind was racing in all directions. 'How is he going to keep Joy safe now? Is this the Great White's plan? What is the water giant thinking? I had asked him to save Joy, not drown him!' The Great White caught Joy in his mouth and dragged him down underwater. Ollie tried following them but the Great White moved with such speed that Ollie lost sight of both of them.

The ocean heaved, moaned and groaned. The wind was screeching all around him, but Ollie felt a different storm brewing inside of him. He was filled with guilt and despair! He knew, in some odd way, that he was responsible for what had happened just now.

The water was churning around him. He needed to swim to safety, but he did not want to live anymore. He was cursing himself for being the idiot who had just gotten his friend killed.

An old man, sitting crossed legged in the aisle, raised his hand. 'I want to know what one can do about the guilt of being the cause of the death of a loved one. I think…in some way…I was responsible for my wife's death and it haunts me. I think I know how Ollie feels.'

He slowly drew his knees up to his chest and buried his head in his hands.

The storyteller walked up to the man and placed his hand on his shoulders and gave him a reassuring squeeze.

'It is normal to feel this way when we focus our anger on ourselves as we grieve over a loss. We feel guilty about having failed to protect our loved ones and regret taking wrong decisions. We feel angry about being unprepared and not being able to control the inevitability of the end. Ancient wisdom says that guilt and regret are two different experiences. Guilt keeps us in bondage and isolates us, while regret keeps us in the past. Both emotions are necessary. In the dark moments of the soul, we start our search for the truth. These moments help us introspect about what went wrong, what was humanly and realistically possible and what was not, and also our emotional response to it.

'It is also a great example of how critical we are of ourselves and our weaknesses. Are we kind to ourselves when we make mistakes? Do we love ourselves enough to forgive ourselves? I have come to understand that we need to use the guilt and regret as a tool. You are not responsible for anyone's death. It was meant to be! You just played a crucial role in it becoming a reality for another, and you also learned a few life lessons in the process.'

He stroked the old man's head gently.

'And I now want you to surrender your pain to the great creator and ask for healing. Trust and know that the universal energy will send people and situations, and direct you to be in places that will heal you. Trust in miracles that will heal us because we all deserve to be happy!'

The old man seemed to have found some comfort in these words. With the storyteller by his side, a sense of calm descended on him. Feeling reassured, the storyteller took a few steps back and turned to his audience. 'Lets take a short break,' he said and then walked out of the stage.

6

A VISION

The storyteller returned, looking rejuvenated. He had clearly washed his face and tidied his hair. He took a few sips of water, cleared his throat, smiled at his audience and continued the story.

The tall Maasai stood in the shade of the palm trees. He was in two minds. He kept wondering whether he should wait for a few more days. He was tired of waiting around by the beach. Over the past few days, boredom had been winning this waiting game. Every day was the same. He saw nothing unusual around him. Even if he left to get a drink or some food at a nearby shack, he would hurry back, worried that he had missed what the sea had to bring forth for his tribe.

Almost a week had passed since Olamayian had arrived at Paje, a small sea-side fishing village on the east coast of Zanzibar. It was breezy and bright on the beach during the day. The sun reflected off the white sandy beach, hurting his eyes as he scanned the length and width of the shore ever so often.

In the beginning, everything had seemed new and entertaining. The Maasai hawker boys who walked up and down the beach, all dressed up in their traditional finery. At first, they had all looked so handsome and enigmatic against the backdrop of white sand and turquoise green waters with their colourful, bright, cotton shukas wrapped around their body and adorned with traditional Maasai jewellery. But they just had to spoil it by wearing cheap, shimmery, metal-rimmed, dark glasses and, worst of all, they had started to give up their cowhide sandals for synthetic shoes made in factories.

Olamayian felt as if these boys were lost between two worlds. They strutted around like peacocks to make a quick buck. They loved being photographed by the foreigners for a price and were getting a bad name for harassing people for a few extra shillings. They sold trinkets and Maasai jewellery that their women would have spent hours making, but very rarely did they share the money with the women.

He felt sad for his people and began to understand the driving force behind his father's vision and the tireless efforts he was making to bring in the next era. They were Maasais: proud warriors, nomads and pastoralists. Their ancestors held their power in their uniqueness; they followed a simple way of life. Maybe some of their customs seemed uncivilized to the rest of the world, but that's what made them who they were. Holding on to their core values and their essence was becoming increasingly essential. He feared that all was lost in the new world that was appearing around them.

Urbanization was good in so many ways, but it had its evils too. Olamayian realized he was overthinking and getting too philosophical again. What he needed the most now was to go back to his boma, the simplicity of village life, the smell of cattle, his bed. He missed the company of his brothers and the other warriors. He missed the face of his woman. She was so beautiful, so gentle and she loved him. But he also knew he could not disappoint his father!

Olamayian did not know if he was even at the right spot, but he had to trust himself, and also the vision he had had recently. In his vision, Olamayian had seen two palm trees and a turtle sitting between them. He had found the two palm trees growing side by side. Now all he needed was for a huge turtle to walk out of the sea to make all this waiting worthwhile.

Olamayian loved and respected his father way too much. He followed him blindly because he believed, like the rest of the village, that his father, Sironka, had the vision. His father was known as the pure one, the village laibon, the most respected village elder, the high priest, the chief diviner and medicine man. His father had recently had a vision and his instructions were very clear. Olamayian had been specially chosen to go to Paje and wait for the sea to wash up an offering and he was to bring that offering back to their tribe.

Olamayian was not that sure about his own vision. He had seen a turtle and that baffled him a bit. 'How can I take a turtle back to my tribe?' The turtle needed the sea to survive and there was no sea anywhere near where he lived. It would be sad if the turtle died away from its natural habitat.

He had not dared to ask his father for some more insight, clues or clarity about his mission; it always came across the wrong way. He just wished his father would be more forthcoming with information. When he went to meet his father, the night before he had left, he had tried one last time, but the old man was silent. He stared at him with his cold, dark beady eyes. Olamayian wanted to kick himself! He should have requested his mother ask his father; she always knew how to get around the old man.

Naserian was his father's first wife. She was not Olamayian's birth mother, but that did not stop her from loving Olamayian and his sister like her own. His father respected Naserian very much and he knew his father would not deny his mother's request. He always felt that his two younger half-brothers were spoilt and he often wondered why he was the one being always put to the test.

He remembered his father's words before they had parted that night. 'Olamayian, if you have the slightest desire to carry on the tradition and be the laibon you are destined to be, then instead of asking me for clues, try to use this as an opportunity to see how you can go inwards and ask Enkai, the powerful knowing one, to guide you and give you a vision. Why do you seek to be spoon-fed by me always?' And with this, his father had gotten up and walked away to his boma, where he lived with his third wife.

Sironka left his sandals outside his boma and went to check on his wife. She was fast asleep. He was still angry with Olamayian. He had told his son repeatedly that he needed to build his intuition. The intuition was like a muscle—the more he exercised it, the more clarity he would have. He had told him to journey within himself, connect to his higher self—his inner voice, to the truth—but the boy always doubted his own abilities and gifts. Sironka already knew what the ocean was going to bring to their village, but he wanted his son to own and seek his visions and follow them.

He missed Lena on such occasions. Lena was his second wife and the mother of his eldest son, Olamayian. She had been his one true love and had passed away many years ago. Their love was strong and wholesome. He would often dream of crossing over the three worlds to be with her, but he knew it was not yet his time as he still had not finished what he was born to do.

Sironka also knew that he had been chosen by the Great Spirit for yet another mission, one that would come from the sea. But it did not make any sense to him. 'Why him?' he thought. He already had his plate full. But it was best not to question the wisdom of the creator. The story had yet to unfold.

Sironka was tall, elegant, well-spoken, knowledgeable, wise and respected by all for his foresight and passion to be the change. He was spearheading a powerful movement, along with the government of Tanzania, and many international and national non-governmental organizations, to integrate the Maasai into a conservation project—as they were the original custodians of the forest and its animals. He had managed to unite all the different Maasai communities and convinced them to come together and fight for their rights and identity.

He attributed his forward-thinking to the exposure he had received while being married to Lena. She taught him about the world outside, which had then sounded so much more civilized than his own. But Lena always pointed out the aspects that made the Maasai so special. She always spoke about how the world needed to know more about the Maasai way of life, their inter-connectedness with nature, and with each other. She had hoped that someday, the misconceptions that surrounded them could be wiped away. She respected his family and culture and followed so many of his traditions. They used to talk during the night about how they hoped to see the emergence of a new world.

Lena was also one of the most outspoken women Sironka had ever met. She was not liked by some of the elders and the women of the tribe, but was loved by his mother, who stood by her and supported her always. The village elders often told him to get a third, younger and healthier wife, but he loved Lena.

Lena was not from his land but from a country called England. She was fair, beautiful, gentle and kind. She had eyes as blue as the kingfisher's feathers. She had hair like the rays of the sun, and was way wiser than him. He had met her as a young Maasai warrior when she and her family had come to Tanzania for a holiday. It was love at first sight for both of them. She had stayed back against her family's wishes, and they had married and had two children. But she succumbed during the birth of their daughter, Nalangu.

With every passing year, she became frail and constant bouts of malaria had started to wreak havoc on her health. When she gave birth to their daughter, her body could not take it anymore. Lack of proper medical attention and a weak immunity led to her death while she was birthing her child. She called out to Sironka many times during her last night at the hospital. He could hear her cry, and he kept asking the nurses if he could be with her. But they would not let him. In the early hours of the morning, they handed him his daughter and informed him about Lena's death.

That was the turning point in Sironka's life. He was heartbroken and wished he would drop dead, but that was not to be. He also knew that he had no right to take his own life. That was not how things were done by the living. If he died this way, he would not have the privilege of being an ancestor for his children or the tribe, nor would he be united with Lena in the after world. He would remain suspended in perpetual darkness. So he decided to find a way to live without her.

While she was alive, Lena had often spoken to him about her dreams for their daughter. When he sat outside the hospital, waiting for them to release her body, he made a promise to her spirit that he would help create a new future and hope for his people, especially for their daughter and the many other Maasai daughters of the tribe. But before he could create something, he needed to first get away from everything to mourn and grieve his loss.

The elders of the tribe urged him to find another wife, but all he wanted in his life at that point had been silence. And after a month or so, he left his tribe and roamed the land. Sometimes, he was spotted by other tribesmen in the bush, sitting quietly under the shade of a tree, surrounded by animals. He slept under the stars, walked with the lions, ate off the land. The sun, the earth, the breeze and the animals were his constant companions. They were his healers and teachers.

He slowly began to connect the dots. The one who created the universe—the powerful one, the womb of the wild—had showed him the truth. Spiritual teachers appeared to him in visions, helping him understand his purpose in life and the secrets of ascension. He was the map-maker, the bringer of light for generations to come. He was responsible for heralding the change and Lena's death was no coincidence.

Meanwhile, back in the boma, the village elders of his tribe asked his first wife to look after his two children. Naserian was happy to do so, as Sironka had always been kind to her, even though she was unable to bear any children. He looked after her, giving her all the respect of being his first wife, even though he had married a white lady.

After several months, Sironka came back to his tribe but he was a different man. He seemed wiser beyond his years, and slowly everyone had started to acknowledge his powers.

When he started to talk about his plans and about changing some of their ways, he was faced with a lot of resistance. Sironka soon realized that the Maasai elders needed more time to understand that change and death were the only constant in life. He needed to be patient, so he started with his children and taught them to think, to be different. He was a very hands-on father, which was rare among the Maasai men. Most fathers believed that they were only responsible when it came to protecting, finding food and grazing the animals and the women looked after the children, cooked and built their homes.

Sironka married again after his wanderings. His mother, who was still alive, felt that marriage would have a grounding effect on him. Maasai men were allowed to marry many times, the one condition being that they had to provide for all their wives and children. Each woman had her own enkaji, where she lived along with her children. The wealth and status of Maasai men was measured in the number of children and cattle they had. When Namelok was chosen to be his third wife, he sought permission to talk to her; he wanted it to be her choice. He felt she needed to know who she was getting married to. Maasai women usually never had a choice. Their fathers chose the man they were to be married off to and they were traded like cattle. When he met her, he was taken aback by how young and beautiful she was, and he wondered why such a beautiful, young girl would want to marry a middle-aged man like him. He sat down near her and told her about Lena, his work, why he was doing what he was doing, how his heart was not in marriage, that she could refuse to marry him if she did not want to be a part of his life and that he would handle everything with her family.

She patiently listened to him. When he had finished speaking, she slowly looked up at him, her eyes glistening with unshed tears, and in a very sweet and clear voice, she told him that she felt very honoured to marry a man like him and bear him children. He was a wise man with a good and pure heart, and deep down she knew he would respect her, look after her, and that their children would be brought up with good values and insights. She felt he would help her grow into a strong, empowered woman. She hesitantly told him that she had the secret desire to read and study and she knew no other man would allow her this freedom.

Sironka was stumped by this young girl's clarity. He spent the night under the sky and stars, he spoke to Lena, he spoke to his ancestors and the next morning, he told her family that he would marry Namelok. But marriage changed nothing much. He would still take off for days into the wild. In the past few years, he had been constantly on the road, meeting people from different government bodies and other tribes. He was a man on a mission. With frequent exposure to the Western world, Sironka realized that in many parts of the world, women had equal rights. He really wished that the Maasai women would also be given respect and freedom. Every human should have the choice to marry whoever they want; and likewise they should also have the liberty to leave, or stay, if they felt like it.

When his daughter, Nalangu, turned thirteen, he sent her across to the missionary school, a few villages away. Naserian accompanied her to look after her. Father Frances and the nuns took good care of her. She had grown up to be a beautiful woman and was now a teacher at the missionary school. He was proud of all his children, especially Olamayian, who had grown up to be a fine man and was going to make an excellent leader for the tribe someday.

Back at Paje, Olamayian was feeling worried and anxious. He had made his bed under the makeshift shelter. It had been raining for the past two days, and the sea was at its roughest tonight. A raging storm had sent everyone scuttling to safety. As he settled down for the night, he prayed for the safety of all creatures in the sea. At some point, early in the morning, he woke up with a start. The rain had stopped. He lay there, trying to gather his thoughts. And then he felt the urge to get out of bed and go for a walk on the beach. He did exactly that. With time and practice, he could distinguish between his voice and a much wiser, stronger voice in his head. His father called it the voice of knowing.

He wrapped his shuka around him, wore his sandals, and walked towards the spot where he spent most of his days. He sat down, leaned against the bark of the palm tree and watched the sea. It was calmer but darker than usual. The sky was getting ready to light up. The slight breeze and the hum of the waves made him sleepy. He must have dozed off because he woke up to the sound of birds chirping in the distance. The sun was rising. It promised to be a beautiful morning.

He rubbed his eyes and stretched, and that's when he saw the turtle! *Was he dreaming or was it real?*

Yes, it was a turtle. It was trying to pull seaweed off a large log washed up by the sea. Olamayian felt so elated that his vision had come true! He whooped and jumped around with excitement and broke out into a song. His father would be so proud of him; he was so proud of himself! Maybe his father was right. He too had the sight and he needed to stop doubting his abilities. He walked carefully towards the turtle. He did not want to scare him back into the sea. 'What am I supposed to do? Am I supposed to help the turtle or capture him?' But when he saw how engrossed the turtle was in getting the seaweed off the log, he decided to help.

As he bent over the log and tried pulling off the slimy weed, he stepped back, shocked. The log twitched and heaved. Under all that weed, something was still alive. A sea creature perhaps. It was still breathing, so he carefully started to yank the weed off with all his might. He was amazed when he saw a human face emerging.

It was a man!

He worked harder now to take off the seaweed from the man's body. When the last of the weeds came off, he bent down to check on the man who was ice cold. His lips were blue. Olamayian pumped the man's chest and water started to gurgle out of his mouth. He slapped his face, thumped his back and decided to give him mouth-to-mouth resuscitation. Still the man lay motionless.

The turtle had not left, and was still next to the man. Olamayian wondered whether the turtle was just curious or if it was trying to help the man?

The young Maasai wondered if it was too late for the human. By now, the turtle was next to the man's head, trying to nudge him awake! *'This is interesting.'* The man and turtle seemed to have a connection because when he looked into the eyes of the turtle, he swore he could see despair. This pushed the young Maasai to try again, and he wasted no time and pumped the man's chest. Finally, some more water gurgled out and that's when the man started to cough and weakly opened his eyes.

His eyes were light in colour and his skin was dark, but not as dark as his. The man lay still; only his eyes moved. He tried sitting up but could not. He noticed the turtle and immediately reached out to pat the creature. The turtle inched himself up, as close as possible, to the man as if wanting to impart some of his strength. The man struggled to sit up and when he did, he vomited the last of the bile and water he had in his gut. He looked around, touching and curling his hand into the sand.

He looked at Olamayian and smiled a weak smile and then, he turned to watch the sea.

The sun was up by now. The hawker boys had come closer to look at the three of them and were trying to poke and prod the turtle. This worried the sea-washed man; he crawled on all fours and reached the turtle and whispered something. He then struggled to get up and he reached out to Olamayian for help. Olamayian helped the man to his feet. The man swayed and stumbled, but he kept walking towards the sea. The turtle followed him. The young Maasai watched in horror as the man walked back into the water along with the turtle. This man seemed to be on a mission to kill himself!

Olamayian ran into the water to find the man. After a few minutes, the man's head bobbed up at a distance. The young Maasai swam to him and pulled him back on to the beach. This time, the turtle was nowhere in sight. *'So he was just trying to keep his turtle safe!'* He now lay sprawled on the beach, and again smiled at the young Maasai in gratitude. Then he passed out.

Olamayian carried the man to his makeshift shelter. He did not know his name, so he decided to call him the turtle man. The turtle man needed food. He needed to rest and recover. He lay the turtle man down gently on the reed mat. He wondered at how the man had managed to get himself wrapped up so tightly, like a parcel, in those slimy weeds. On second thought, the weeds had a really thick layer of mucous on them. That too was odd! He wondered whether the turtle had done this to him. He shook his head. It did not make any sense, but at this point all that mattered was that he had to keep the turtle man alive.

The Maasai cleaned the man like he would for a baby. He took off his wet clothes, sponged his body clean, tried to comb his matted hair, and then, he wrapped a red shuka around him. He was filled with so many questions. 'Is he a fisherman who got lost at sea, or a tourist who fell overboard after a party?' He was eager to know this man's story. His father often said that all humans have stories that can alter our reality for a lifetime.

The turtle man must be special. He had survived raging storms and the sea had not killed him. The young Maasai hoped he spoke English, else it would be very difficult to communicate. Olamayian had gone to the missionary school when he turned eight. His father was insistent that he learned everything from language to history and literature, and be a man who could walk in the world with his head held high. He was so glad that he took his father's advice because now he was a university graduate. He could communicate with the foreigners as well as he could with his people, on any subject.

The young Maasai allowed the turtle man to sleep off his exhaustion and managed to feed him at regular intervals to keep him nourished. He would leave the man's side in the evenings to take a long walk along the beach. That's when he noticed that the turtle with three flippers emerged from the sea late in the evenings every day, slowly walking the beach searching for his friend. When he did not find his friend, he would slip back into the ocean. Olamayian's heart went out to the turtle. He had seen this sort of connection and loyalty in the case of domestic animals, but not in the wild. He was certain that this turtle needed to see his friend to be reassured.

Two evenings later, he carried the turtle man, who was still fast asleep, to the beach and laid him on the sand, at a spot where he knew the turtle could see him. Like clockwork, the turtle emerged from the sea and made his way to his friend. He nudged the man's head, tried putting his head under the man's hand and the Maasai could see that this encounter was distressing for the turtle as he was unable to get a response. Finally, Olamayian lifted the man's hand and placed it on the turtle's head and stroked the turtle. The turtle visibly calmed down and chose to stay close to his friend. After a while, he slowly made his way back into the ocean and Olamayian carried the man back to their shelter.

The next day, around mid-morning, the man woke up

after having slept for four days straight and asked for water. The young Maasai was overjoyed. The man could speak! And he spoke English with an accent, like the foreigners who came visiting Zanzibar. The man gulped down the water and then moved back to lay down again. He kept staring straight ahead, looking into space. He did not speak the entire day, and late in the evening, the Maasai shook the man gently and asked him to follow him and took him to the beach. Olamayian gestured to the turtle man to sit down next to him on the sand.

After a while, the turtle made his way out of the water like he always did. The young Maasai could see that the man was overjoyed when he saw his turtle. He could not stop smiling. The turtle man shakily walked up to the turtle and stroked him, he knelt and hugged his friend. Both men sat on the beach with the turtle in silence for a long time. The ocean surface was alive and shimmering in the moonlight and, after a while, the turtle made its way back into the ocean and the men walked back.

Olamayian asked the turtle man if he was hungry, and the man nodded. They walked to a shack that looked cosy, inviting and crowded. They took a table at the far end, where it was relatively quiet. Olamayian watched as the turtle man scrolled through the menu with his long, thin fingers.

He cleared his throat and said, 'I will have a vegetable sandwich.'

The Maasai was concerned and asked, 'Don't you think you need to eat some kind of meat to regain your strength?'

The turtle man refused politely saying, 'I'll stick to vegetarian fare.'

Olamayian placed their order. Then he smiled. 'I have

been calling you the turtle man. My name is Olamayian. I am the son of Sironka, the laibon, the wise, the elder of my tribe.'

'My name is Joy, son of a simple village fool,' said Joy.

The Maasai smiled at that introduction and asked, 'Where are you from, Joy?'

'I am from India, from a small seaside village called Galgibaga. Please can you tell me, where am I now? What is this place called?' asked Joy.

Olamayian replied, 'You are at Paje, a small seaside town on an island called Zanzibar, part of Tanzania in Africa.'

Joy wished he had paid more attention in class when Mrs Pinto had taught them geography. All he knew about Africa was its location on the world map. How had he reached so far? This had turned out to be a very long journey!

'I had no clue where my boat was headed! I was told Africa was close by when I was picked up by a fishing trawler a few weeks ago. I simply decided to follow Ollie, because Ollie seemed to know where to go...' Joy paused when he saw the puzzled look on Olamayian's face. 'Ollie is my turtle. He kept me alive, fed me, and looked after me.'

Joy paused as their food had arrived.

He picked up his sandwich, took a bite and his eyes misted over with tears. 'I was so hungry. This is heaven,' Joy said with a mouthful of food.

Olamayian laughed. 'Eat up then! I need to hear your story and then I need to sleep today. Looking after you was a full-time job.'

The two men ate heartily. After returning to the shelter, Joy settled down on his mat for the night and the young Maasai sprawled himself out in the hammock.

'Joy, how did you come from India to Africa? I thought we need big steamers and ships to accomplish such a journey,' asked Olamayian.

Joy was hesitant at first, but eventually he decided to share his story with Olamayian. 'What if he thinks it is too far-fetched?' he thought. As he started to talk, he wondered whether the young Maasai would think that he had made it all up. But with every word, Olamayian seemed more and more fascinated by Joy's journey. He got off his hammock and came to sit near Joy so as to not miss a word. He now knew why Sironka wanted him to bring Joy to the village.

Slowly, Joy started to piece the last bits of his story together. It sounded as if he was doing this for the first time, even for himself. He remembered falling off his boat, which had capsized in the storm. He also recalled seeing a huge, white whale emerging out of the waters, right in front of him. When the whale crashed into the heaving ocean, it created such a large wave that it pushed him off the boat and down into the ocean. That's when he lost consciousness. The next thing he remembered was waking up on the beach, with the young Maasai staring down at him and Ollie next to him.

'Olamayian, I do not expect you to believe me...but that's my story,' said Joy.

'Joy, we have the free will and choice to really listen to a story and allow it to have an impact on our lives. Or we can just brush it off as a stupid story. I have imbibed so much energy and learning from your story tonight. I am happy that I am the first to have heard it. Our ancestors said that each story is alive, and it has its own energy, spirit and lifespan. Some stories last for centuries, some last a few days, and each story we hear imparts many lessons for those who are true seekers and to those who have taken it upon themselves to awaken from slumber.

'When we are told a story, it's no coincidence! The story chooses the person it wants to be told to. There is always a divine plan and a time to hear it. You know, Joy, the same story may be told to several people, but each will have something different to take from it. If you don't tell your story, you will get very sad because the story has come to you and it has to be told. Tell your story without any shame, guilt or fear of being judged. You will do humankind a favour by telling your story, it is precious.' Then Olamayian slowly got up and walked back to his hammock.

'My brother, it's time we both catch up on some sleep. I know you have been sleeping all this time, but I need to sleep and you need to rest.' The Maasai closed his eyes.

Joy lay on his mat, staring at the sky. The young man was right! His story was special and he should not doubt its truth; in fact, a movie could be made about it! He smiled, and slowly, the sound of the waves lulled him back into a deep sleep again. Sleep was healing for him.

The next morning, when the young Maasai woke up, he realized he had overslept. The turtle man was nowhere to be seen and so, he jumped out of his hammock. He hurriedly put on his sandals and started to walk towards the beach but he could not spot Joy anywhere. He walked back to his hammock and sat there, wondering what he was going to tell his father.

An hour later, he felt someone's hand on his shoulder. He looked up to see a smiling face. It was Joy!

'Where were you? I was looking for you!' asked Olamayian with relief written all over his face.

'I went to meet a shack owner. There was a sign outside his shack advertising the job of a waiter and he was kind enough to give me the job. I think it is because I am an Indian, and so is he,' said Joy.

'Why do you wish to stay here? You can come with me to my village! It's in Tanzania, bordering the Selous Game Reserve! It's nice there, and we are one of the few villages that are a part of the eco-tourism project. My family and I will look after you,' offered Olamayian.

'Olamayian, I am so indebted to you already for saving my life and looking after me. You have even fed me these past few days. I need to stay here, this place feels right at this moment. Ollie is here too, and I do not feel like leaving him or travelling any more. I would like to be here with my turtle. Also, this is a seaside town and it feels a lot like my village back in India,' said Joy.

The young Maasai looked into Joy's eyes. He knew instantly that the only thing he could do now was to respect his wishes. By now, the young Maasai was certain that it was Joy who was the sea's offering, not the turtle from his vision. His father would understand his failure to bring Joy with him. He always said that every human is born with a free will and a destiny, and everyone else had to respect that. Though Olamayian felt Joy's destiny was tied to his village, it may not be time yet. Maybe Sironka had an answer.

All he knew, with certainty at this point, was that Joy and the turtle would not make the journey back to his village. Oddly, he was okay with that. His job may have simply been to come here to rescue Joy and get him back on his feet. It was best to let Joy do what he wanted. Acknowledging all this, Olamayian felt peaceful.

Joy could see that his new friend was worried about him. But Sunny, his new boss, had been kind enough to give him a week's trial as a waiter. And Joy also needed to figure out what he wanted to do now. He had the chance to create a new life all over again. No one from his past was here, with the exception of Ollie. Africa was so far away from home; he could just leave behind his terrible memories since there was no one waiting back in India for him anymore! All he cared, at this point, was about Ollie, his next meal and a roof over his head—and all three were right here in Paje.

'I understand your decision to stay here, Joy. Keep yourself safe and someday, we may meet again. You have been given a second chance to live life. You are blessed.' With that, Olamayian extended his hand, offering a parting handshake, but Joy reached out and gave him a big hug.

Joy helped the Maasai pack up his belongings and asked. 'I forgot to ask, why are you here in Paje?'

The young Maasai paused for a moment. 'I had come here to meet a friend!'

'Oh! Have you met your friend? Or did I keep you busy? Thank you for being here to save me!'

Olamayian replied with a cryptic smile. 'Yes, I did actually meet my friend! And now it's time to go back home.' The Maasai slung his small cloth bag over his shoulders and walked to the highway to catch a ride to Dar-es-Salaam. It was a long way back home!

Joy watched Olamayian walk away till he was just a speck in the distance, and then he got down to basics. First on his list was clothes. All he had on him was this extremely worn out pair of shorts that he had propped up with a reed rope, which the young Maasai had given him. He had lost so much weight. His hair was an unruly mop, his beard was long and shapeless. He had even lost his shirt and sandals somewhere in the sea. The only thing he had was a mat and a red cloth that Olamayian had left him.

His boss had not only been kind enough to give him an advance on his salary, but had also offered him a bed at the back of the shack to sleep at night as well as three basic meals. Joy was told that the best place to get himself clean and ready for work was Stone Town. Joy got a ride on an open-air mini truck.

Stone Town made him feel as if he was back in Goa. It had the same vibe—small lanes, balconies overlooking the busy crowded streets, people bustling around, vendors selling their wares and spices. Joy managed to find a barber who worked his magic on him. Then he bought a few clothes, slippers and other necessary items. He found a restaurant that served Indian food and had a hearty meal. Then, late in the evening, he caught a bus back to Paje.

He walked towards the beach to a spot that had become Ollie and his meeting point. Like clockwork, Ollie emerged from the sea. They sat side by side. Joy whistled a song and stroked Ollie's head, and it felt like old times again. Later, Ollie swam back into the sea and Joy rolled out his mat and slept under the palm trees.

He woke up early, got ready, and arrived at the shack for work. He was familiar with the workings of a shack and settled in quickly. Days turned into weeks and Joy was soon enjoying his new life. He felt so grateful to have three square meals and a fulfilling job. He found himself smiling more often. He was happy and peaceful. He was an instant hit with the tourists who visited the shack as he spoke English and was quite the charmer.

Sunny, the owner of the shack, had soon realized that Joy had excellent managerial skills. Joy was hardworking and trustworthy, and Sunny could blindly leave the shack to Joy. Within a few months, he gave Joy a promotion and a hefty pay hike. Joy could have lived in the town, but he still chose to live in the shack so that he could be near Ollie and the sea. When Sunny enquired about how he came to Zanzibar, Joy had fleetingly told him about his journey across the sea, which was intriguing to Sunny but not believable. And when Sunny enquired about his family, Joy informed him that he had none.

7

ALIGNMENT

Meanwhile, after saying goodbye to Joy, Olamayian got himself a window seat on the local bus to Stone Town. During the journey, the bus broke down. While some of the passengers, along with their chickens and children, got down and waited, Olamayian sat in his seat, lost in thought. He recalled how he came to be called Olamayian. His parents had given him the name Leboo when he was born, which meant the one who was born outside. He was not born in the village, but in England, in his mother's homeland.

He was a mix of his parents. He was not as dark as a Maasai and his eyes were like his mother's—blue, calm and wise. He was a tall and handsome man with aquiline features and looked a lot like his father. While growing up, he was like any other Maasai boy, wanting to become a warrior. He waited eagerly for the day when he would finally be a part of the Maasai garrison. He hated being teased by the senior warriors for not being circumcised, and knew when his time would come to become a man, he would not flinch. On that day, he would bring great honour to his family.

Like all the young warriors, he too was eager to be a part of a legendary lion hunt, even though his father was not in favour of it. He dreamed of oiling the dead lion's mane to honour it and wanted to become a proud owner of the prized lion tail. He used to daydream of being the village hero, like Mingati, his father's friend, who often regaled him and the other young warriors with lion-hunt stories around a bonfire. He knew every story as he had heard them since he was a young boy. What he loved most about these stories was how the tribe celebrated for a week after the first lion was killed, like Mingati had managed to do. All the young girls of the village wanted to mate with the warrior who speared the lion and dreamed of having his baby. The news of Mingati's victory had even spread across all tribes.

Empikas, the group in charge of the hunt, had been planning the lion hunt for days. Only some of the elders and senior warriors, who were in favour of safeguarding the age-old traditions, knew about the exact day of the hunt. Before the actual hunt, they had practice sessions in secrecy as many opposed the tradition. Those who were caught were punished severely.

Since ancient times, the Maasai had believed that the experience of hunting a lion built the character of young men. It was considered a sign of bravery and personal achievement if the Maasai warrior managed to kill one. Facing a lion was one of the most challenging experiences a man could ever be blessed with, and he would never come out of it unscathed. His soul was transformed in those few seconds of the encounter. Many warriors became addicted to that experience and wanted more of such moments of pure fear, bravery and victory. But then, many Maasai warriors had also lost a fight while many lions had lost their lives during these 'man versus lion' combats.

Lions had been hunted for so many years by the Maasai that they now feared the colour red. Unfortunately, the lion population was also declining. Thus, instead of solo hunts, the Maasai warriors had started to hunt in groups. Young Leboo was unaware of the lion hunt that was being planned, as the other warriors feared that he would tell his father who opposed such practices. Yet, Leboo was one of the best warriors of the Maasai garrison. They all knew it would be good fortune to have him in the hunting party.

That night, Leboo went to bed, and at around 3 a.m., his cousin brother woke him up. They quietly stepped out of the boma. There he saw a few senior warriors waiting. They told him to get ready to join them in their hunt. For the next two hours, they walked and tracked the lions down. They had chosen a pack of eight, consisting of three lions and two lionesses with young cubs. The Maasai never killed lionesses as they were givers of life. Early in the morning, they spotted two of the male lions sitting under a bush. Everyone in the hunting party agreed that it was best to chase the lions out of the bush, away from the lionesses and the cubs, on to the open plain. It was way safer for them there, as the lions were masters at manoeuvring through the African bushes.

They started the hunt and chose to anger and provoke the lions with their rattles, bells and loud hollering. This, they believed, gave the hunted lion a fair chance to defend itself. Suddenly, an electric charge transformed the atmosphere, changing it from a situation of peace to one where they fought to survive. The two lions charged. The warriors could hear the lions' roar rumbling across the forest. The warriors and the lions were on the verge of reaching the clearing, when suddenly, out of the blue, the hunting party saw the third lion to their left. He had been stalking them silently through the bushes, and when a few turned their gaze towards him, he charged at them. At that very moment, something snapped in young Leboo. He broke away from the group and ran towards the lion, his spear held high in the air, with only his shield to protect him.

The lion roared and charged at Leboo. He reached out and clawed Leboo on his thigh, but the young warrior was in a trance. He did not feel the pain. His heart beat like a drum—loud and fast. His mouth had gone dry. The lion's roar was deafening, but Leboo thrust the spear at him and managed to give the beast a nasty scar on his back. He knew that if he failed to spear the lion in the next few minutes, he would be killed. He was so close to the lion and then, something happened.

Everything slowed down and fell silent around him. He could hear his heart beating steadily, but there was no longer any fear in him.

The air was pulsating with energy. At that moment, the young Maasai could feel that everything—from stone to the dried piece of wood and the lion—was a part of one pulsating mass of energy. The lion and Leboo, it seemed, had merged into one body of energy, each knowing and feeling what the other was thinking. It was a dance of life, and at that moment, he heard the lion's heartbeat. It was loud and clear and sounded a lot like his own. He could feel the lion's fearlessness, his will to survive, his power. He looked into the lion's eyes, golden green with flecks of brown; they were the most magnetic eyes he had seen! 'How can I kill such a magnificent creation of God and why am I killing it? For its tail?' He hesitated and the lion took a step back too.

Both man and animal looked at each other, and something changed forever in Leboo that moment. He understood, with absolute clarity, what his father had been teaching him about the inter-connectedness of life on earth. He knew if he killed the lion today, he would be killing something very sacred and beautiful. The young warrior did something unthinkable. He slowly put his spear down. All the warriors who were watching knew that the young warrior had made an error in judgement. It was suicidal! But then, something even stranger happened. The lion stood still. He stopped roaring, and both man and beast stared at each other for a while. It was clear to both that the fight was over.

The lion turned around and took off with great speed to join his pride. When he had covered some distance, the lion turned around and looked back at the hunting party, checking to see if they were following him.

As he felt safe, he sauntered off at a slower space and disappeared into the dark canopy of trees. Leboo then turned to face the other warriors. Everyone was silently watching his every move. He knew that he would be the butt of all jokes from now on. But he did not care. All he wanted was to go back home and apologise to his father. That's when he spotted his father, standing silently and watching him from a distance. Sironka had followed his son when he found out about the hunt. His face was pale and his eyes moist. Leboo walked towards him, knelt in front of him and offered his shield and spear to his father.

'Sorry father! I know you never wanted me to be a part of a lion hunt. I guess I needed to be a part of a hunting party to understand what you have been trying to teach me all these years. I promise you today, that I will preserve the circle of life. I will guard it with my own life. But first, I deserve to be punished for what I have done,' said Leboo.

Sironka took the spear and shield and put it aside and then, he asked his son to stand up and hugged him tightly. In a relieved voice, Sironka said, 'You are alive and that's what matters. You are my son, my blood runs through your veins. I would have been very surprised if you killed the lion. Who am I to forgive or punish you, my son! You did what you were supposed to do, and you learned what you were meant to learn. We all do things that are not right, but in the end, if we can learn to understand and forgive ourselves, it justifies our actions.'

Sironka continued, 'One of the most important lessons I have learned in life is to live each day with a deep awareness. It's so easy to lose your connection with the world, but the creator works in mysterious ways. This, I feel, you have learned today. We all think we are the powerful ones but there is a force way bigger than us, directing things for us. Today you have realized a few core spiritual truths and I hope you will do justice to this lifetime of yours by not thinking just about yourself, but doing something for the world around you.'

'Today, my son, you have taught all of us who have watched your fight a lesson. What you did today will make us think twice before we take another's life. You taught us that we always have a choice. We don't always have to kill.'

Sironka lifted his son's shield and spear and handed it back to him. He said, 'Let's go back home to celebrate because today, the lion has accepted you as his equal. You are his keeper. You have earned his respect and trust. From today, everyone will know you as Olamayian, the one who speared the lion first. You do not need to kill a lion to get a lion's name.'

From that day on, Olamayian honoured the lion. The lion's spirit lived within him, and over time, he developed special abilities to communicate with them. He knew when the lions were in distress and needed his help. He would go to them and they too had learned to trust him. He knew how to track them down within minutes—a feat that no other tracker had been able to achieve so far. Whenever he was nearby, the lions came to him. Everyone in his tribe and the other tribes were aware of this deep connection and they respected him for it.

Like his father, he too started to work actively with the government agencies. He wanted to stop the killing of lions by poachers and the other Maasai tribesmen. He travelled far and wide to help educate the young warriors about the necessity of protecting the lion. He was now the lion keeper.

That was why Olamayian understood the importance of the turtle in Joy's life. Ollie was Joy's spirit animal, but the new world that Joy came from did not know the importance of having and honouring a spirit animal. He realized that Joy feared losing his connection with his turtle if he moved away, and he believed that they needed to meet every day to keep their special connection strong. Maybe someday, Joy would learn the ways of the spirit world.

Olamayian knew that Joy was blessed, he just had to become aware of his blessings.

Olamayian had to travel a long and difficult route to reach his village. After the ride on the bus, he took a ferry and then a train. Then he waited to hitch a ride on a safari van to reach his village. But no one came to the pick-up point, because, this year, the tourist season had taken a hit due to a pandemic. However, on the bright side, the animals now thrived without human intervention. Some of the elders believed this too had been written down millions of years ago in the earth's fortune. This was the way Mother Earth could stop the humans in their track and take time to revive herself. He decided to trek to his village, and the long walk did him good. He had needed to stretch his limbs after all that waiting at Paje.

When he entered his father's boma, Sironka was sitting by the fire. He looked up and like an excited child, he asked, 'Did you meet the turtle?'

Olamayian was slightly taken aback. He had never told anyone about his vision. But then, Sironka always knew.

'Yes, I met the turtle, but I also met a man. I could not get them to come back to the village with me,' he said.

Sironka did not look upset by that information. 'It's alright that you could not bring them back. They are safe and you ensured that. Tell me their story. I have been eagerly waiting for you. Where is the man from? What language does he speak?'

Olamayian smiled. It was so good to see his father like this after a long time, so full of childlike curiosity. He told his father the story of a man called Joy and his turtle, and how they had crossed the Indian Ocean on a small boat. He filled him in on the details that had made the journey so surreal and magical. His father smiled as the story progressed.

Sironka placed his hand over his son's arm. 'Olamayian, did he tell you about the white whale?' he asked.

Olamayian could not hide his surprise. 'How do you know that he saw a white whale, father?'

Sironka smiled and replied, 'The ocean keeps letting me in on the details that even the man does not know about. It is such a blessing to hear you and the spirits of the ocean talk to me at the same time. I am not sure who has a more interesting story to tell.'

Olamayian knew better than to question the ways of the spirit world. It was late in the night when he finished telling his story. Finally, he walked back to the hut that he shared with his friends and slept.

◆

Six months had passed since the day Joy had washed up on the beach.

Joy had, by now, realized that it was healing to do simple, mundane, repetitive actions in a day. It was a boring routine to follow, but it gave his life some order, something he lacked before he had gotten on that boat. He loved waking up early in the morning, when it was still dark, to the sound of the waves. He lay in bed, waiting for the birds to start chirping. He loved morning walks along the beach. The feel of sand underneath his feet, the breeze through his hair, the smell of the sea, salt and seaweed in the air. He felt all of it deeply and knew he was lucky to be alive!

After his walk, he would get the shack ready for business. He worked the whole day and would catch a few minutes of peace late in the afternoon. His mind had stopped dwelling on the past. He had still made no friends, but he was one of the friendliest people around the shack. Ollie was still his only constant. Every evening, when the beach would get quiet and dark, he went to their favourite spot and always found Ollie there, waiting for him. They would sit or lie next to each other. After a while, Ollie would signal that their time was up by waddling away into the sea, and Joy walked back to take a shower. Then he would slip into bed and another day would dawn, just like the previous one.

> 'Have you noticed that there is a certain peace and calm in a routine? It may seem repetitive to do the same things over and over again, for days on end. But, like Joy has realized, this very repetition can be healing, especially after you have overcome a huge challenge.
>
> 'The interesting thing I have noticed is that somewhere in the space between one breath and the next, we find some peace.'

Sunny often urged Joy to make some friends, but he did not feel the need. When he craved Indian food, he would catch the local bus to Stone Town. He had not touched alcohol or drugs, even though both were found abundantly around the shack. He was in a good space and he did not want to spoil it. All the other guys who worked at the shack often joked about Joy needing a few vices. They said that his life was way too clean, simple and boring.

Joy happened to mention to Sunny that his birthday was just a few days away. Sunny thought it would be good to do something special. He and the boys got down to planning a big surprise party for Joy. Sunny got some of his friends in the shack business to rustle up some food for the party.

The day arrived. That evening, Sunny told Joy to close the shack early. As Joy had some extra time on hand, he decided to take a dip in the ocean. After a refreshing swim, he sat on the beach. He wondered where his life was headed—from a top corporate job in London he had become a manager of one the smallest of shacks on the beach of Paje. His future was in a limbo and suddenly, he started to feel very low and disheartened. It hit him that he was now all alone in the world. He had no friends and family back in Goa, no one was missing him or waiting for him. Professionally, he was finished. Despite the years of hardwork, he had created nothing substantial, nothing that he could be proud of!

He brushed aside these thoughts and walked back to the shack. As he drew closer to the shack, to his surprise, there was music. All the boys were there along with some guests whom he had seen around occasionally. When they wished him happy birthday, he realized that they were all there to celebrate him. Even as he smiled, he felt like an utter failure. The thoughts that had stirred up after the swim still lingered.

Despite his feelings, he turned around to Sunny and smiled a shy, boyish smile. 'You did this for me?'

'Yes, Joy, we planned this surprise birthday party for you.' Sunny hugged Joy, patted his back, and then in a loud voice, declared the party open.

The music system pelted out some really good local dance numbers, and everyone was merrily dancing and eating. Some women walked in. They did not seem to be guests. One of the prettier women stuck to Joy the whole evening and fixed him a drink. He did not know when or how, but she got him to have the drink. *It had been inevitable!*

All the music, dancing and food made him sadder. Instead of enjoying himself, he started to spiral down into an abyss of darkness. Joy could not stop at just one drink.

He drank, he danced all by himself, he sang his Goan songs! The party carried on late into the night, and on the beach, Ollie waited for Joy for a long time and then, finally, swam back into the ocean.

After that eventful night, Joy's life again took a turn. The old Joy was back!

As weeks went by, Sunny watched with sadness how they had all lost Joy to the bottle. Sunny knew Joy was a good man, but now he also knew that Joy had been an alcoholic at some point in his life. He was back to his old ways. Joy was getting worse with every passing day. The happy Joy, who was always smiling, had disappeared. He was replaced by a very sullen Joy, always preoccupied and angry about something. His clothes were dirty and crumpled, his eyes had this watery, glazed look that addicts had and his hands shook. He would wake up late, long after the shack had opened up for business, and drink till late at night.

He had stopped going to the beach in the evening to meet Ollie. He had drowned himself in alcohol, yet again!

> 'I guess...it's time to call it a night. We meet tomorrow for another evening of storytelling,' the narrator said. There were a few grunts from the audience. But they all knew it was pretty late and it was wise to go home.

8

THE WISE ONE

The next evening when the storyteller entered the hall, he found that his audience had grown. Word had spread that an unusual story was being told here. Everyone greeted the storyteller with applause.

He smiled and settled down. 'I see new faces. I believe you must have heard the gist of yesterday's story from your friends who have brought you here. I will now continue with the story.'

Ollie, like a loyal friend, kept visiting the spot daily. Weeks went by, but Joy did not turn up. Ollie was worried and he hoped that nothing terrible had happened to Joy.

That day too, like always, Ollie made his way to the beach. Like all the other days, Joy was not there. Ollie stayed longer than usual, hoping and wishing to see Joy. Disappointed, he swam back into the ocean. Ollie's heart was so heavy and sad. He knew these night trips to the beach would have to stop. Joy was not coming back to meet him. He had to come to terms with this separation.

Ollie must have swum far out into the sea that night and gone deeper than usual, because suddenly, he could feel the water rippling and vibrating around him. Something big was around him. The water was darker and denser at this depth and he could not see clearly. He swam a few feet upwards to get to safety, and that's when he bumped into something solid. He looked up and realized that he was under the belly of a very large fish. He took a sharp turn to swim away but then he stopped. He was tired of always running away. A sudden calmness descended over him and he slowly turned around to face his biggest demon—the fear of death.

There, in front of him, was a white whale. It was Great White who had helped him keep Joy safe during the storm. The Great White swam around Ollie, creating a circular current to prevent him from escaping. As Ollie twirled and whirled in the current, he looked into the eyes of the Great White and realized they were gentle and kind. He saw the entire ocean reflected in those eyes and for some odd reason, he felt happy.

'It's been a task trying to find you,' said the Great White.

Ollie was confused and wondered what the Great White wanted from him. Ollie cleared his throat, and in a very clear voice, thanked the whale for keeping Joy safe.

'By the way, I know you are the one who wrapped Joy in all those weeds.' Ollie scratched his head with his flipper and asked, 'Why the weeds? And you wrapped him so tight that he was blue when we unwound him. I remember seeing you emerge from the ocean and the huge wave that you created destroyed the boat. I saw Joy disappear in the water. You took him deep under. I lost both of you quite quickly,' said Ollie.

The Great White smiled. 'I was just doing what you requested. I kept your friend safe.'

Ollie was mesmerized by the Great White's smile. He saw thousands of teeth glistening in glee.

'Yes, I had to wrap him up in seaweed because there was no other way to keep him safe in my stomach. It prevented him from becoming mulch in there. I knew the rubbery weeds would protect him. How is your human friend doing?' asked the whale.

Ollie looked away. 'He is alive, I can feel it. His fellow humans helped him recover from the ordeal. I stayed around in these parts to be with him. He came every day to meet me for many months, but then stopped a few weeks back. I guess he must be preoccupied.'

The Great White could see the sadness in Ollie's eyes and asked, 'Little turtle, what is truly upsetting you?'

'I don't know why Joy gave up on our friendship! Did I do something wrong? I keep feeling like it's my fault. What if it's true...what some of the sea folks say—humans and wild animals can never be friends. I am such a fool that I believed our friendship was special. I believed that we had gone through so much together that it could withstand the test of time and events. On most nights, I have been swimming back into the ocean without meeting him. It feels like he has left me.' Ollie cried with a broken spirit.

The Great White stroked Ollie's head. 'Don't be sad, little one. Joy is still your friend, and you will never part from each other, not until your last breath. Always know that. You will always carry a part of each other deep in your hearts. Close your eyes and go within, because he is there, deep within you. There are no partings or endings inside of you. Sometimes, some ties need to be untied. We need to drift away for us to reach where we are supposed to go.'

The turtle closed his eyes and after a few minutes, opened them. 'I cannot see or feel him,' said Ollie, almost crying.

'Don't despair! You need to train yourself to see beyond the veil of physical reality. You have come so far, don't give up hope. Master this way of communicating, not only with Joy but with the whole ocean. Ollie, that's your name, is it not?' asked the Great White.

Ollie nodded. 'How odd that you know my name! I do not remember telling you.'

'The entire ocean knows your name. You have achieved the impossible, little one!' said the Great White.

'Me? Achieved the impossible?' Ollie looked surprised.

'You have to ask yourself, are you now the same turtle who left the shores of India to save your childhood human friend? You struggled to adjust to his moods, became his caregiver. You, the sea-dweller and he, the land-walker, crossed the ocean together. You learned how to communicate with him, you fed him, kept him safe. You healed him with your presence, love and loyalty. You taught the sea creatures about so many ways of being constant in our feelings, irrespective of this ever-changing world around us. Take a few moments to give yourself some credit, little one!'

The Great White continued. 'The ocean asked you to bring the human to the shores of Africa, and you were resourceful enough to do that by taking the advice you were given along the way. You taught us how to listen to the universal call and align ourself with our life's purpose. Unfortunately, many of the sea creatures had stopped listening and following their life's purpose. You taught us to have compassion and love for the species that is killing us and our habitat. You made us all realize that no meeting is a coincidence and that in the end, only love is real.'

'You had the courage to do what was asked of you, just like your mother. She would be so proud of you. Your parents were chosen by the ocean mother because each was so unique, strong and beautiful. You are a good mix of both your parents. Your father crossed many oceans, unlike all turtles. He was a fearless traveller, while your mother was a bundle of pure love and courage. You have faced your fears and your weaknesses, and your metamorphosis has given us so much hope,' said the Great White, his voice booming with energy.

'You have a bigger task at hand. You, my little one, are the wise one from the clan of Olive Ridley turtles,' the Great White said.

Ollie's world stood still as the words echoed around him.

Ollie seemed dazed by the knowledge. The Great White nudged him back to the present moment and said, 'Each sea clan has a wise one. These wise ones are guided by the ocean mother and other sentinels in different galaxies, all to help lead their clan and those around to an awakened life. They will herald a change and help others adjust and survive in the new world. You need to travel the world like your father, spreading the word and hope.' Even as the Great White spoke, Ollie was a sight to watch as he tried his best to digest and assimilate all the information.

His jaw dropped, his eyes widened like little teacups, his flippers folded in front of his neck.

'Me? The wise one! I truly respect you, just as the whole ocean does, but I feel as if you've got this one wrong! One of my brothers is the wise one. Have you seen me? I only have three flippers. I get scared and I am nervous most of the time. I get sad, I cry, I hurt. I don't understand things! How can I be the wise one? I am so attached to things. I need help most of the time! Look at how many sea creatures the ocean had to send to help me bring Joy to Africa,' ranted Ollie in disbelief.

'Yes, I guess you are exactly the way you have described yourself to be. I don't think wise ones are supposed to be perfect. The wise ones laugh, need, cry, feel, dislike or like everyone else, but they somehow end up having a large quotient of compassion and love in them. Love is the closest description of what our creator is. This ancient wisdom is coded in the wise ones of different clans. This same wisdom is also coded in the water molecules around them. When the time is right, this wisdom comes alive and that's when the wise ones start to fulfil their destiny.'

The Great White was now revealing the ancient secret.

'The wise ones are so unique that they understand what others feel. They are ready to learn more about themselves and the world around them. They are ready to question, to keep seeking and to move beyond limiting beliefs, blocks and fears. They agree to know nothing, but then, little one, from nothingness comes everything. It's time to align yourself to your true purpose,' said the Great White.

Ollie was silent for a while. 'What am I supposed to do, now that I am the chosen wise one?' he asked.

'You just need to be Ollie and be super receptive and grateful, and every day, the ocean will polish you into magnificence. Your presence will inspire, regenerate and give hope to many,' said the Great White.

'If I have to reach out to many more of my kind, I will have to travel far and wide,' said Ollie.

'Ollie, even if you touch ten lives and inspire them to be the change and the promise for tomorrow, you have done what you were born to do. Ten sea creatures will change twenty, and in turn, they will change and inspire many more lives. Little one, know that we all are the same energy and energy moves very fast, and know that goodwill ripples through the ocean. It has to become a force so strong that it can counter the ripples of negativity. Yes, you make a very small part of the cosmos, but also know that you are immensely powerful,' the Great White reassured Ollie.

'What about Joy? I can't just leave him!' asked Ollie.

'I guess that, Ollie, it's time you allowed him to figure his way out himself. He has to find how to live purposefully in this world. Let the humans take over now. We, sea creatures, can connect telepathically, so use your will and connect to his soul and when you do, you can inspire him to live a beautiful, purposeful life. I have said to you what I needed to, and now it's time to part. Make me proud and don't lose your goofiness. It's quite endearing,' the Great White said as he swam away.

Ollie decided to take the advice of the Great White and try his flipper at being a wise one. But he was still doubtful. All this information was still sinking in. Before he took off on his big adventure, he decided to visit the beach the next evening one last time. As always, there was no one there.

And so, he set off.

Many weeks passed since he last met the Great White. Ollie, in his heart, now knew that he had an important role to play as the wise one of the Olive Ridley clan. Gone was the shy turtle who ran away from forging new friendships and confronting the unknown. Now he was a turtle driven by a purpose. He had a broader perspective and an understanding of the tasks that lay ahead.

But not a day would pass by without missing and thinking of Joy. He always wondered what Joy was doing and if all was well with him. Every day he was moving further away from Zanzibar, which meant further away from Joy. He was now closer to the southern tip of Africa. The water was cleaner and cooler here.

It was early in the afternoon when he caught sight of a beautiful patch that had just the right amount of light and shade, and he felt that the weeds around would keep him safe from predators. He desperately needed to catch a few winks as he had been travelling for many hours now. Suddenly, something bumped into him from behind. When he turned around, he nearly got run over by sea creatures, a whole lot of them of different sizes and shapes. They rushed as if they were on a mission of some sort. He tried stopping a Clownfish.

'Excuse me, I see all of you are in a rush to go somewhere. Can you please tell me what is happening? Are we in some kind of danger?'

The Clownfish stopped and turned around. He watched Ollie intently, 'Looks like you are new around here.'

'Yes, I am,' said Ollie.

'Well, a legendary storyteller has come to our part of the world and today is our lucky day. She is going to tell us all a story!' said the fish.

'This rush is all for a story?' asked Ollie, perplexed.

'Are you doing something very important right now?' asked the Clownfish.

'No, I was just settling down to sleep,' said Ollie.

'I think you need to hear the stories,' urged the Clownfish.

'Okay. Can I come with you?' enquired Ollie.

'Sure, just hurry! I have waited for three years for this day. The last time she came, she told us a story about the giant octopus that got itself stuck in a huge ship along with a little star fish,' said the fish as she swam away furiously.

Ollie followed the Clownfish through the maze of sea creatures. They both pushed and shoved and managed to squeeze themselves into a good vantage position from where they could clearly see a huge killer whale taking centre stage.

A big, black Musselcracker was giving a long speech on how privileged they all felt to have the orca with them. His grumpy old face would occasionally break into a childlike smile when he looked at the killer whale. He was excited about the story she was going to tell them.

'And now, I present to you, the magnificent story teller from the North Atlantic Ocean!'

He bowed and moved aside.

The orca cleared her throat, winked and smiled at her audience. 'So, it's been a while since I last came to these waters.'

Someone from the audience shouted. 'And we all have waited and waited for you.'

'I came back like I promised,' said the orca, smiling.

'Yes, you did,' chorused the audience.

'Now let's not waste any more time on useless pleasantries. Today I am going to tell you the story of a wise old turtle. We all need to know that the great spirit has a plan for all of us and we need to trust in that plan,' said the orca. Ollie was all ears now. It was a story of his kind.

'Once upon a time, there was a wise old turtle,' the orca began the story. 'The story begins on the day she first saw my mother and me...'

It was a windy day and the sun had lit up every corner of the world around the turtle. She could feel life buzzing around. The sea sparkled and glimmered and it felt like the stars had decided to rest on her instead of the night sky.

The seagulls were creating a racket, like always. It was their feeding time. But today, their chatter did not bother her as there was so much beauty around. She sighed deeply, as she was filled with gratitude for a life well-lived.

The rock-face was warm. She had managed to get the best spot to sun and watched on lazily as a fish or two happily somersaulted out of the water. That's when she caught sight of two black fins in the distance. These were a new addition to the sea around here. And then, an orca emerged out of the water, followed by her calf.

She shook her petite turtle head in surprise. Orcas rarely came to this part of the world. These two must have lost their way in a storm. Whatever the reason, they were here and were strangely swimming too close to the shoreline. If they did not watch out, they could get beached and would surely die, she thought.

All the other turtles had left for the arribada that was to take place in a few months on the west coast of a country called India. The adult turtles fed and nested in two different locations in the world, and every year, they moved between these two spots. This unique mass nesting phenomenon of the Olive Ridley turtles had taken place for centuries. It was considered a sacred event for the turtles, held during the darkest night just before the new moon.

Her friends and family were part of the group of turtles that had moved on, but she had decided not to join the arribada this season as she did not want to be a part of the mad rush. She could not take all the pushing and shoving when turtles congregated in the sea before they came ashore to lay their eggs on the beach. Her old bones were weary.

It all seemed pointless to her now because she felt that her time was coming to an end. Nowadays all she wanted was to feel the breeze, hear the waves and feel the sun on her back without worrying about getting ready to drop her next clutch of eggs.

Over the past forty odd years, she had laid many a clutch of eggs and prayed that every little one that hatched from her clutch would make it alive. But she knew that was not likely. Only a few lucky ones would survive. Many of the young ones met their end in the first few hours after they had hatched and others when they emerged from under their sandy nest. They were eaten by dogs or pecked on by birds.

The sea was as treacherous as she was loving. The little hatchlings swam blindly once they entered the sea, not knowing what was in store for them or where they were headed. But they instinctively knew that their safety lay in swimming to deeper waters. It was a secret whispered to them by their mothers when she carried them as eggs.

The old turtle knew how important a link her species was in the marine ecosystem. The turtles were the ocean keepers. They were quiet, mysterious and time-honoured creatures, not just for the sea but for the ancient humans as well. Her kind ensured that seagrass beds were grazed and kept short at all times, that corals were healthy since the survival of other species depended on them. They had roamed the seas for over a hundred million years, and the sea knew that if this link broke, it meant trouble for not just the sea creatures, but also humans.

She was hearing hushed whispers in the sea all around her. The wise ones of the sea were predicting a major shift and were teaching their kind to adjust and adapt to the new, broken world. A change was on its way, they said and this might just be the sixth mass extinction over the past 400 million years, an era where the environment of the planet changes so much that most animal and plant species die.

She heard that the humans were the cause of this extinction this time. The ocean spirit was worried and was making all efforts to keep sea creatures safe from the chaos that may be unleashed if a solution was not found soon. As they all knew, from experience, that it would take over three million years to recover from this catastrophe, they all had to act speedily.

The sea urchins told her that for the sea council, this was the least of their worries at the moment. Climate change had started and it was going to be the new killer. Everyone was feeling the heat and this was one of the main reasons that the sea turtle numbers were decreasing too. Cooler sands meant more male turtles were born and warmer sands resulted in female turtles being born, but an equal quantity of both were needed for them to successfully reproduce.

Humans had further made the situation worse for the turtles as they had started to level dunes around the beaches. The waves were rushing in and eroding the beaches, washing their eggs into the sea. Over the past few years, it was becoming increasingly difficult for the turtles to stay alive on their journey to their nesting beach due to all the excessive fishing activities.

She felt that it was safer to while away her last days on this beach where there was enough to eat, ample sunny spots to warm her body, and except for the noisy seagulls, everything was perfect.

The turtle slowly waddled off into the sea; she needed to swim to clear her head.

The turtle spent the next few days in peace and in the sheer bliss of feeding. The orca and her calf were still around, and she always made it a point to watch out for those two before she went into the sea. It was tiring, having to be on guard always, but today she decided to enjoy herself. If it was her day to die, she was ready. It felt like a good day to die.

She felt the urge to go deep into the sea.

The silence of the water was healing, and the slow hum of the sea creatures was music to her ears and soothed her nerves. She floated, flipped and tossed around playfully.

But suddenly, she felt the water ripple around her. She opened her eyes and saw the orca right in front of her. She stayed rooted to the spot, mesmerized by the sheer magnificence of the killer whale, who was beautiful and grand with her black and white markings glistening under the water. No wonder so many called them the guardians of the sea.

The mother orca and calf circled around her, and then the mother spoke. 'Please do not be scared. We have been waiting to talk to you,' the orca said.

'Oh! You want to talk to me? I thought you had other plans for me!' the turtle exclaimed.

'I want to talk to you because the ocean spirit wants you to join the rest of the turtles on the arribada. You will have to lay your last clutch of eggs. From that clutch, the wise one will be born!' the orca said.

'Join the arribada? It's too late! All the turtles left days ago. I will never be able to catch up. And why me?' the old turtle objected.

'Well, I thought the same way too. A younger female turtle would have been a better choice, but as you and I know, the Great One has a sense of humour. At the moment, it looks like the old ones are now the chosen ones,' the orca said with a twinkle in her eye.

'So are you also a chosen one?' the turtle asked.

'Yes, I am. I am an old one too. Initially, I also questioned why I had been chosen but I have come to realize that we, the old ones, have a strong essence in our souls. We have seen, felt and experienced more than the rest. The little ones who are made from us will carry that in them even when we are long gone. Maybe there is something special about you and me, something that no one else has. It is futile for us to waste our time questioning it. I allowed myself to follow the call. If my calf will be the beacon of hope for all the orcas, the ocean and the sea creatures, I will go out of my way to do what is needed,' said the orca.

'I need to think. Also, as you know, I need a male turtle to mate with. This can't be done alone. I am so tired of all the mating games,' sighed the turtle.

The orca could see that the old turtle was still full of fears and doubts. 'Once you know what you want, surrender and all will fall into place. Think about it.' And with that, the orca and the calf swam away.

The turtle swam back to the shallow waters and wedged herself between two rocks for the night. She needed space to think over what the orca had said.

She dozed off, but at some point in the night, she heard whispers around her. She woke up with a start, but there was no one around. She was settling back to go to sleep again when she heard the whisper again. This time, it was louder. A little ahead she saw something twinkling. She moved out of her safe spot, curious to see what it was.

The sea was alive with magic!

Just ahead of her was a patch of sea glowing and lit. It was calling out to her and soon, she found herself in the midst of the shimmering patch. Her mind stilled and she could understand the murmurs of the sea—it was urging her to take the advice of the orca. Amidst the glowing, glimmering patch, she saw images float by—of her past, her birth, her family gone by, and then those images faded and were replaced with images of all that had happened to mother earth in the past millions of years and all that may happen in the future. She saw possibilities, she saw hope and she also saw destruction. At that moment, she knew that she had to answer the call of the ocean spirit.

She woke up to the seagulls screeching overhead. She was still wedged between the rocks, but this morning, she felt different—much younger and stronger.

She wondered if the shimmering patch had been a dream, but a deeper knowing propelled her to follow the orca's advice. It was meant to be. She surrendered herself to the sea and the Great One and waddled off into the ocean.

From a distance, the orca watched the turtle swimming far out into the sea. She hoped the turtle had finally decided to follow her advice. She kept away from the turtle, following and keeping an eye on her. After a day or so of observing her, the orca could see that the turtle was swimming, but she was not fast enough to be able to catch up with her group. She obviously needed help. As the orca swam towards her, she was greeted by the turtle friend with glee. The turtle was relieved. The orca had kept her promise to help her speed things up on this journey.

'Now hold on to my tail tightly,' said the orca.

The turtle held onto the orca's tail as tightly as she could with her two flippers and the orca swished away. Everything was a blur. The turtle could feel the water rush, gurgle and bubble past her as they moved ahead with a speed that she had never experienced in her entire life. She understood now how the big fish swam.

The killer whale occasionally flipped out of the water and took in air through her blowhole, but she was a turtle and she was finding it difficult to breathe. By now, she was feeling nauseous. Everything was moving too fast for her and it was proving to be difficult to hold on to the orca's tail. And so, she let go.

The orca stopped suddenly and turned around to see her calf and the turtle staring accusingly at her.

The young one confronted her mother. 'Can we just slow down a little? I know we are on a mission, but we need to figure out how we all can travel together,' the calf said with sincerity.

'Yes, I agree with the young one,' the turtle said breathlessly.

'So how would you both like to take this journey with me?' the orca asked.

The little calf perked up. 'A little speed, a little rest, a little feeding time, a little sunning, a little talking, loads of stories and please, can you not be so serious about the whole thing?'

Both the older ones laughed. Then the three swam and after a while, fell into a good rhythm.

As days went by, the turtle realized that the little calf

was surely a storyteller. The child was already showing signs of being the wise orca her mother was training her to be. The turtle understood what a free spirit was when she got to know the calf. The little one oozed happiness, curiosity and alertness; she always overflowed with ideas on how to reach their destination without stressing too much. And, in her childlike way she was teaching the older two how to be in the present moment.

'Turtle, can I tell you another story?' The young orca did not wait for an answer and in the next breath, carried on talking. 'Do you know why the orcas are black and white in colour and not entirely black?'

'No, I really do not know. I thought you were born this colour,' said the turtle.

'Well, legend says that there were never ever any whales in the sea that had black and white marking. Even the humans sing this song on their sea journeys when they honour us.' This obviously was the calf's favourite story because her eyes twinkled with delight as she narrated it.

'Once upon a time, there was a great big black whale who was the reincarnation of a great chief who lived on earth. The chief's ship caught fire while trying to save his people from being conquered by evil forces and he drowned, but the sea granted him his wish of being a guardian for his village. He reincarnated as the big black whale and watched over his village from the sea. He would warn the villagers of dangers by appearing to them in their dreams or by blessing them with a sighting on festivals where they honoured him.'

'As time went by, he fell in love with an osprey, a sea hawk. She was a beautiful, big bird with large wings and intelligent eyes that missed nothing. Her belly was white as snow. When he first saw her, she was perched on a tree near the shore and she looked so regal with her wings folded in. He was so in love with the osprey that he often jumped into the air to be closer to her. She too would respond by swooping down closer to ocean to meet the whale. Seeing their love for each other, the sea blessed them with a baby that had black and white markings, and the first orca was born as a symbol of romance, harmony, protection, family and community.' The little orca finished her story with a smile.

'That was a beautiful legend, little one. Thank you so much,' said the turtle.

'Turtle, can I ask you something? What is the difference between a legend and a story? I get confused. I thought I was telling you a story, and you say it's a legend!' asked the calf.

'In my understanding, a legend always starts off as a story and then, as it is passed down the ages from one generation to the next, it gains bits and pieces of their energy. These legends also remind us that we should not lose hope; we should, instead, believe that the extraordinary is possible, and dream to keep our imagination and creativity always alive. No one knows the origin of the legends, but I am glad they are there. Some parts of the legend may be made up, and some parts are historic and must have actually happened,' the turtle said.

The orca could see that her friend had a gentle, but persistent strength. She had grown fond of the turtle.

The turtle was now determined to lay her eggs and she hung on to dear life on their rides across the sea. She ate and rested, picking up strength. It had been raining for the past few days and the water was murky, but the three of them kept plodding on. And soon, the day came when they had to part ways.

Around mid-noon, the orca stopped and called out for her calf. It was time to say goodbye. All three had known that the journey would come to an end soon, but parting was proving to be difficult.

The calf was distressed and started to cry, and the turtle's heart broke on seeing that. She had started to love the little one like her own. She swam to the calf and stroked her with her front flippers. 'Do not be sad, little one! If it is destined, we will meet again. But you should always know that we were supposed to meet and part in this lifetime. Please remember, separation is just an illusion. We all are beings of energy and we will always be connected.' As she spoke, she wiped away the tears that had rolled down the calf's eyes. 'You will meet my little one someday, and promise me, you will keep an eye on my baby.'

'I promise you, turtle. I will always seek and try to find the wise one from the Olive Ridley turtle clan. I will always look after your baby,' promised the calf.

The turtle stroked and caressed the calf for the last time, and then, she swam to the mother orca and nudged her lovingly. 'My friend, I'll always be grateful to you for helping me align myself to the larger picture. I had given up and was preparing for the end to come, but you came and gave meaning to the rest of my life. I feel proud of being chosen by the sea to bear the wise one,' she said.

The two friends parted. Closure was painful, but it was also healing in some odd way.

Slowly, the orca swam away with her calf.

9

FLIPPER TO FLIPPER

The turtle swam alone for the next two days. She kept enquiring from the various schools of fish about the progress of the other Olive Ridley turtles, and she realized she was still behind. She wondered if she would be able to make it on time. More importantly, she worried, being unsure as to whether she would find a male turtle to mate with; and there were none around.

She steadfastly swam towards the beach where she was born. She could feel that the currents were stronger than usual. It was dark and raining by now, and she was growing tired of swimming.

She had started to feel extremely dizzy and tired, and must have passed out at some point. Then, she faintly heard someone coaxing her to hold on tight. It just felt so good to lean into something stronger than her.

When she woke, she saw a large Olive Ridley male turtle at some distance from her.

As he saw her emerging from her resting spot, he swam up to her. 'It's good to see that you are awake at last! I thought I had lost you.' He had a clear, strong voice with a twang and clearly, he was not from around here. She took a good look at him. He was younger, for sure, but also weather-beaten, scarred and nice-looking, in a turtle kind of way.

'So if you are feeling better, I think we both should be on our way to put you back on track on your journey. Are you a part of the arribada?' he asked.

'Yes, but I decided a little late in the day to be a part of it,' she said.

'Hmm.' The male turtle scratched himself under the chin. 'If you are going to lay your clutch of eggs, you better hurry.' He nudged her on.

She thought for a while and decided that he was right. She needed a little help and he seemed harmless.

'Okay, let's go. But please note, I am not much of a talker.' And even as she said that, she remembered the orca and her calf.

But he was not one to be quiet. He told her all about himself. He said that he was called the lone wanderer. When he was very young, he had decided to swim out into the open sea, travel around all the oceans. Babies, girls, and rowdy boy romps never really fascinated him. His adventures took him across the oceans and he had travelled far and wide and seen so many fascinating sea creatures and undersea worlds. He took pride in being so well-travelled.

As they both swam towards the western coast of India, he realized that she was really on a mission. Most of the time, the turtle was lost in her own thoughts and very focused on wanting to reach her beach.

He decided to break the silence at some point. 'You make me feel nervous, but I am going to tell you the story that inspired me.' He swam closer to her. 'Across many seas, there is an island called Hawaii, a magical land. It was believed that there was a very powerful demigod there called Maui, who was huge, much larger than the humans we see walking on Mother Earth. His special powers were strength and foresight. One day, he went fishing with his brothers and threw his fishing hook into the sea. Can you imagine how big his fishing hook was? Big enough that he fished out islands from the sea!

'Anyway, even the waters around this island—Hawaii—held special powers of healing and wisdom. The humans who lived on these islands often talked and worshiped the mystical turtle called Kauila born on the black sand beach of Punalu'u.

'She was born of two sea turtles who were blessed by the sea gods with ancient wisdom and magic. Her mother, Honupo'okea, buried her egg in the black sand and it was a special egg because it was of the same colour and shape as the Kauila wood. Before going back into the sea, Kauila's father, Honuea, dug deep into the earth with his flippers, creating a freshwater pond near the egg.'

'Why did her father dig a pond near the egg?' she interrupted. 'What does Kauila wood look like? And why was the sand black?'

He smiled because he finally had her attention and she had asked not one but three questions, all in a row. 'Wait, lady! Have patience!' He smiled his slow, lazy, charming smile again. She realized that he was really good at telling stories and his voice had a dream-like quality. She felt as if she was in Hawaii herself.

'Well, the sand is black because the mountains on the island and inside the sea are always gurgling and hissing, and Mother Earth would often erupt through their mouths in a melted, angry, fiery form. She, in her melted glory, is usually black in colour, and when she cools down, most of the land and beaches are created. But I have seen that the beaches on the island are not just black but red, green and yellow too.

'So after a while, both her parents returned to the shore and they saw that the egg was ready to crack open. From it emerged their beautiful baby daughter. She was dark and glossy, like Kauila wood, unlike any other turtle. And they called her Kauila. Mother and daughter made their way into the pond and they stayed there until Kauila was old enough to be left on her own. Kauila made the island her home. She would rest at the bottom of the freshwater pond and air bubbles from her breath would rise to the top of the pond and delight the children who would play around the waterbody.

'She loved children and would often transform into a beautiful little girl so she could play with the village children. She also watched over them and kept them safe. The humans honoured her. So this is how the ancient sea turtles ensured that turtles would walk on the earth among the humans, to help them and look after them, to be their soul guides and become their power animals.' His eyes turned a bit sad as he continued.

'But when I look at how we are hunted, killed and eaten by the humans, I am confused. We were supposed to live in harmony and look after each other. But it seems that they don't care about us.' He looked heartbroken, she noted and her heart went out to her new friend. She realized he was a gentle soul.

'Don't lose heart! I have seen that there are a group of humans who are fighting to save our kind,' she reassured him. 'But I just hope it's not too late, for them and for us. The ocean spirit is also preparing for future changes.' Something in her voice made him look at her and he saw tears in her eyes.

'Why are you crying? Did my story make you sad?' He said, concerned.

'No! In fact, I am surprised that you told me this story. I am not sure if I should share this with you. You may just laugh and think I am going cuckoo in my old age, but I just feel you have been sent to help me too. I have been told by the ocean spirit to lay my last clutch of eggs. From this clutch, the wise one will be born,' she said.

'The wise one? The wise one for our clan or the ocean? That's interesting!' He was very excited at the news and was swimming around her in circles.

'For both, I guess! But I still have not found a mate,' she said as tears rolled from her eyes in sheer desperation.

Mating in sea turtles could be dangerous, especially for the female. The male would have to mount her and hold on to her shell with his front flippers for quite a while. Sometimes mating took hours. She would have to keep swimming to the surface with him on her back to ensure that they could both breathe. Also, other male turtles would keep trying to dislodge the mounted male turtle off her back, which could get bloody, painful and dangerous at times.

'Let's find you a male for the job,' he said encouragingly, tugging at her. Thus reassured, the turtle agreed. They both swam ahead, laughing and giggling.

They travelled together, learning from and adjusting to each other's eccentricities and their natural ways of being. He helped her see things with a new perspective and she looked after him, helping him realize the simple pleasures of togetherness. She found him the best spot to lie down or the juiciest jelly fish to feast on. Flipper to flipper, they slept together as friends, but there were days when both of them needed their space. She needed to go within herself to introspect and he needed to roam alone. The first time he disappeared on her, she thought he had gone away for good. But she kept swimming towards her destination and then, when the sea began to turn dark, he appeared next to her. She got quite used to him disappearing, and after he had his fill of wandering, he would swim back to her. She called him the wild roamer.

They had grown very fond of each other. He was proving to be a good friend. She wondered, if he was open to the idea, maybe, he could be her mate. But that depended on him. On second thoughts, she was just not his type at all. And how could she forget? She was way older than him.

One day, she decided to talk to him. 'I have come to realize a few things about relationships. It is a lot about how we feel when we are with the other and I feel happy and safe around you, even though you and I are imperfect in many ways.'

Her eyes were twinkling with mirth and she was chuckling; but she knew that time was slipping away from her and it was better to just say what was on her mind than beat around the bush.

'I am asking…if you could consider being my mate. I am much older than you, and you may prefer a younger mate. But I need help, and over the days I have spent with you, I feel that you are perfect for the job.' Then she laughed and giggled.

He could not stop looking at her as she spoke. She was so beautiful!

'You make it sound so cut and dry! If you laced it with

a little romance, I would be your mate in the blink of an eye. I like myself better when I am with you, I see a better version of myself. I always thought that I was perfectly fine alone, but with you, the journey is more fun,' said the wild roamer, smiling wider than he ever had before.

She laughed and swam towards him. She nuzzled him lovingly. 'You know, you are imperfectly perfect for me. I love you in an odd sort of fuzzy, heartfelt way.'

'Now, that's better.' The wild roamer embraced her gently with his flippers.

As the days and weeks passed by, they swam together towards the nesting beach, each knowing very well that the clutch of eggs that she carried inside her was blessed. Never in turtle history were little hatchlings created out of so much love. They both spoke to the future hatchlings, infusing them with their wisdom and their insight, letting them know that they all needed to look out for the other, to seek and help each other align to their own greater purpose in this lifetime. They were told to not be loners like most of their kind but to instead try to be a family of some sort, to find a way to save the sea and to always hear the call of the sea, no matter what.

As they neared the beach, after weeks of swimming, they bumped into more of their kind. Some of the female turtles had already laid their first clutch of more than a hundred eggs and were getting ready to lay their next. She knew she only had one clutch of eggs in her. Some of her younger friends were surprised to see her and they wondered what an old girl like her was doing here. The rest of the turtles were taken aback that she had a faithful escort with her and did not want to have a little fun on the side.

A few kilometres away from the beach, she turned around and held the wild roamer with her flipper. 'I need to do this alone now. I think it's the right time tonight,' she said.

'I'll wait for you out here,' he said gently.

10

TIME TO LET GO

She waited till it was dark and slowly made her way to the farthest end of the beach. This was the beach she was born on and these grains of sand held many memories for her. She had laid numerous clutches of eggs, year after year, on the beach. Now this was her last.

This part of the beach was more secluded since it was rockier than the rest of the land. Turtles were creatures of habit and used only one side of the beach, often disturbing previously laid nests. With her years of experience, she knew which spot to choose to keep her eggs safe. This year, the sand and weather were cooler, so most of the hatchlings would be males.

She slowly started to dig a conical pit with her hind flippers, and when it was one and a half feet deep, she went into a trance-like state and slowly started the laborious process of laying her eggs. It was a small clutch with only seventy eggs and she felt a wave of relief wash over her once the last egg fell into the nest. She had done what she had been asked to do by the ocean spirit. Her heart was filled with so much gratitude for all the help, love and learning she had received on this journey. She slowly covered her nest with sand. She was tired, but she was happy. All she wanted now was to find the wild roamer. But she still had one last thing to do before they left the beach.

It was early in the morning and the crab lady emerged from the crevices of the rocks near the waterfront. She gingerly walked across the rocks and took a dip in the water. The water was shallow and was the right temperature for her arthritic limbs. She had been living on this part of the beach for many years now.

She saw a turtle emerging from the water. This was rare, she thought. The females always came out to roam when it was dark. As the turtle drew closer, she recognized the turtle to be an old friend of hers, one who came here often to lay her eggs on this beach.

'It's so good to see you, crab lady! I was hoping that you had not moved away!' said the turtle, visibly relieved.

'Me and move? Nah! This is my beach! It's good to see you here so early in the morning!' the crab lady said.

The turtle pointed to the nest. 'By the way, this nest holds my last clutch of eggs. I want you to please help me and promise me that you will look after this nest and ensure that all the hatchlings have a safe passage into the sea when they emerge from the sand.'

'You don't have to worry, turtle! I'll keep an eye on them,' said the crab lady earnestly.

'I am so grateful to you for helping me out. I have travelled far to lay these eggs and it's been a tough journey. Every hatchling needs to make it to the ocean because one of them is the wise one from our clan of turtles. In the coming times, this special turtle, the wise one, will help my clan of turtles, the ocean and the sea creatures get through tough times.' The turtle told her story about being helped by the orca and finding true love with the roamer.

The crab lady listened intently. She had been so oblivious before, living in her little heaven, but she knew that the world around her, including the sea, was changing for the worse. Her friend, the raven, often went on and on about it, but she had just put it down to him being an old grump. If a solution was coming into being, then she would definitely help, without a second thought.

'My dear friend, I entrust you with these eggs and will now be on my way. Please look after my babies for me,' said the turtle.

The crab lady could see that the turtle's eyes were moist with unshed tears. Normally, the turtles laid their eggs and left the hatchlings to fend for themselves. This clutch of eggs meant a lot to the turtle, she saw. She was not going to disappoint her friend. She nodded and the turtle slowly made her way back into the sea.

The crab lady walked towards the nest and looked at it. She was not the maternal kind and now, in this old age, she had other worries. But what needed to be done had to be done. She could enlist the raven into the scheme of things; she had to come up with a plan to keep the eggs safe till they hatched, and it meant fifty days of being responsible for something that was not her own. She slowly walked to the tree that the raven perched on.

'...And then, after a few years, the wise old turtle and her partner came to meet me and my mother, and we had countless adventures together. Those stories are for some other time,' said the orca.

The orca was a master storyteller and with this story, she had everyone enthralled. Ollie, in the first few moments, realized that the orca had known his mother for this was the same story that the crab lady had told him before. And then, the orca had spoken of the parts that he did not know.

Someone in the audience perked up. 'So there are many wise ones?'

'Yes, every sea clan has their own wise one who will guide the rest of their species to a higher awareness and help them become the grandest version of themselves. Soon, it will not only be a wise one of the clan but one of many thousand wise ones,' said the orca.

'Have you ever met the wise one from the clan of Olive Ridleys?' asked a massive stingray in a childlike voice.

'No, I haven't but I have heard the initiation has taken place. That is why I swam all the way from the shores of Norway to find the wise one, just like I had promised his mother,' said the orca.

The sea creatures asked her innumerable questions. The orca patiently answered all of them; then she recited poetry and sang songs of the sea monsters she had encountered on the way. She was an entertainer par excellence, but everything she said held a greater meaning. Ollie could see that none of the sea creatures had realized that they were not just hearing a story but were being mentally cajoled into becoming grander than what they thought they were.

The Musselcracker took the stage again and announced the end of the event and thanked the orca profusely. Slowly, the party broke up and the sea folks reluctantly started to swim away. Many rushed towards the orca and surrounded her, asking questions.

The Clownfish turned around to Ollie. 'You deciding to stick around?'

Ollie nodded. 'Right now I want to speak to the orca.'

Ollie then thanked the Clownfish. He decided to wait it out till he saw the last fish leave. The orca was just turning around to swim away when she caught sight of Ollie watching her.

'Are you waiting for me?' asked the orca.

Ollie nodded.

'You are an Olive Ridley turtle. I never knew your kind were seen around these waters,' said the orca, puzzled.

'Actually, I have travelled all the way from the shores of India to drop a friend off at the east coast of Africa,' said Ollie. 'Goa, to be more precise, is where I was before I left its shores. The same beach your friend laid her last clutch of eggs.'

He could see that he had the orca's attention now.

'That's interesting! So just curious, have you met the wise one of your clan?' asked the orca earnestly.

Ollie smiled. 'Yes, I have! I am getting to know him better every day!'

'Where is he?' asked the orca with hope and eagerness shimmering in her eyes.

'Right in front of you!' Ollie said with a broad grin.

The orca whooped with happiness. She swam around in circles and clapped her fins.

'We have found each other! Did you know that I was on my way to look for you in this big, wide ocean?' said the orca. 'Look at the miracle, you came to me instead! Like I told everyone, my mother and I met your mother and father. We travelled together for a while. But forget about me. I would like to know what happened to you after you hatched?'

'Well, it did not go as planned. You can see that I have three and a half good flippers,' said Ollie.

Recalling what the crab lady had told him, Ollie then narrated what happened after his mother had left the beach. And the story went like this...

So, after her friend, the turtle, left the clutch in her care, the crab lady went looking for the raven. Finally, she spotted him, perched on a branch far up the tree in a shady spot. He was busy chewing on something.

He flew down to meet his friend. The crab lady beckoned him closer and whispered. 'Now listen carefully! My old friend, the sea turtle, has laid her last clutch of eggs behind the rocks. I promised her that I will guard the nest.' She patiently told him about her conversation with the turtle. 'You've got to help me with this. Raven, for once, let's do something for someone else! I have a plan to keep the nest safe,' she said.

'Okay, if that's what you want, Crabby! I'll help you with your plan,' he promised.

The two friends went over the plan many times and soon, they set about protecting the nest. The crab lady guarded the nest in the night and the days belonged to the raven's care. He pecked and cawed away at humans, dogs and other birds. He had even developed a kind of mad, exhaustive dance to keep them all away.

And then, one day, early in the morning, the crab lady saw the first hatchling appear from the sand. Then, another. And more came forward in a few hours. It was going to be daylight soon, and that would get dangerous for the young ones as they could fall prey to other wild animals. Usually, they are born at night and follow the moon rays shimmering on the ocean. These little hatchlings had gotten the timing all wrong, she thought. This was not good, not good at all!

The raven cawed like an excited old grandpa and flapped his wings loudly, almost scaring the little ones.

But the crab lady did not have it in her heart to stop him. She was as excited about the little hatchlings as he was.

Some of the babies had a few bits of eggshell still stuck on them, and she picked and dusted them clean and guided them towards the sea. An hour or so later, no more little ones emerged from the cavity in the sand. The nest looked all sad and empty and it was just a pit with broken eggshells.

'I think this is it, Crabby!' said the raven.

She agreed and they were both a little sad and lost because their little adventure had come to an end. They would now have to go back to their normal lives. As they both walked away from the nest, the raven turned around and gently stroked the crab lady with his wing.

When they walked back to the nest after a few hours, they saw the head of an animal bobbing up and down behind the rocks where the nest was. As they got closer, the crab lady screamed in fright as the dog had a small hatchling in his mouth. The little one was bleeding profusely.

'Raven, do something! Quick! Please do something, save the little one. I made a promise to the turtle,' the crab lady cried.

The raven flew down and started to peck the dog all over. The dog yelped and dropped the hatchling back on to the sand and ran away. But the hatchling was a mess. The raven turned the little one over and saw that one of his flippers was torn, there were cuts at many places and his shell was a bit crushed.

'Crabby, let the little one go! This cannot be the wise one for the turtle clan,' said the raven.

'No, Raven. I promised my friend that all her hatchlings

would reach the waters safely. Please, help me! Now take him to the ocean. The salt water is healing for us sea creatures,' begged the crab lady.

The raven carefully picked up the little one. He could feel the little body shuddering from the pain and shock. He flew to a spot where the crab lady spent most of her days and dropped the little one in the shallow pool of salt water. The water turned red with blood. The crab lady rushed and washed the wounds off the little one and tried nudging the injured flipper into place.

After a while, the raven anxiously asked if the little one was still alive. The crab lady looked worried. 'I hope so. I can see little air bubbles around his head. I'll keep an eye on it.'

Both of them took turns nursing the little one. The baby turtle barely moved. The crab lady kept it safe from the waves and tried feeding it tit-bits of food.

After a few weeks, the little one gained some strength and decided to try and swim out of the shallow pool. He was initially so clumsy, but slowly and steadily with practice, the little turtle could swim around a little. Both the raven and the crab lady decided that the little one needed more time to heal. So in the night, the crab lady talked to the little turtle about the ways of the sea and during the day, the little one was taught how turtles survive deep in the ocean. It was always kept under the crab lady's supervision.

In the evening, when there were no humans around, the little one was allowed to play on the beach. One day, while he was clumsily waddling up and down the beach, a young boy walked past him. He stopped, picked up the turtle, tickled him, laughed and played with him for a while and then, he gently let him down again on the beach. The little turtle was left with a wonderful feeling that whole evening. He waited to see his human friend the next day too, and every evening, this boy would show up and play with the little turtle. He had even started to bring him small treats. Their friendship grew over the next few weeks.

The raven had noticed this growing friendship and one day he brought it up with the crab lady. 'I am very nervous about the little boy and turtle being friends.'

'Raven, you have always been suspicious of humans. He is just a boy, a human child. He means no harm.' The crab lady tried to reason with him.

'Human children are idiots! Sea turtles can only survive in sea and salt water. The child might just decide to pick him up and take him home one day and then what? The little turtle will die. Human children take a long time to gather survival intelligence. Unlike us in the animal kingdom, they know very little about the environment. See what they are doing to the earth and us,' the raven ranted.

The crab lady was silent. She knew that, for once, the raven was talking sense.

'Crabby, do you think the little turtle is strong enough to survive in the ocean now, or would he need more exercise? Should we feed him more? I fought off the dog to save him, but the boy is way bigger.' The raven rambled. He was not going to trust the boy.

'The little turtle has only three functional flippers and the ocean is merciless. I am a sea dweller, and I know this better than anyone else. I have been a coward and have never left this beach. But I cannot dump my fear on the little one. He has to make his own way at some point,' she said.

The raven could see that the crab lady was worried. 'We both know that the little one cannot live with us forever. This was not the deal, Crabby. We were supposed to look after him till he was strong enough, and I feel that he is strong enough now! I do not know if the little turtle can survive in the ocean, but each of us have our own luck and destiny.' The raven kept reasoning with the crab lady.

The crab lady agreed. Though she had grown fond of the little turtle, she knew that he would be safer in the ocean. It was time to part ways with the little turtle.

The next morning, the crab lady was close to tears as she thought about the impending goodbye. She kept fussing over him. All these days she had been a hard taskmaster. She had exercised with him every few hours in order to get some mobility back into his injured flipper.

The little turtle also knew that something was amiss today. Even the raven was not his usual chirpy self. After an hour or so, the crab lady could not hold her tears back. She hugged the little one. She told him how the raven had helped her save him, she told him about his mother and the story she had told her before she swam into the sea. She shared the promise she had made to the turtle's mother. She also told him how his mother believed that the wise one was going to be born from her last clutch of eggs, from which he came.

'Raven and I have grown to love you, but it's time for you to find your own way now. Remember to find the wise one. Stick together with your kind and watch how the other turtles live to survive and copy them,' she said. Then she gave him one last, tight hug.

Before the little one could protest, the raven gently wrapped his claws around him and flew across the ocean.

He could feel the little turtle sobbing and shuddering in despair.

'Raven, I promise you that I'll be a good, little turtle. Please take me back to the beach, take me back to the crab lady. The ocean is very vast and scary and I want to live with both of you...'

But as he was speaking, the raven opened his claws and let go of the little turtle.

The little one turned around to catch one last glimpse of the raven and realized that even the raven was crying. The little turtle then entered the big wide ocean. And thus began his fight to survive.

'...And that, my friend, is how I survived.' Ollie completed his story.

'One day, I will tell you the story of how I went back to that beach, after many years, to meet my human friend and was told by Mother Ocean to take him to Africa,' said Ollie.

'What a journey! It is so wonderful we found each other!' said the orca in a relieved voice. 'What are your future plans now?'

'I plan to travel as much as I can,' said Ollie. 'And of course, to help my kind survive and thrive.'

'Hmm. Would you mind if we both travel together? I can be your guide through these waters. I have done this wise-one thingy for a longer time than you, and my mother has groomed me for the position. Maybe I can be of some help.'

Ollie smiled gleefully. 'That would be wonderful.'

'But right now,' the orca added, 'I need to find something to eat. My tummy is rumbling.'

'Well, I am not lunch, dinner or breakfast for you,'

chuckled Ollie nervously. 'Just know that I am off limits for this whole trip!'

The two laughed and giggled like two old lost friends, and together, they swam deeper into the ocean.

11

SECOND TIME LUCKY

Everyone had just returned to their seats after a quick round of refreshments. The air was still thick with the aroma of freshly brewed tea when the storyteller appeared on the stage and took his position. He cleared his throat, indicating to the audience that he wanted them to quieten down.

Soon, Joy started to crave a drink earlier in the day. Sunny felt so responsible for Joy's situation. One day, after dinner, he walked back to the shack and he saw Joy, like always, sitting in one corner of the shack, drinking alone. He took a chair opposite Joy and in a voice gruff with emotions asked, 'Why? Why, my friend, are you doing this to yourself? I curse the day I threw that party for you. I do not recognize you anymore.'

Joy looked at him and then poured himself another drink. He tried to speak, but he mumbled and slurred his way through a few lines that made no sense.

'You will stop working in my shack from tomorrow, Joy. I can't see you like this anymore,' said Sunny in a matter-of-fact voice and walked away.

Later, when he opened the shack the next morning, Sunny found Joy fast asleep under a table. He gently shook him awake, handed him a cup of coffee, and told Joy that he was fired. It took Joy sometime to register the fact that

Sunny was actually asking him to leave. He was flustered! He had nowhere to go! Suddenly, he felt like the same old Joy with the same old problems. He felt the same despair and helplessness, except this time it was more intense. After all, this was not his country or his people or family. He hated himself more than ever. He was so angry with himself for having gone back to square one.

He had sorted himself out on the boat, he had been happy and living a normal life like others. He was here again now. He had messed up his life, yet again. Every time he got closer to creating a good life, he would sabotage it. He had to accept and acknowledge that he was an alcoholic. He was the son of an alcoholic; alcoholism and failure ran in his blood!

Joy was heartbroken. He sat down and hung his head in despair. He knew now, for certain, that he had no good left in him anymore! There was no hope for a man like him and he had no one to reach out to for help. His new and only human friend, Sunny, was giving up on him. And in his drunken haze, he had forgotten to meet Ollie. He did not even remember when he had met Ollie last. He had lost track of time. All he wanted to do now was to go and find his turtle, but first, he had to get through the whole day and not drink before he met Ollie again. 'How am I going to do that?' he wondered.

> 'The worst fear of an ex-addict is returning to substance abuse and being in a situation where they absolutely lack control over their own lives. Unfortunately, there are triggers and situations that may push them back into addiction. Joy had triggers that made him feel worthless, lonely, not worthy of love or happiness, and it pushed him into various situations where he lost control over himself and his life. We, humans,

> sabotage our own happiness and success because the mind
> is addicted to suffering. It keeps us bound and limited.'

Joy asked Sunny if he could stay in the room at the back of the shack—just for a few days, just till he found another place to stash his stuff away. Sunny was kind enough to grant him his request.

Joy sat down on the bed, lost in thought and not sure as to what he would do next. He dozed off and woke up late in the evening, craving a drink. He tried dousing the urge by drinking large amounts of water. He went for a walk, he tried eating something in one of the shacks and then, he waited for Ollie on the beach. But his friend did not turn up.

He must have fallen asleep on the beach again, because the next morning, one of the Maasai hawker boys woke him up. He walked back to the shack, looking like a mess. He had not bathed or changed in two days. He had managed a day without a drink and it had put him in the foulest of moods. When Sunny saw Joy in such a dishevelled state, he lost his cool. Joy screamed back at Sunny. Then one thing led to another, and Sunny had shoved Joy out of the shack. He told one of the boys to fetch Joy's belongings and threw them at Joy.

Joy stood outside the shack, staring at his belongings all strewn around him. He was angry and flustered. He slowly went about collecting his belongings and walked to a shady part of the beach. He sat there with his back against the trunk of a palm tree. He noticed that people had started to stare at him. 'I must look like a mad man.' He noticed an old Maasai man looking intently at him.

Joy decided to swim to clean himself up. He left his stuff under a bush, took some money from his pouch, a fresh change of clothes and had a long swim. He then found a shack with a good washroom and took a shower. He ordered eggs and toast and tried eating some, but it tasted like sawdust. The need for a drink was kicking in again. He had managed a day without a drop of alcohol. He even told himself that maybe today could be a turning point. After this, he would be on the road to recovery again.

By mid-afternoon, the urge to drink won the battle. He went into a shack, found a dark, shady corner and ordered his first drink for the day. And as the day progressed, the alcohol took over.

> 'While all this was happening with Joy, just a day earlier something mystical was happening in the Masaai village.'

Sironka's dream woke him up. He looked out of his window to see the moon. Tomorrow would be a moonless night. The dream had been a vision. He knew it was time to find the turtle man named Joy. He got dressed and packed up a few belongings at the crack of dawn and went to find his son. He reached Olamayian's enkaji and called out to him. The young Maasai came out, rubbing his eyes, looking dishevelled and still sleepy.

'We need to go and find the turtle man and bring him back with us. We have to leave now,' Sironka said this with an urgency that was enough to shake Olamayian out of his slumber.

'Are you sure about this father?' Olamayian asked.

Sironka nodded.

Then, Sironka patiently waited under a tree while his son freshened up and packed. Both father and son set out on their journey to find Joy.

They first took a cargo train and settled amongst crates

of grain. When they boarded their next mode of transport, the ferry, Olamayian noticed that Sironka was unusually quiet. The young Maasai allowed his father the privacy of his thoughts.

Sironka hated going to Stone Town because for a forest dweller like him, being among crowds of people was extremely overwhelming. They reached the town late at night and decided to take a small room to rest and wash up. The owner of the guesthouse helped arrange a pick up to Paje that left at 6 a.m. the next morning.

They reached Paje the next day and walked to the beach. Olamayian found a shady spot under a few palm trees. He helped his father settle at the spot, and then sat down as well. With experience, he knew it would get really hot as the day proceeded, so he created a temporary shelter with fallen palm leaves. As they munched on their breakfast of ugali, a thick maize porridge, Olamayian gathered the courage to ask his father if he was sure that the turtle man was still in Paje. Sironka, in a clipped voice, informed him that the turtle man was indeed still there. However, Sironka also said something else—that on a moonless night, the man would leave; and after that, there was no way they would be able to find him.

'Father, you know tonight is the moonless night,' said Olamayian.

Sironka nodded. Olamayian waited for an hour after his meal, and then he decided to try to look for Joy. He started enquiring at the shacks but no one had seen him. Sironka, on the other hand, was sitting under the makeshift shelter, waiting for his son to come back with some news when he noticed a dishevelled looking man walking towards the clump of palm trees.

Soon, Olamayian found the shack where Joy had worked for a while. He spoke to Sunny, who told him the sad story of how Joy had taken to drinking and about their latest scuffle that morning. This news filled the young Maasai with some hope of finding Joy. He had to be around; maybe he had gone to town. By late afternoon, he again took another round of the place and wondered. 'How could a man of Joy's size just disappear into thin air?' When he came back, he saw, for the first time, extreme worry creasing his father's face. Sironka was visibly growing more restless by the minute.

'Olamayian, if we do not find him in a few hours, I fear we will lose him forever,' said Sironka.

The young Maasai was taken aback by this information. Now he was sure that Joy was in trouble. 'What does forever mean, father?' he asked hesitantly.

Sironka did not mince his words. 'I mean that he will cross over to the other side.'

This news visibly shocked the young Maasai and he got up immediately. Sironka could see how agitated he was. In a voice riddled with fear, sadness and frustration, Olamayian said, 'Father, I had asked you so many times during the past few months whether it was time to bring Joy back to our boma, but you always said that we had to wait. Now I feel that we waited a little too long. You miscalculated, which may already have cost the man his life. I really like the man. I saved him, looked after him and have been looking forward to bringing him back to our home someday, and now I get to know that he only has a few hours left to live? I have tried to find him all morning. How will we find him in the next three hours?' he lamented.

He got up and walked away from Sironka. He felt as if he was choking with unspoken anger. He feared that he would lash out at his father, which would be disrespectful. Olamayian decided that he would search all the shacks that were still open one last time. When he came out of the last shack, he saw Sironka waiting for him at a distance. Olamayian shook his head in disappointment. They walked back to their makeshift shelter in silence, each lost in their own thoughts.

Meanwhile, Joy had slipped off his chair in a drunken stupor and had curled up under a table in the shack. Late in the evening, the owner of the place found him, shook him awake and asked him to leave. Joy walked out of the shack and again tried to see if he could find Ollie. He hoped that Ollie would come to meet him today. He waited, and after an hour or so of watching the waves crash against the shore, he knew, somewhere deep inside of him, that Ollie had finally left him, just like everyone else in his life had done.

This thought, ever so fleeting and small, managed to crush the last shred of hope Joy felt. He curled up into a ball on the sand and lay there for a long time. He had no thoughts, but his heart was racing and beating loudly. Something must have snapped inside of him because he could not get up anymore. He knew, with certainty, that it was the right time to end his life. He could not fight this battle with addiction alone anymore, and no one really cared if he lived or died.

After a while, he mustered all the strength he had and walked towards the sea. The water was cool, and so, he walked deeper into the sea in a trance. The water reached his chest. The waves pushed him back, but he stumbled on. Finally, he came to a point where he suddenly could not feel the ocean floor beneath his feet. He knew it was time for him to let go of his life.

He allowed the water to gather over his face and head. He momentarily struggled to come up for a breath of air. But at some point, he pushed away the urge to save himself. He said a little prayer. Then he asked his mother to find it in her heart to forgive him. She had given him life, but he could not find it in him to live anymore. He felt the water beginning to fill his lungs and slowly, he knew that the icy cold darkness of death was wrapping him in her arms.

On the beach, Sironka took out his medicine bag and started to hum and chant. The sound put Olamayian to sleep. It must have been around midnight when Sironka shook his son awake. Even before the young Maasai could wake up properly, he noticed that his father had taken off in the direction of the ocean. Sironka must have seen something because he was running now. The young Maasai followed his father into the dark moonless night. When he caught up with him, he saw his father standing very still and looking out to the sea.

He turned towards his son and in a very sad voice, he declared. 'Joy is in the sea.'

Olamayian was stunned. 'What do you mean? Has he taken his own life? Are you sure, father?'

'Yes, I am,' said Sironka, and he walked into the sea as well. Olamayian saw this and felt worried. He knew his father was not a strong swimmer.

He heard Sironka's voice. His father had started to sing a song so mournful and yet, so powerful, that it shook and melted something inside Olamayian's heart. He did not realize that he had tears running down his cheeks. Sironka continued singing; his voice had the sound and essence of the sun, the breeze, the waves and their ancestors. It was a song requesting the sea gods, the great thunderous one, to be kind to a man called Joy, to give him and his boy one more chance to make things right. He acknowledged that they were humans with faults and limitations. He sang of mistakes, forgiveness, love and gratitude and when he had finished, he walked back to the beach and sat down, exhausted.

The young Maasai had followed his father into the water. If the man had pointed him in a direction, he would have dived into the ocean to find Joy. However, something calmer inside of him urged him to go sit with his father on the beach.

Slowly, he reached out and held his father's hand. He remembered having done this when he was scared as a young boy. His father's hand was warm and reassuring. They sat like this for an hour or so, and slowly, Olamayian noticed that the sea had started to recede. The sky was getting lighter. Paje was known to have low tides early in the morning. On most days, the water moved back by almost a kilometre or so.

Sironka rose and started to walk along the beach. He turned around and asked Olamayian to follow him. Soon, in the distance, they saw a rock jutting out of the sand on the beach. As they both got closer, they knew it was not a rock but a man. He was curled up, lying motionless. Olamayian knew it was Joy. He ran towards the slumped, unconscious figure and turned him over.

Sironka reached there and asked, 'Is it him, my son?'

Olamayian looked up and nodded. 'Yes, it is Joy. You

did it, father, you saved him!'

Sironka shook his head and said, 'The womb of the sea, the creator Enkai, had mercy on all of us. But first, let's check if he is actually alive!' Sironka knelt down by Joy's side and touched the side of his neck, then a smile finally crossed his lips.

He could feel a faint pulse.

Once again, Olamayian got down to the job and tried to empty the contents of Joy's stomach. Sironka started to massage Joy's body to increase the heat. As he did so, he hummed and sang. In a few minutes, Olamayian saw life seeping back into Joy's inert body. His fingers moved, his eyes tried to flicker open, his lips twitched and then, he slowly opened his eyes.

The young Maasai felt a sense of déjà vu hit him. 'Joy! You okay, brother?' he asked.

Joy tried to register who was talking to him. Everything was blurry. As things came into focus, he clearly saw the Maasai's face.

Olamayian held Joy's ice-cold hands and gave it a reassuring squeeze. 'I guess it is time! I am not going to take no for an answer. Now you must come back home with me.'

Joy said nothing. He nodded and closed his eyes.

Olamayian carried Joy back to their shelter. He saw that Sironka was trying to pull some things out from under a bush.

'These are his belongings,' he told Olamayian.

'How do you know that?' asked his son.

'I saw him put it there in the morning!' replied Sironka.

'You saw him and did not stop him!' exclaimed Olamayian.

'I was not sure it was Joy. In my vision I had seen a man with a turtle sitting on the beach. The man looked much cleaner, not like a messy drunk,' said Sironka.

'Father, you are the great Sironka, the man whose visions propel our tribes forward. This is insane! Are your visions not clear and precise? You could have saved us so much worry, pain and anguish, if you had told me that you saw Joy earlier in the day,' Olamayian said.

He looked exasperated as he lowered Joy to the sand.

Sironka was watching his son intently. 'Olamayian, I have a small request. Please do not put me up on a pedestal like everyone else does. Yes, I am the laibon of our tribe, but I am also your father. Do not expect me to know everything, every time. I make mistakes too. I often don't have complete clarity about my visions. Over time, I have realized that I am given clues by the creator. I pick one up and I am led to another, and that's how I unravel the quest. If I go with the flow and not fret and resist, then Enkai, the great one, will take me where I am supposed to go.

'I am not ashamed of being a human with failings, so please be kind to me and find the compassion in your heart for an old man like me. Children often think parents know it all, but we don't! I am sorry to burst that little bubble of yours. I am human, as human as anyone else. I too learn from you and people around me. That's the cycle of knowledge. That is how wisdom is transferred. Help me and I will teach you what I have learnt, and one day, you will know more than I do at your age. Hold space for me to tell you my fears, my worries. I need you to be a friend as well as a son. I take you as my equal in so many ways as you have blossomed into a wise man, with a pure heart!'

Olamayain hung his head and nodded. 'I am sorry, father. I have been slightly on edge over the past few hours. But I hear you, father, and I'll keep this in mind for our future together.'

He went to help Sironka gather Joy's belongings. There was not much to pack, just a few clothes and personal items. He tied them into a bundle in the shuka he had given Joy when they had last met.

After a few hours, Joy stirred. He opened his eyes and looked around. Olamayian was not around, but the old Maasai he had seen before was sitting opposite him. Joy still felt foggy but he sat up and asked for some water. Sironka uncorked a calabash with cold drinking water in it and gave it to Joy.

'Where is Olamayian?' Joy asked in a raspy, gruff voice.

'My son has gone to find some food for all of us,' said Sironka.

Joy sat down with his back against the tree trunk; his whole body hurt so much.

The old man held out his hand to Joy. 'My name is Sironka,' he said.

Joy shook his hand and said, 'I am Joy.'

Sironka smiled, his eyes twinkled. 'I have known you, Joy, for quite a while now. It's good to finally meet you.'

Joy looked at Sironka, not knowing what to make of what the old man was saying. But he noted that the father and son looked a lot like each other. Olamayian came back with some packed food for all three of them and was happy to see Joy propped up against a tree trunk.

Sironka placed some food on a crumpled newspaper and offered it to Joy. 'Eat this, you will feel better. Just chew on it till it melts into your mouth and only then should you swallow it. Be careful, your insides must be raw after gulping in all that salt water.'

Joy looked at Sironka. The old man's eyes were wise and his voice was calming.

After their dinner, Olamayain spoke to Joy. 'I heard that you have an issue with alcohol.'

Joy looked down upon his folded hands and nodded. 'When I was in India, I was an alcoholic. I managed to quit the habit while on the boat, but now I have started to drink again.' Joy seemed defeated.

Sironka spoke in a very calm voice. 'It's okay, don't beat yourself up because you fell back on a habit. Be kind to yourself. Smile, my boy! You are still alive and you still have a chance to work through this challenge. The ocean really wants you to live. Once you know why that is the case, you will take that reason and fly, create and expand. But before you can start, you must also fall to the ground. You will have to learn to get up, dust yourself and spread your wings again.'

Joy looked on, doubtful, but he felt too weak to argue.

'One day,' the man continued, 'you will learn to cross all dimensions of the human mind, free from the shackles of thoughts that bind you. But for right now, I'll make you a potion that will numb the urge for alcohol. But you will also have to fight the urge to drink yourself. The herbs are intelligent, they work better when their vibration matches your resolve to heal yourself. My son and I are both willing to stand by you and help you. We will pull through this together.' Sironka spoke in a gentle, reassuring voice.

He then asked Olamayain to bring him a few herbs from the market and started to collect a few stones and dried palm leaves to build a fire. He took out a small earthen pot from his cloth bag, placed it on top of the fire and put some water and dried herbs from a small leather pouch in it. He allowed the concoction to simmer for quite a while, and later, he added the fresh herbs that his son brought back. That gave the liquid a dark green colour. It looked a lot like slime, and Joy was asked to gulp it down once it was ready.

Joy calmly held his nose and gulped the liquid down. In no time, he felt extremely drowsy and slept.

Early next morning, they left for Dar-es-Salaam. Joy was extremely exhausted, and so he followed the two men and did everything they asked him to do. Wherever he found a comfortable spot, he lay down and fell asleep. It was only the next day, when he sat in the train that travelled across Tanzania, that he started to notice the world around him. He saw wildlife scuttle past, he saw a herd of elephants peacefully grazing. The train chugged along and meandered through a coastal jungle, and slowly, the canopy of trees eased out to open grasslands. He could see an odd trail or two disappearing into the bush, sometimes a spiral of smoke was a tell-tale sign of human settlement.

Sironka kept feeding Joy small bits of food. He also made him take a few sips of that foul concoction. When he showed signs of withdrawal symptoms, Sironka would wipe his brow with a wet, cool cloth and calm him down, making him smell some herbs and salt. He even diverted him with stories and songs. Olamayian would often catch Joy wiping his tears, and he would say something to lighten things and make Joy laugh.

Late at night, they reached their destination. They were

met by a young woman in the central family compound, which Joy later got to know was called a boma by the Maasais. Sironka introduced the woman as his wife. In a sweet childlike voice, she informed her husband that the kids were fast asleep. He instructed his wife to make an extra bed in their enkaji for Joy and he asked his son to string up a mosquito net around Joy's bed.

Joy had to bend his head to enter the hut. It was quite dark inside and it had a musty, woody aroma that permeated every corner. In some odd way, the smell was comforting. It reminded him of his mother's kitchen. The dying bonfire at the centre of the hut cast a few shadows around the room, creating a cosy and lived-in atmosphere. There were two or three very small holes in the walls, and they were covered sparingly with twigs. He saw that those were the only windows. He saw the children fast asleep in a small room, but then, suddenly out of the darkness, he heard a goat bleating. It came from inside the hut. He hoped he was not going to sleep next to a goat! He saw Sironka leaning over and patting something in the dark. Yes, it was a goat!

Sironka bent down and touched the goat's stomach. 'She is due to deliver her kid any day now,' he explained. 'So we keep her inside, in case the lions decide to feast on her.'

This simple sentence sent shudders down Joy's spine. He was not fond of all animals, and the wilder they got, the more he wanted to run far away.

'Lions?' he asked in a worried voice.

Sironka said, 'Yes, lions! We are very close to the Selous Game Reserve, so when you sleep, you will hear their call at night. Sometimes they roar and sometimes they just meow.'

He grinned cheekily when he saw how uncomfortable Joy was with this information.

Olamayian came in and asked Joy to follow him. He showed Joy a small enclosure at the back of the hut where he could clean himself before he went to bed. Joy enquired if Olamayian would sleep in the same hut.

'No, I live in another enkaji, but in the same boma. I stay with the other warrior friends and cousins, but soon I will be getting married and then my wife will build her own enkaji and I will live with her,' said the young Maasai.

Joy understood.

He was soon gladdened by the wash and he crept under the mosquito net and slowly, the sounds of the night lulled him into a deep sleep.

Sironka heard Joy come in and settle down. He knew the young man had fallen asleep. Then he slowly turned around and looked at Joy carefully. A lot needed to be done. How was he going to get Joy to break his patterns and stop hurting himself? How was he going to teach him to live an extraordinary life? His head was filled with so many questions, but something wiser spoke to him and told him to crack open Joy's heart. He had to enable Joy to receive and give love, he had to heal the hurt, the pain, the loss and fill every crack in Joy with hope and light. That would empower him to dream again and help him understand the ways of the universe. Sironka smiled. It was amazing how the great spirit always had all the answers. He now knew how Joy could begin his journey to becoming whole again.

When Joy woke the next morning, sunlight was streaming into the hut. He remembered that Olamayian had called the hut an enkaji. He saw three children watching him intently, and when they saw him awake, they burst into loud giggles. They clapped their hands and spoke in a language that he was unable to understand. One of the little boys ran away, and in a few minutes, brought back Sironka's wife.

'So you are finally awake! I was getting worried by the minute, but my husband said that you needed all the sleep that you could get. He has gone for some meetings today and will be back in the evening. You must be hungry. I have kept a little something for you to eat and drink,' she said in English.

Joy nodded. After freshening up and a meal of rice and fresh milk, Joy stepped out. He saw that it was a bright morning. Children were running around, women were busy cleaning and milking the cows. Many villagers stopped and stared at him. He sat under a tree, watching the Maasai dressed in their colourful wraps, going about their daily life. In some odd way, it was calming the storm within him. Soon, Olamayian dropped by and asked him if he was ready to go down to the village well to take a bath and wash his clothes.

Olamayian gave him a bar of soap. 'A small gift for you,' he said with a smile.

Joy laughed. 'Thank you, this is the best gift I have received in a while.'

He gathered his clothes and followed Olamayian out of the boma. On the way, they passed a large enclosure in the centre of the settlement with thorny brambles around its edges. It looked like a small fortress, except that the walls were alive; they were trees and shrubs that were growing and encased tightly together in a metal mesh. A strong smell of dung permeated the air.

The young Maasai pointed to it, and in a very proud voice, he informed Joy that this was one of his father's new projects. 'Our wealth is our cattle, our goats and our children. This enclosure is where we keep our livestock safe from wild animal attacks. This is the best practice that we, as a tribe, have taught ourselves. We don't cut down any trees to create the fence, and if we move, we leave something that will blend into the environment rather than taking away from it. We also have a well assigned to our tribe. Supply of water is extremely limited due to the frequent droughts that we experience. Two years ago, we had to walk five kilometres, one way, to fetch water from a waterhole that was also used by the wild animals. It was very dangerous. A number of lives were lost. But now, a few tribes share one well. It has made our lives so much easier.'

They reached the well and Joy could count around ten tall, young Maasais sitting around it, chatting away. All of them were wearing red robes and some had painted their body and hair with a red paint. They wore more jewellery than Olamayian did. After a round of introductions, the young warriors immediately made Joy feel like he was a part of their group. They switched to English, although not too well. Soon they put down their spears, took off their sandals and undressed.

This was a little unnerving for Joy, he had never ever participated in communal baths before. He asked Olamayian if he could go behind a bush to undress or if there was another place where he could have a bath in private.

Olamayian laughed aloud. 'You will end up being dinner for some wild animal. Joy, relax! We all are men here. No women or strangers will come this way. Wash your clothes and then have a bath in peace,' he assured him.

Joy hesitantly did what Olamayian had suggested, and after a while, being naked felt like the new normal around the others. The young men laughed, teased each other, and a large part of their day went by as they waited for their clothes to dry. Many of the young Maasai men caught a few winks under the trees while the others kept watch.

Joy felt extremely light and happy as he spent time with his new friends. He realized that he had not felt the urge to have a drink the entire time that he had been with them.

On the way back, as they neared their boma, there was a massive rush at the entrance of the enclosure. Goats, cattle, and their young herders were coming back home for the night. Shouts and sticks were swung through the air, tongues were clicked and a chorus of low hisses managed to get all the livestock safely back into the enclosure. The thorny branches were put back into place. Many of the young men raised their hand in greeting to Olamayian and also acknowledged Joy with a smile. Then they walked back, laughing and joking, full of stories about their near misses and adventures of the day.

Olamayian and Joy were standing on one side, waiting for the dust to settle down. 'These are all my cousins, my family and some friends. One day, you will know them all by name. Joy, I can take you to graze the animals someday,' said the young Maasai. 'I know you will enjoy the experience.'

Joy nodded.

As Joy walked further into the boma, he saw Sironka sitting under the only tree in their family compound with a few other older men, smoking their pipes.

Sironka called out to Joy. 'How was your day today? You look well rested and clean,' he said.

Joy smiled and told Sironka how much he had enjoyed the day. In the same breath, he added that as the evening was approaching, the urge to have a drink and be alone was growing stronger.

Sironka saw the worried look in Joy's eyes and he reached out and patted his back.

'Do not worry! Everything will slowly be set right again. I have left some of the concoction near your bed. Drink that and put your efforts into feeding yourself. We got you some rice and some spices from Stone Town. A friend brought in a few vegetables for you from the mission school. I hope it will work for you. We realized that our food may not go down well with you. Go in and ask Namelok if you can cook dinner on her stove,' Sironka said in a gentle, coaxing voice.

Joy nodded.

He then entered the enkaji. Namelok was busy feeding the children. The kids did look dusty and messy, but when they saw him, they gave him the biggest, toothless smiles. It melted his heart.

He asked Namelok if he could cook his meal, and she was relieved. 'I was worried. I did not know what to feed you,' she said.

Joy laughed.

He first drank the concoction, and when he had calmed down, he slowly got down to figuring out how to cook a meal for himself on a wood stove. He remembered his mother using such a fireplace to cook their meals. He was clumsy at first, but soon got the hang of it and quite enjoyed the process. One of the boys handed him a calabash filled with fresh milk for him to have along with his meal. As his food cooked, he rested against the wall, watching the children eat and play in the warm glow of the fire.

It was quite dark in the hut. Very little light filtered through the small holes in the wall and the wood fired stove created a hazy smoke screen around the hut. He watched Namelok getting the space ready for the night. She was a beautiful woman with a purposeful air about her. She wore the right amount of Maasai beads, which made her look quite regal. She seemed like the perfect companion for Sironka.

She handed him a small glass bottle of mosquito repellent. 'Please use this, we don't want you falling sick,' Namelok said. He noted that she had a twinkle in her eyes.

Joy ate his meal in silence, relishing every morsel. He drank some milk, cleaned up the pots and then, he stepped outside. The evening air was cool, and he sat out for quite a while, going over his day. This was a far cry from the life he had known. Today had been a day so different from any other. He had spent most of his time cleaning, grooming and caring for himself. It felt like a ritual of self-care that he had never, ever, indulged in his regular life.

After a while, he turned in for the night.

Later, when Sironka came into the enkaji to sleep, Namelok was awake and she enquired gently. 'How long will he stay with us? If it's for a while, I'll make some more space for him to keep his stuff. Or will you shift him into Olamayian's enkaji?'

'That is not an option. He is still fighting his addictions and he needs supervision. It will take him time to heal. I will need your help here. He needs to learn how to be a part of a family again. He has been a loner for way too long. He needs to feel needed, loved and accepted and made a part of something. He needs to start dreaming again,' Sironka shared.

Namelok looked at Joy curled under his net, fast asleep. 'My instincts tell me that he is a good, simple man. When I see him sleep, I can see the child in him. I will look after him,' she promised.

12

SPIRIT ANIMAL

Joy woke up. It was still dark in the hut, and he wrapped the blanket around himself. He heard Namelok trying to wake one of the children, who mumbled his protests. He felt safe in here, in this little hut in the middle of nowhere, with a family he barely knew. He sat up and saw Namelok in a corner of the hut, breastfeeding one of the younger children under a colourful sheet. She looked up and smiled. Joy looked away self-consciously but Namelok did not mind the intrusion. He was coming to realize that the Maasai were very comfortable in their skin and nudity was not such a big issue.

Namelok was soon busy instructing her older son in Maa, the language spoken by the Maasai. The boy grudgingly picked up a few empty calabashes, strung them around his neck and slipped his feet into his sandals.

'He milks some of the cows for me before he leaves for school, so the family has some milk to drink when they all wake up. Would you like to help him?' Namelok asked Joy.

Joy hesitated for a minute and then, he smiled. 'Why not? But I do not know how to milk cows,' he said sheepishly.

'Don't worry. He will teach you. It's easy,' Namelok assured him.

She looked at her son, he smiled and beckoned for Joy to follow him. The young boy made his way to the cattle enclosure, with Joy behind him.

'My name is Legishon. I am Namelok's eldest son and Olamayian's half-brother. I know your name is Joy. You have a nice smile, by the way. We can be friends,' said the young boy with a cheeky grin.

Legishon had a soft, steady voice. He encouraged and guided Joy while he tried to milk the cows. He smiled when he noticed Joy's inability to get the cows to listen to him. Through fits of giggles, he showed Joy how to wash the cow's udders before expressing their milk. All Joy could manage were a few painful kicks on his shins and half a calabash of milk for himself. His knuckles and fingers were red and sore, his feet were covered in dung, and he felt like a complete mess. By the time he got back to the enkaji, he was sweaty, sticky and ready to collapse.

Namelok looked at him and burst out laughing. 'I guess you need to have a bath, you look and smell like a cow,' she said.

Joy laughed, handed her the calabash and asked, 'Would you please warm it up for me, Namelok? I have earned every drop of it. Legishon is a professional milker, but soon I will be one too!'

In that instance, Namelok realized what her husband wanted her to do for Joy. This man needed both feminine and masculine energies to nurture him back to being whole again. Sironka would do what he had to, and now, she too knew what she had to do.

Joy was still busy scrapping the dung off his slippers as he followed Legishon to the village well.

'Joy, how often do you bathe in India?' asked Legishon.

'Twice a day,' said Joy in a reasoned tone.

Legishon stopped, stared at Joy and burst out laughing. 'That's such a waste of water. Here we all have to use water carefully. My father will soon install water tanks in our boma, yet for us, water is so very precious.'

As they walked back and entered the family enkaji, Joy was curious to know more about this thirteen-year-old and asked him a few questions about what he was studying in school.

'Legishon, I will be happy to help you with your studies any time,' said Joy.

'Brother, my mother can hear every word we speak. She understands English quite well. I know she will take you up on this offer and the little free time I have after school will now be gone.' The young boy was smiling and shaking his head. 'I cannot miss the evening gatherings! I learn so much about being a Maasai,' said the young man.

Joy curiously enquired about these gatherings.

'I am learning to become a man, a warrior! I spend time with senior and junior warriors. We learn, sing our songs, dance, tell stories. You are welcome to join us. Olamayian will be there too,' he offered.

After the boy left for school, Namelok showed Joy a place to put his belongings and then, she left for the day to collect firewood, milk the cows and do a whole lot of washing. Joy swept, dusted and cleaned up his spot in the hut. And when he looked around, he decided to clean and sort out the whole hut. He huffed and puffed, sorted and dusted the whole place down. Sironka dropped by and he saw Joy busy with his new project, so he smiled and left. He guessed it was not just Joy who needed them, they all needed a little of Joy in their lives too.

The enkaji looked amazing after he had cleaned and scrubbed the place spotless. When Namelok returned, she was thrilled to enter such a clean hut and could not stop herself from hugging Joy fondly, even though he looked dusty and dishevelled.

'Thank you so much for helping me out. I have been meaning to do this, but could not find the time,' she said.

Joy blushed. 'I have all the time in the world. I was wondering...can I start teaching the children from tomorrow? I need to do something!' Joy pleaded with her.

'That would be wonderful! Joy, you know it's okay not to do anything and nothing sometimes,' she said. 'Anyway, it's soon going to be time for the gathering. Today is boys' night out, you will like it. You better cook up a meal for yourself and remember to rub yourself down with the mosquito lotion. It will be good for you to meet up the other warriors there,' she told Joy.

Later in the evening, Joy followed the sound of singing and saw a bunch of young and old warriors huddled around a large bonfire. Some faces were familiar, but most were new. Olamayian was sitting cross legged, relaxed and happy. He called out to Joy and asked him to come and sit next to him.

The Maasai warriors were dressed in their tribal finery. Some were standing comfortably and some were leaning on their spears, their left foot hooked around the back of their right knee. The rest sat around the fire. They were singing in a hypnotic tone. They moved their heads, clicked their tongues in a rhythmic manner, and soon, one warrior would break free and start to jump high up in the air, his feet barely touching the ground, casting tall shadows around. The younger boys were clapping and hooting. All the people seemed so happy and were smiling. Few of the elders even used rattles and horns as musical instruments.

There was a sudden change in energy and Joy saw that someone important had joined the circle. The man wore a big headdress made of feathers and beads, and a robe made of animal hide. When Joy looked closely, he realized it was Sironka! He looked so grand and regal; he had an air of mystery about him. It felt as if he knew something that all of them did not, but Joy had already realized that this man was different.

Sironka sat down on a large wooden stump, cleared his throat and then, in a voice that could have calmed the storms, started to talk to all in Maa. Olamayian softly translated what Sironka was saying for Joy. It was a story about how the elephant came to be.

So the legend goes.

There was once a poor man who was tired of being poor. He heard that Ivonya-Ngai, the one who feeds the poor, would do anything to ease the poor's plight. So he decided to find Ivonya-Ngai. He went on a long journey, and one day, he came across a beautiful mansion, surrounded by lush green pastures, abundant herds of cattle and sheep grazing. He had found all this in the middle of the desert.

He knocked on the door of the mansion and Ivonya-Ngai generously opened the doors to paradise. When the poor man cried his heart out, he was offered a hundred sheep and a hundred cows. The poor man refused, demanding no charity but only wanting to know Ivonya-Nagai's secret to success. So, he was given an ointment to rub on his wife's canine teeth. The man left with it, and he convinced his wife to willingly participate because it would make them rich. She started using the ointment and soon, they noticed that her teeth had started to grow quite long.

Joy could see that the youngsters were completely engrossed in the story. Sironka's voice had a hypnotic effect. He was now standing in the middle of the circle and walking slowly, to and fro, his every action was followed by the rattles of his head dress and the swishing of his robe. He used his voice well. One moment he was loud, another moment he dropped it to a whisper. He made them gasp, he made them wince. He was a good storyteller and he had cast a spell on all of them.

When the wife's teeth had toughened the man decided to cut it. It hurt her so much; she cried out in pain, but he did not listen to her pleas. He took the ivory to the market and it fetched a good price. And so, his greed grew. He wanted to rub the ointment on his wife's teeth again, but she did not allow it. She begged him to spare her as she was carrying their child. He was beyond caring, and he did not listen to her. One night, when she was asleep, he rubbed the ointment on her teeth again. Slowly, her teeth started to grow and that's when she realized that her husband had tricked her.

Heartbroken, she ran far away from him, and went deep into the forest to keep herself and her unborn child safe. She fed on berries and fruits; she learnt the ways of the forest. But loneliness would often get to her. One night, she was restless and kept tossing and turning. At some point, she opened her eyes and saw that she was encircled by all her feminine ancestors. They had come to console her and she felt happy. She knew she was not alone anymore. She was protected. She was guided and she learnt the ancient wisdom of the earth, the sky and the galaxies. As time went by, she noticed her skin was changing its texture. It was now rough and dry and had turned muddy grey. She was growing bigger in size and had transformed into a mammoth.

One day, she saw her reflection in the water. She no longer looked like a human. She wondered why she had to suffer so much. That night, she cried herself to sleep.

She dreamt of her ancestors and they told her not to worry. Her transformation was a necessity for generations to come. She needed to accept and love herself, to look beyond her colour and size. She was far wiser than all the people on this earth. She needed to acknowledge who she had become for the whole world to revere her.

The next day, she went back to the waterhole and saw her reflection in the water. She saw how wise her eyes were, how white and long her teeth were, how well she could hear the sound of the jungle. She felt as though the earth was talking to her through her feet. She smiled. She knew she had transformed into true magnificence. Then the day arrived when she gave birth to the first baby elephant.

'So remember, always, that the elephant is the wise old lady of the jungle. The lion is the king, but she is the queen of the jungle. She too was once human. Elephants understand us more than we realize. They like to eat the food we eat and they like to come near our houses. So instead of shooing them away, know they come to meet us because they miss the feeling of home and the memory of the food that runs in their blood. Learn to be kind to them,' said Sironka.

By now, there was a hushed silence around the bonfire.

Suddenly, one of the younger boys cheekily perked up. 'I understand about the teeth, but how did the elephant get such a long nose?' he asked.

A young warrior sitting next to him smacked his head playfully and said, 'Don't you remember the story he told us about how the elephant got into a fight with a crocodile?'

The young boy rubbed the back of his head. 'I was not there that night. I had caught a fever. Maybe you can tell me that story later,' he said to the warrior.

Joy was listening intently and he realized that these storytelling evenings were a regular event, much like movie nights back home.

The evening carried on, and Sironka and the youngsters kept talking about the hidden lessons and messages in the story. There were debates, some healthy verbal disagreements. It was an enlightening experience. Joy wished he had grown up like this in Galgibaga. Everything he knew was so fragmented. Television, smartphones and the internet had taken over family time. It had put people into bubbles. People like him got so sucked into the virtual world that they had lost their connection with everything around them. Most of the youngsters wanted to leave Goa, their home, and go overseas. He too had done exactly that. Now he had no home or family left to go back to.

Joy walked back with Legishon, and as he got ready for bed, the evening was still alive in his head. He had learnt so much about the need to give the young a space to learn, to talk with the older generations in a non-condescending way. He had also learned so much about the gentle, wise elephant who is devoted to protecting the tribe, the reincarnation of ancestors and about community.

Days turned into weeks. Joy had quickly gotten into

a routine. He had not felt the urge to drink, thanks to Sironka's concoction and the busy schedule he was keeping. The addiction would rear its ugly head once in a while, but over the past few weeks, it had felt negligible. Every day he experienced a small victory when he lay back in his bed without having fed his addiction. He was quite proud of himself, but then, he could not discount the efforts made by Sironka, his family and the tribe who had made him feel at home. They kept an eye on him, and upon any sign of him acting a little out of sorts, Sironka would appear with one of his herbal remedies, few wise words and ways to heal.

His days now started early. He would help Legishon milk the cows and was slowly proving to be good at it, though he had a lot of catching up to do considering the little Maasai's skills. He came to realize that the cows loved music, so he sang songs till he was hoarse. He could now collect a full bucket or two of milk without getting kicked. He helped Namelok clean up the house, he cooked his meals and taught the children. He had taken to repairing some odd things around the house, and on seeing this, some of Namelok's friends had started to request his help with fixing things in their huts.

Gradually, he had become the official handyman of their tribe. The rest of the Maasai men in the tribe would often tease Joy about being the only man in demand around the boma. He spent the late afternoons with Olamayian and his friends. Often, Sironka would chat with him in the evenings. One such evening, Olamayian had come to his father's boma with a few friends. It was a special night as Joy was cooking them an Indian meal. A forest ranger had managed to pick up some spices for him from town, on Olamayian's request. Everyone was excited to eat an Indian meal, and it was quite a crowd in the boma by the time Joy served the food.

They all sat around the fire, eagerly awaiting their meal. They chatted and laughed; many backs and heads were slapped in jest but when they were handed their plates full of food, silence descended. They waited till Sironka put the first morsel of food in his mouth, and then the rest started eating. It was a simple rice and vegetable dish topped with dollops of clarified butter, which he had spent hours making.

Their silence bothered Joy. 'If it's not something you like, I really apologise. We Indians eat this often. The next time, I can make an Indian curry,' he said in a worried voice.

Sironka looked up. 'Joy, it's amazing.' Everyone else nodded in agreement and smiled at him.

They all went back to eating their meal in silence, savouring every morsel. Everyone deemed the meal a big success and wanted it to be a monthly event; they would even pitch in with supplies. Joy was so happy that he was able to do something to give back to his new family. In fact, he realized he had really enjoyed feeding people. It made him feel connected. He wondered why he had never done this before, but he never had many friends or felt like he was a part of a community. No one ever really came over to his and his ex-wife's house.

While Joy was helping Namelok clean up, Olamayian looked at Sironka and smiled. 'Father, this feels like magic. It's so good to see Joy smiling and happy. I can't imagine that a few weeks ago he had tried to kill himself. His energies have shifted. Do you feel his healing is complete now?' he asked.

Sironka laughed and said, 'His healing has just begun. I feel it's time now that you start taking him with you on your trips into the forest, along with the rangers.'

'What good will that do, father? These trips can be boring to watch. When I track, I am lost in my own world,' said the young Maasai.

Sironka smiled, 'You have to teach him nothing. He will learn just by being in nature. Like he has been learning to be a family man by living with us. He has been a loner all his life, so all this is a first for him and he is really making an effort. Most importantly, he is learning to belong to a tribe, a community and I have also noticed recently that he is learning to tell stories. I heard him tell the kids a bedtime story yesterday.'

Olamayian nodded. But he was still quite doubtful. He followed his father's instructions and took Joy into the forest to graze the cows for a start.

Joy saw how the young Maasai effortlessly manoeuvred the cows and hummed a song as they walked. The bells around the cows' neck rang a merry tune and the buzzing of the heat flies set the mood for the day. After a while, they found a clearing with enough juicy vegetation for the cows to feast on. The young Maasai found a place to settle down for the day, under a tree from where he had a vantage view.

The cows spread around and started to graze. The two men chatted about mundane stuff. Then Olamayian started to talk about his conservation work and his mission to keep the lions safe. He talked of his many trips into the forest with the rangers. He told Joy about the first time he saw a female elephant that had been killed by the poachers. They had left her a mess, having mercilessly mutilated her face to remove the ivory. Her three-month-old calf would go into hiding every time there was a human around. Olamayian remembered how he had seethed with so much anger and rage for days. But as he worked with the rangers, he realized that animal killing was a business. Many international flights landed on the game reserve with a bunch of rich foreigners who would hunt the lions down for a bit of sport and trophy pictures. He initially thought that his tribesmen were the problem, but the Maasai only killed to protect themselves now. The Maasai themselves were worried about the declining numbers of lions and often wondered why they were being made a scapegoat by the government. In fact, the government could use their knowledge and wisdom to protect their habitat. So, he had decided to put his efforts into protecting the wildlife and fighting for the rights of his people.

'I soon realized my anger had to become a constructive force. I would really like you to come with me, Joy. You can try your hand at being a conservationist, rather than being the handyman of the tribe. All the men are sceptical about you being so useful because they do not feel needed by their women anymore,' said Olamayian with a laugh.

Joy laughed too. 'I guess you are right! No harm in having a change of scenery.'

The heat, the occasional breeze and the hum of buzzing flies lulled Joy into a deep sleep. Olamayian let Joy sleep. He walked around to ensure that none of the cattle strayed away, and also to let the wild animals hiding in the bush know that the cattle belonged to him. When he got back, he heard Joy mumble. Olamayian also noticed that Joy's cheeks were streaked with tears.

He gently shook Joy awake. 'Joy, are you okay?'

Joy woke and he wiped his tears. 'I was dreaming of Ollie. I was swimming deep down in the ocean and I saw him in the distance, but as soon as I got closer, he would disappear. This is the first time I have dreamt of Ollie since we have parted. I miss him, Olamayian. I know he must have come to the beach to meet me but I was always too drunk to care. I feel that I have let him down and I cannot forgive myself for this.' Joy was so overcome with emotion that he started to cry again.

'I don't know where he is or where to find him. I am filled with so much regret. I feel lost when I think of my failure as a friend and about our lost connection. I keep myself occupied every day, because my whole life, I have only worked. If I get a few moments to myself, I start to worry about the fact that I am wasting my life, just like I did in India. I start to feel guilty. I wonder how I am supposed to live my life now. Should I go back to my country? I do not know what I am supposed to do anymore!'

The dream had stripped him off his armour. The vulnerable, lost child in Joy was visible.

Olamayian sat down next to Joy, patted him on the back gently, like he would for a child and said, 'I think you need to cry, Joy. My grandfather said that we need to let the tears flow in order to make space for the smiles in our hearts. These cows have been witnesses to my tears so many times.'

Joy nodded in agreement. When his mind calmed down, he felt the urge to talk to Olamayian about his childhood. He told Olamayian about how he had felt homeless for so many years, especially after his mother had died. And he felt it more so now.

Olamayian took Joy's hands and placed them on his friend's chest. Then, he said, 'Home is where your heart is! When you feel sad, scared or broken, close your eyes, slow your breath down and put your hand where I have placed it now. Know you are home. A heart filled with love has all the wisdom of the universe and it has the power to guide you to do the right thing. It will ease your hurt, calm your fears, you will realize that you have never been alone. The whole universe is in you, helping you to be magnificent. But you need to connect, ask and believe. Let's both do it now.'

Joy closed his eyes and slowed his breath. Soon, he felt calmer.

'What does your wise heart say, Joy? Say the first thing that comes to your mind,' Olamayian prompted.

'It's saying that Ollie loves me, no matter what I did or did not do,' replied Joy.

'I want you to know that today you choose to meet him again,' said Olamayian.

Later that evening, Joy sat in Olamayian's enkaji around the fire, along with the other warriors. They had just finished a meal of ugali, a thick maize porridge, which he ate with a green plant stew. The rest of the men had large helpings of meat that they had cooked specially for themselves. To him, it looked a little raw, but they relished it. It was a fun evening! Most of the warriors were young and Joy felt light and happy as he watched them fooling around, singing and dancing.

Olamayian requested Joy to go back to his father's hut. 'I don't want you getting bitten by insects. Namelok is very particular about you not falling sick. So, we have all been warned to look after you.'

Later, Olamayian met Sironka and told him about Joy's emotional breakdown.

'He is not proud of his roots, father! He does not know what he is expected to do in this lifetime, and he has some unfinished business with his father. To top it all, he misses his turtle too. I can't find his turtle for him, but I will introduce him to a friend of mine,' said Olamayain.

Sironka reached out, hugged his son and kissed him on the forehead. 'You did good.'

The next few weeks, Joy woke up early every morning, helped around the house, wore the ranger's uniform that Olamayian lent him and accompanied the young Maasai and other rangers in a jeep. The whole day was spent tracking wild animals, helping ones in distress, keeping a tab on the game reserve boundaries and ensuring that poachers were at bay. Then, there were days with casualties, where he saw animals trapped and butchered by the poachers. That made him feel sick and angry. Joy understood what the young Maasai had told him about focusing on the positive aspects. The first few days after these sightings, he was unable to eat food at night. But then in the days that followed, Olamayian and the rangers would talk him into refocusing on their mission.

Joy saw how the rangers doubled their efforts to keep the animals safe. They made it a point to go deeper into the game reserve and intensify their watch. One such day, while they were on one of their patrols, another Maasai tracker reached out to Olamayian on the radio. Joy had started to pick up on words and knew the difference between Swahili, which was the official language of Tanzania, and Maa, spoken only by the Maasai. Olamayian was visibly excited and gave the coordinates to the ranger who was driving.

'I just found out that an old friend is close by. I would like to introduce him to you,' he told Joy.

They drove deeper into the forest and they saw a zeal of zebras running helter-skelter. Suddenly, a lion came streaking out of the canopy of trees, chased a zebra and took it down with ease. The zebra struggled to break free, but could not. Olamayian put his hand on the ranger's forearm, a sign for him to cut the engine. Two other lions sauntered out from the bush and walked towards the fresh kill and started to feast on it. The lion who had killed the zebra sniffed the air, and then he started walking towards the jeep.

'The lion is walking towards us and this is an open jeep!' Joy visibly started to panic.

Olamayian got off and started to walk towards the lion. Joy heard the ranger taking in a deep breath and saw beads of sweat appearing on his forehead. Then something strange happened. Both man and lion stood, watching each other, for a few minutes. The lion sniffed the air again and walked to Olamayian. He rubbed his head against Olamayian's legs, just like a pet cat would do. Then he purred, and it sounded like a deep rumble. The young Maasai stroked the lion's head and rubbed it behind the ears. Both man and animal watched the other lions eat the zebra. After a while, Olamayian bent down and whispered something into the lion's ear. The lion licked his hand, slowly walked back to join the feast and the young Maasai walked back to the jeep.

No one spoke on the ride back. Olamayian was very quiet, lost in his thoughts. Although Joy was brimming with questions, he let the young Maasai be. The ranger dropped them off at the entrance of their boma.

Olamayian and Joy settled down under the tree where the elders sat. No one else was there.

'He is my Ollie,' Olamayian explained. Then, he went on to tell him the story of their first encounter.

'Every time we meet, I am moved beyond words and my heart fills with so much love and respect for him. He is my greatest teacher and friend. He talks to me in my dreams about things that may happen. He guides me when I am confused, he helps me remain balanced and do the right thing. He keeps me aligned to my purpose, protects me and my family from any harm. He gives me strength to be the best warrior of my tribe and the best tracker for the rangers. I attribute most of my tracking skills to him.' The young Maasai appeared overwhelmed as he spoke about the lion.

Joy looked confused. 'The lion is your friend, like Ollie and I are friends, but I don't understand the rest. How does he teach you? How do you understand him?'

Olamayian smiled. 'He talks to me, just like we are both talking right now. In our physical reality, he roars and purrs like a lion, but in my heart, he talks like a human would. My father has taught me that there are two worlds, one that we see and the one that we don't.'

Joy shook his head in confusion, still trying to comprehend what Olamayian was saying.

'When it's time, my father will guide you. All I can tell you at this point is my reality, my connection with my lion. I don't expect people living in the urban world to understand our ways, but your soul has chosen to be in our world. We cannot choose which animal becomes our spirit helper. They choose us on the day we are born. The animal will present itself to us when the time is right, either in a physical or spiritual form. We need to imbibe their attributes. I know that no matter what happens to me in this lifetime, I am not standing alone; my lion is with me all the time,' said Olamayian.

'What if our spirit helper is killed or dies? They live in the wild and anything could happen.' Joy expressed his biggest fear. He always worried about something happening to Ollie.

'Even then we are connected! I close my eyes and connect to his spirit form. Even if he ever passes on to the next world, he will still be there with me,' said the young Maasai.

Joy was silent for a few minutes and then asked, 'Do you think Ollie is my spirit helper?'

Olamayian looked at him and asked back, 'What do you feel, Joy? You watched me and my lion today.'

Joy's eyes were brimming with tears. 'I guess he is, and I am heartbroken that I did not treat him well. Now he has gone.'

'He has not gone away, Joy. If you dreamt of him, he is trying to connect back to you. We are taught to always honour our animal spirit. We sing about their powers, we wear a part of them on us,' said Olamayian as he showed Joy the tooth he was wearing on his neck. 'This belongs to a lion who was killed by a poacher. Every time I touch it, it strengthens my resolve to do my bit to protect the king and his forest. So you need to find a way to honour Ollie. Close your eyes, calm your mind and talk to him. Ask him to show you how to honour him and your friendship, and one day, he will start talking to you. Just don't give up till he does.'

Having said this, Olamayian could see that Joy was

already feeling better.

Joy entered the hut and went to his things. He looked at the stash of bits and odds that he had collected. He found what he was looking for—a broken seashell that had stuck to Ollie's shell when he had come out of the sea in Paje. He asked Namelok to help him string the shell up into a nice neckpiece that he could wear. In no time, she had made one for him. He wore it.

That night, he felt peaceful and he spoke to Ollie before he closed his eyes. But Ollie still did not say a word to him. Joy did not give up. From that night onwards, every night, for the next few weeks, he kept talking to Ollie. Early one morning, he dreamt of Ollie and him swimming in the middle of the ocean. Ollie was playfully nudging him, and they were both laughing and happy. He reached out and held Ollie's flipper. Everything felt so real that when he woke up, it took him some time to get his bearings. He could feel his hand tingling. He touched it and smiled. Ollie was alive, and so was he!

> 'So I guess I'll leave you tonight at a point where Joy needs to rest, just like all of us here. Tomorrow is another evening of storytelling. Rest, eat, feel the breeze, taste the salt in the air, be mindful of every moment and remember to smile! Don't dwell too much on the story. Just allow it to settle inside you. Goodnight, and see you all tomorrow.'
>
> The day's session had been a very long one, but nobody seemed to mind that it was quite late.

13

THE PROMISE

The next day. The same place, same people. The storyteller settled down in his chair and the audience got comfortable in their chosen spots. He continued with the story...

One afternoon, when Joy came back to the boma, he saw a bunch of women dressed in their Maasai finery, sitting in a circle around a foreigner. Namelok asked him to join the circle and help them understand what the foreigner was saying.

They went on to tell him about the new project that Sironka had enrolled the women into. It was about rearing bees and collecting honey, explained the American woman. They were going to train the Maasai women to become bee keepers, which in turn, would help the flora and fauna of the forest to flourish. Besides, the women could sell the honey in the local markets to tourists in resorts around the game reserves. But first, they would need to construct bee boxes for the activity to commence.

Joy smiled when he heard the excited voices and saw their childlike enthusiasm. He knew that the Maasai women were not going to construct anything, nor were the men. As he was their glorified handyman, he would have to do it for them. So he asked all the right questions. The American woman handed him the drawings for the box.

She too had realized his role.

All the women left, except for an elderly lady who sat in a corner, chatting with Namelok. She looked at Joy and smiled. Namelok informed him that she was Sironka's first wife! She noted the puzzled look on Joy's face.

'In our world, a man can have many wives. It is normal. In fact, we never have an issue with our co-wives. We live as one big family, as friends. Naserian is a very wise woman. She helps me bring up my children and guides me through difficult times. She often says that she is blessed with such a good friend in Sironka, but has a better friend in me.' Namelok laughed and gently stroked Naserian's hand.

'Naserian feels that it's best if you move to the mission school to construct the boxes, since you are the only one in the tribe who can help us. We know if Sironka puts in a word, Father Frances, the mission in-charge, will lend his tools to you. We can get someone to get the wood together for you,' informed Namelok.

Two weeks later, Joy was asked to pack few clothes and essentials. All the material he needed to construct the bee boxes had arrived. He was going on a trip, along with Sironka, and Joy was really excited. It was a change of scene and a new challenge that he was really looking forward to. He was game to do anything to keep his mind active.

Early next morning, a ranger came to pick them up in a jeep. Namelok and her friends seemed sad to see Joy go.

Sironka burst out laughing on seeing the women fuss over Joy. 'Ladies, please stop sulking. He is just going away for a few days. What would you do if he decided to go back to his country?'

He saw the look of absolute horror cross their faces. He patted Joy on his back. 'Just know you are much loved and will be missed by our women if you ever decide to go back to India.'

They reached the mission after quite a few hours. It took a while because after every few kilometres, someone would hail them to talk to Sironka. Soon enough, Joy realized that Sironka was truly an important man in the community. When they entered the mission gates, the jeep slowed down. They were being followed by a bunch of children. They stopped outside a large white building with a thatched roof. A short, stout man with a sun-burnt face came to greet them.

He had a warm smile and sparkling eyes. His shock of white hair gave him the appearance of a teddy bear. He gently asked the children to go to their classes. 'Sironka, my friend! I have missed you,' he said in a French accent.

The friends met each other affectionately. Sironka looked like a tall, ebony pillar next to the French man.

'Father Frances, meet Joy. He is from India and will be helping the tribe with the new beekeeping project,' said Sironka proudly.

Joy shook hands with Father Frances. 'Good to meet you finally, Joy. I have heard a lot about you and the project from Naserian.'

They all walked into the building, it was cool inside. Joy could see a number of classrooms where children were studying. Father Frances ushered them into a large office and they sat on the wooden chairs that had been offered to them.

'I hope you will be spending some time with us, Sironka,' asked Father Frances.

'Yes, I will be. I need to discuss a few things with you,' Sironka assured his friend. The priest looked pleased.

A girl entered the room and walked up to Sironka. She touched him on the shoulder and smiled at him. 'So good to see you, father!'

Joy looked at Sironka's daughter. He was faced with a beautiful woman. Her hair, skin and eyes were much lighter than that of the other Maasais, but the family resemblance was striking. She had Olamayian's smile and Sironka's nose and bone structure. She was not very tall. Her hands and arms were delicate. She was wearing a khaki jumpsuit that matched the colour of her curly hair. She had tamed the tight corkscrew curls by pulling them away from her face into a ponytail. She had one of the most transparent faces Joy had ever seen. A person could read her mind by just looking at her large, light-brown eyes.

Sironka introduced her to Joy. 'Nalangu this is Joy, our friend from India.'

Joy smiled self-consciously and shyly mumbled a greeting.

'I have heard a lot about you from my brother, Olamayian, when he dropped by...and also from Naserian, my mother. She has been waiting for you and has a lot of work lined up here. Be forewarned, the fence of the vegetable garden needs repairing and my mother complains that Father Frances is too lazy to help her,' Nalangu said with a giggle.

Father Frances smiled. 'Please tell Naserian that I am getting too old for this. She did the right thing by finding a younger man to do her bidding'.

All of them burst out laughing and Joy felt at ease immediately.

Father Frances looked at Joy. 'Young man, we have a room ready for you. Sironka always sleeps under the stars.

Dinner is at six, at my house.'

Then, Nalangu asked Joy to follow her. They walked out of the school building, crossed a large playground, and went towards a long row of rooms. All of them had thatched roofs. His room had a large window that looked out into the thicket of trees, and he could see a watering hole in the distance.

'In the early mornings and evenings, you will see the animals come for a drink,' said Nalangu. 'After you have freshened up, come to the third room down the verandah. Father Frances lives there and you can have some tea and cakes.' With that, she left.

Joy sat on the bed and tested the mattress with his hands. After many months, he was going to sleep on a bed again. It felt strange. He looked out of the window and wondered where his life was going. He remembered the days when he would meticulously plan everything. His life had taken an odd curve. From being an investment banker to a shack owner, to now making bee boxes for the Maasai! He shook his head as he realized it was best to go with the flow and not overanalyse things.

He rested for a while. Then he freshened up and walked across to Father Frances' room. Sironka and the priest were chatting animatedly, both oblivious to the fact that Joy had joined them. Joy listened and heard about how Sironka had enrolled his semi-nomadic tribe into so many new projects. His vision was to turn their Maasai settlement into an eco-retreat where people could come and stay with them, learn about their way of living and methods of conservation. He was creating semi-permanent housing structures for it, keeping the Maasai way of living in mind, except for the piping and plumbing for the water tanks.

Joy was quite fascinated by the eco-retreat project. He also heard about the soap-making project headed and run by the women of the boma, which was already being replicated by other Maasai tribes. Lack of personal hygiene was often a cause of sickness and death among the Maasai. Many foreign reporters had come to cover the cause. Sironka hoped that the beekeeping and honey-making project would work the same magic. The success of these projects brought in a steady stream of income into the hands of the women and so they did not have to be dependent on the men. Joy realized that Sironka really wanted to empower women and wanted them to start playing an important role in the development of the tribe. He kept repeating that he had to keep his promise to his wife, he had to ensure that his daughter and many other daughters born into the Maasai tribes live a self-sufficient, happy and abundant life.

The women were also going to build new enkajis, under the supervision of Father Frances, for visitors to stay in. Joy thought this was a brilliant idea. In his experience, the Maasai had a really different way of living and the world needed to experience it as well.

It was different and varied. On some occasions, he had even seen them drink cow's blood mixed into their morning milk. The milk took on a pretty pink hue. But he just could not get himself to taste it, even though Olamayian told him that it would boost his immunity. He had accepted this as a part of their culture. Very rarely did the Masaai eat vegetables. Their diet consisted more of a plain rice and maize porridge, unlike Indians who could not live without curry, flavouring their food with spices and chilli. He was the only one, along with the cows, consuming all the plants and vegetables in the tribe. He was often made fun of for it. He had started to cook quite regularly for them and he frequently incorporated different edible plants, berries and vegetables into their diet. They all ate it with relish.

Nalangu offered him some tea and cakes, which tasted like a slice of heaven. The sugar rush made him feel slightly light-headed and left him smiling. He watched as the children finished their football game and realized that there were very few girls around. When he enquired about it, Nalangu informed him that it was a struggle to convince the Maasai families to send their girls to be educated at the mission school. They felt that the main role of women was to tend to the cattle, produce babies, and do the housework; education was a waste of time. But mindsets were changing, and she was seeing a lot of progress.

After a hearty dinner and unending cups of sweet tea, they all retired to bed. On the way back to his room, Joy heard Sironka calling out to him. Sironka was sitting under a tree. He spread out a shuka and asked Joy to sit with him for a while. He had a humble air to him, but his eyes were sharp and wise.

'Joy, how old was your father when he died?' asked Sironka out of the blue.

Joy was taken aback by Sironka's sudden interest in his father. He remained silent for a few minutes. 'He was sixty-eight years old,' he finally replied.

'Do you miss your father?' enquired Sironka.

'I do not miss him as much as I miss my mother, but he has been on my mind a lot, especially since I was on the boat,' Joy said nonchalantly.

'What did you not like about him?' Sironka asked.

'I did not like the fact that he was an alcoholic, a stubborn man, even violent at times. I hated how he would always create a situation that would lead to a fight. He was never happy with anything I did—no words of encouragement ever. I wish he had not made my childhood a living hell!' Joy replied vehemently.

Sironka laughed. 'We are the creators of whatever happens in our life. You created your own living hell,' he said.

Joy looked puzzled. 'How am I responsible for my father being a violent alcoholic and a stubborn old fool? I was just a young boy. How did I create all that unpleasantness in my life?' His voice had taken on an irritated tone.

Sironka could see that his words had unsettled Joy. Sironka gently patted his back to calm him. 'Joy, when I went walking about in the forest, many ancient enlightened beings showed me priceless secrets. They told me that before we decide to take birth on earth, we choose our parents and all the people we want in our life. We choose our life's purpose and the situations that will help us reach it. Once we take birth, we forget about all our choices and our purpose in life. Some of us wander around aimlessly, not knowing what we are looking for, while some of us get our act together. Incidents keep happening to propel us towards our life's purpose. So instead of blaming our luck or fate, we must understand why we chose the people and situations in our life. It will bring us clarity. We can learn to move to higher levels of spiritual consciousness,' Sironka explained in a calm voice.

'It's beautiful in paradise where all souls live, and it is hard for a soul to come to earth as a human. Life on earth is not easy, but once you get better at it, it will become easier. Understand this, my son, every experience, good or bad, is part of a bigger plan that will collectively push us to fulfil our life's purpose and to contribute to the evolution of humankind. We are not living just for ourselves, but for others as well.' Sironka smiled gently.

'So Sironka, let me get this straight, what you are saying is that earth is just one big school for us? We graduate as humans, and if I graduate with honours, I will help humanity?' asked Joy.

'Yes, Joy! But you need not be an honours student. You just need to be a happy, flexible and a curious student. And the journey is all about becoming something magnificent. Along this journey, what matters is how many lives we touch, how many people we inspire! Many don't get the formula right. We think life is about possessions: my house, my money, my land, my emotions, my feelings. We fail to realize that all of these things are transient. Not many of us know that we have the key to unlock the door to pure bliss. It lies within us, not in another person or thing. Once we know it, then even the worst thing, even hurt or loss of our most precious objects, will not shake our foundation.' Sironka paused as he saw Joy struggling to make sense of this.

'Joy, let me tell you a secret. We always have to improve ourselves and bridge the gap between ourselves and our divine selves. We all are divine beings with human experiences. It's tough in the beginning. You will make mistakes, you will hurt, you will cry. But you know you will never be destroyed because nothing can destroy you,' Sironka said.

That finally eased Joy's confusion and he broke into a smile. 'I seem to have chosen a tough course. I am not sure if I will ever graduate. Most of the time I feel lost,

I just want to give up and drop out. But looks like the headmaster or head mistress is adamant and sends me teachers to help me with my work. You surely are one such teacher, Sironka.'

Sironka laughed heartily. 'I am just one of them, you have others. Your turtle, and even Legishon is one. Hasn't he turned you into a master milker?'

'But honestly, Sironka, I don't know what I am supposed to do or achieve in life anymore. These days, I just live so aimlessly. I am confused because what drove me before holds no ground now,' Joy confessed.

Sironka ruffled his hair. 'You are doing just what you are supposed to do, and sometimes, that means doing nothing. You have no idea how much you have learnt and grown in the last few months just by being aimless. You are making space within you to recreate your future. I know it's something that you cannot understand now, but trust the process. One day you will be so glad for this period of nothingness. At times it's good to not have an agenda, to stop doing and just being. Whatever you are doing now, will one day make sense. Trust the process and surrender. Take it one day at a time.'

Sironka pointed to the sky and said, 'Somewhere up there, your ancestors reside and they are watching over you. Ask them to help you, be your guides. It is important to honour your father's memory, Joy. We have to find it in our hearts to respect, accept and love the people who have not made great life choices. Your father was a child of the creator and did the best he could have done.'

'But Sironka, because of his mistakes and weaknesses, my mother and I went through so much hurt and pain,' Joy protested.

Sironka smiled. 'Joy, he was doing and being exactly as he was meant to do and be. This is how it really goes: when your soul chose him as a father, you both knew he was going to be an alcoholic. As you grew up, you had the choice to not become one, but you also took the path of addiction. I am sure you now realize how an alcoholic person feels. Your father must have felt like this too, he must have also tried to get rid of the addiction, felt heartbroken for hurting you and your mother. When we are immature, we notice actions. When we become wiser, we notice the emotions behind those actions. Joy, you are being helped by the creator to end your addiction. You are truly blessed, so concentrate and focus on your blessing instead of what went wrong in the past.'

Joy nodded in agreement. 'Yes, on the boat I was forced to give up my drinking and now I have you to help me. I am very grateful.'

'Try finding the magic in both the bad and the good in life! Anyway, enough talking now,' Sironka said. He got up and stretched himself. 'I need to rest my old bones now. Tomorrow is another beautiful day and if I don't wake up, just bury me under this tree.'

When Sironka noticed the shocked expression on Joy's face, he laughed out loud. 'At the right time, you will understand.'

Sironka then rolled out of his bed under the tree and lay down. 'Before you go, I want you to know why I love this tree so much. This is a grandfather tree. There are many grandfather trees spaced out at a comfortable distance from each other. Countless trees are connected to this tree by a very intricate network of roots under the soil. If a grandfather tree is cut, many other trees will perish and die without reason. This tree has a very strong life source coursing through every part of it, and when I sleep under it, I can hear the trees talking to each other. I can feel its energy flowing through me. It pains me when I visit the urban world. I see them thoughtlessly chopping down trees to make space for their constructions without giving any thought to the trees, soil or wind or asking permission. Our ancestors often said, "Sit under a grandfather tree and you will imbibe ancient wisdom. Dip your feet into a grandmother river and she will wash your soul clean."'

They were both silent for some time and then Joy wished Sironka goodnight and left for his room. As Joy lay in bed, he decided to be grateful for the good and the bad in his life. Some of what Sironka had said made sense, while some of it still seemed too complicated.

Joy spent most of the next day setting up his carpentry workshop. By evening, Olamayian and his friends came by to pick up Sironka and the plumbers who were going to lay some pipelines for the new washrooms and water storage tanks in their boma. After they drove off, Joy went to the back to help Nalangu cook dinner. It was easy being around her. They laughed, talked about their family, life and why the moon shone brighter on cloudy nights. Joy was happy to have found another friend.

Days went by quickly. Joy was busy creating bee homes. They looked like small masterpieces. He had fallen into a routine of making the bee boxes, helping Father Frances with computer-related work, cooking meals with Nalangu, and playing football with the children. Sometimes, he taught Nalangu how to cook some Indian food with the limited spices and condiments they had in Father Frances's pantry.

After dinner, Joy walked Nalangu back to her boma. It was a long walk and they talked on the way. They discussed books, conservation and other random fun things that friends share. She told him about her life and how, when she turned thirteen, she was sent with Naserian to live in the mission. Young Maasai girls were not allowed to stay in the same enkaji as their father after a certain age. But her father was very clear. He did not want her to be left unattended and unsupervised in another hut where the other girls of her age usually stayed.

Sironka wanted Nalangu to receive a well-rounded education and enough exposure to be self-employed. He went against tradition and did not get her circumcised. 'I think one of the most significant causes my father is still fighting against is female circumcision as a rite of passage. What is surprising is that many elders in the Maasai tribes are supporting him, but he has made enemies too. Many of the Maasai traditionalists don't want this tradition to be changed as they believe that the uncut woman is unlucky and needs to be shunned.'

The more Joy learnt about Sironka, the more he loved and respected him.

At other times, Joy helped Naserian extend and tend the herb and vegetable garden. He soon realized that he enjoyed getting his hands dirty in the soil. Evenings that he spent with Nalangu and her mother were quite relaxing and peaceful for him.

As days turned to weeks, Naserian noticed a growing affection between Joy and her daughter. Nalangu looked radiant and happy in Joy's company. She teased him, and she would laugh like she never had before. Naserian was growing worried at this, and she knew that a time would come when a few hard decisions would have to be made.

Meanwhile, at some point, Joy had come to realize that he had fallen in love with Nalangu. Nalangu was a simple, happy soul. Her innocence and childlike purity radiated through her very being. She was truly beautiful, inside and out. Her smile could light up his day. Her eyes twinkled when she teased him and would tear up if she heard a sad story. She had a soft heart, and he could see that she was way wiser than her years. She was indeed Sironka's daughter!

He found many excuses in the day to be around her. She smelt of fresh roses. Her soft, feminine fragrance made him want to hold and kiss her, but he kept his feelings in check. He did not want to scare her away. She was much younger than him. And while she had never mentioned any other man in her life, he was still a married man. Getting involved in a relationship was the last thing he wanted.

One day, Joy told her about his life in India. She silently heard him and when he dropped her outside her boma, she reached out and held his hand.

'Don't be sad, Joy. There is always a bigger plan and reason,' she said innocently. He smiled and nodded.

Soon, a month and two weeks had passed. Joy had finished making all the bee boxes. Naserian's vegetable garden looked well organized. A ranger dropped by to let Joy know that Olamayian was coming in a day or two to pick him up. That night, Father Frances insisted on cooking dinner to thank Joy. After dinner, they all sat out in the verandah and spoke about the future. Father Frances inquired whether Joy would ever consider going back to his country and Joy said he was not sure yet.

'At this point in my life, I just take each day as it comes, just as Sironka has taught me,' Joy said with a smile.

'You are good at computers, a great cow milker, a ranger in the making, a carpenter, a good farmer too... The list is endless!' said Father Frances.

Joy laughed and added to the list. 'I ran a shack back in India, I now cook regularly for the tribe. I am a jack of all trades and master of none, and yes, I enjoy telling stories these days, but I am not as good as Sironka is at it.'

Father Frances laughed out loud. 'No one is as good as the old goat. He is also an amazing visionary. I feel one of the best things that he and a few elders have done is to create the Maasai Olympics. Someday I hope you get the chance to see it.'

Joy was surprised. 'Maasai Olympics?' he asked.

'Yes. For the young Maasai men, the easiest way to achieve warrior status was to kill a lion single-handedly. Now, there are too many people and too few lions. So, the Maasai Olympics was created to celebrate Maasai culture. The winners receive cash prizes and medals of honour. Over the years, they have added many new categories, the latest being for best conservation efforts by a boma or a community. I like that one. Then there are trophies for bull breeding. The young warriors now have a way to show off their warrior skill sets, they have something to train for, they get university scholarships for being the best runners and we sponsor them to run marathons around the world.' Father Frances sounded so proud and enthusiastic about the whole concept.

'I know, Father! I have come to know that our boma is very progressive. I am absolutely fascinated by the live tree walls Sironka has built to safeguard the cattle,' said Joy.

'When I first met Sironka, many years ago, I remember driving to the boma. All the enkajis were built in a wide circle and the lifestock stayed in the centre. So I had to walk through slush, dung and flies to get to Sironka's enkaji. He informed me that they kept their livestock and themselves safe from wild animal attacks by erecting these flimsy, tall, thorny, dried bushes around their boma. So these living and ever-growing wall fences are a blessing. I am amazed at how civilized the boma looks now. It has become a shining example for the government to show other Maasai tribes,' Father Frances said with pride.

Joy was curious about the man he had come to respect over the past few months. He wondered what drove him, but he also wanted to get to know more about the Maasai. 'Father Frances, don't you feel that the Maasai are a semi-nomadic, pastoral tribe and settling down in one area could be limiting for them? They will become bound to a place and may lose their essence,' Joy pointed out, a little worried.

'I agree, but the Maasai are the best people to evaluate what needs to be kept and what needs to be shed with changing times. Their stake on the land is reducing. It is either being taken by urban development, farming, conservation projects or national reserves. They need to limit their wandering, which is sad. In the past, the animals and the Maasai coexisted, but now the balance has tipped. Efforts are being made to teach the Maasai the economic value of wildlife in their land, so rather than killing, they can conserve. They are the best conservationists, but the government is taking away their rights,' said the priest.

Joy realized that the problem was deeper than he had perceived.

'The world is moving forward with such speed that the Maasai will need to embrace change. Unfortunately— or fortunately—the national reserve boundaries will need to be respected. The interesting thing is that everything Sironka has created is temporary. They can move within no time and set up camp anywhere, anytime! Men like him are rare.'

Joy could see that Father Frances had immense respect for Sironka. He was silent. The conversation was insightful and it took him down memory lane. He remembered Chandrakant and his green tribune buddies in Galgibaga. He had been insensitive to their repeated requests to shut down his shack as it was too close to the beach. They had offered to help him shift his business to someplace else, but Joy had gotten it in him to stand up and not be bullied by these men. Not only had he been insensitive, but he was rude as well. Joy was lost in thought. He did not realize that Nalangu had cleared the cups and plates.

Father Frances got up to retire for the night. 'Joy, you will be leaving us soon and we will all miss you. I wondered why Sironka bent the rules to accommodate you into his life. You know by now that the Maasai have some very strict rules that they live by. Uncircumcised men are not allowed in their homes. And yet, you live with him in his enkaji. Sironka mentioned that you are on a quest and you needed to be with him and the family. I wish you all the best and may you find what you need.'

Nalangu informed both the men that she would be sleeping in one of the rooms next to Joy's because it was too late to go back to her enkaji now. As she reached her door, she turned around and hugged Joy. 'Father Frances was right in saying that we all will miss you when you leave,' she said.

Although Joy was tempted to hold her close, he did not do so.

Early the next afternoon, Sironka arrived. Joy hugged Sironka and could not stop smiling.

'You look happy, my boy! I hope you are ready to come back with us now?' asked Sironka.

Joy smiled and nodded. Sironka spent most of the day with Father Frances and early in the evening, he went to meet Naserian and Nalangu. Joy met Olamayian and caught up on news of the boma and the new, improved tourist huts. Joy was looking forward to seeing these traditional Maasai enkajis redesigned by Father Frances and built under Namelok's supervision.

A group of wildlife researchers were arriving in a month to live in their boma. The water pipes had been laid by the plumbers and they had also constructed their first set of eco-washrooms and toilets. They no longer needed to walk to the bush. However, some members of the tribe refused to use these toilets.

The only thing that still had to be constructed was the cooking hut, and Father Frances, the main architect of the project, needed to make a final trip to set the ball rolling for them.

Meanwhile, Sironka shared a meal with his wife and daughter. While Nalangu cleaned up the remains of the dinner, Naserian asked to speak to Sironka privately. They both walked out of the enkaji. He lit up his pipe and they found a comfortable spot under the night sky.

'I hear from Olamayian that you are constantly meeting people and are on the move. Please rest well and look after your health,' Naserian told Sironka in a worried tone.

'Naserian, you and I both know that I am not getting any younger and I have to settle a lot of things for the tribe,' Sironka said.

Naserian nodded in agreement. 'Yes, I know that you are a man driven by your visions.' She paused, and then took a deep breath. 'Sironka, we have a slight issue that we need to address before it gets out of hand. Joy has fallen in love with Nalangu, and I am quite sure she loves him too. However, our daughter is yet to register what has been going on between the two of them.'

Sironka was silent for a while. 'Naserian, she knows that she is promised to Koinet. They both had decided that he will go to the university in Europe to study, work and gain experience. He has now come back and has taken up a well-paying government job. His father recently told me that he now wants to settle down and marry Nalangu. Has she told Joy about Koinet?' he asked in a perturbed voice.

'I don't think she has. You need to talk to our daughter. She has to decide. Even though you can take the decision for her, I know you won't. You have always given women our right to choose what we want for ourselves' said Naserian.

Then, they saw Nalangu walking out of the boma, dressed in traditional Maasai clothes. She looked beautiful and delicate. Naserian got up and walked back inside, creating space for the father and daughter to talk. Sironka patted the space next to him and asked Nalangu to sit with him.

He decided immediately that he would get straight to the point.

'Nalangu, I met Koinet's parents a few days ago. They told me that he has come back home. They were wondering if we could do a ceremony to take your relationship to the next level. I spoke to Father Frances and he would like a European engagement ceremony, like he had promised your mother.'

While Sironka spoke, Nalangu was silently staring at her feet.

'My dear child, do you still want to marry Koinet or has there been a change of heart?' Sironka asked her gently.

'No father, I have been true to Koinet,' said Nalangu.

'I am not doubting your loyalty to Koinet, but love sometimes creeps into our hearts when we are not looking. Naserian, who has brought you up like her own, is very worried because she feels that Joy has fallen in love with you. And we both want to know if you love him too.'

Nalangu looked up, shocked. 'But he has not told me that, nor have I said or done anything to lead him on,' she said.

'Nalangu, you both have done nothing wrong. Love is such a powerful and expansive emotion. When it enters your life, it lights you up, and I guess that's what your mother has noticed in you. So I just want you to know that there is another man who loves you, besides Koinet. It is for you to decide if you still want to marry Koinet or if you would rather explore another relationship. Whatever you decide involves your whole life and I will stand by whatever choice you make,' Sironka said kindly.

'Father, I do not know what to do anymore! I am confused. When I am with Joy, I am happy. I feel alive. Koinet is an amazing man, well-educated and travelled. He is a good and simple man, and he loves me and will be a good father and caregiver. Joy, on the other hand, is so unsure about everything in life and he is still legally married. If I give a second thought to my future with Joy, it feels extremely fragile and I cannot bear leaving my country and family. I have so much to do and accomplish here, but yes, I will not deny that when I am with Joy, I laugh a lot. We both love being in each other's company. He is a friend, unlike any friend I have ever had in all my life.' Nalangu was crying as she spoke about her worst fears to her father.

Sironka was distressed to see her crying. 'Take your time. Whoever you chose to be with, you have my blessings.' He wiped Nalangu's tears and hugged her.

Sironka walked back to the mission and made his bed under his tree. His heart was heavy. He just hoped his daughter would make the right decision. Free will was a funny thing. Even though he knew what needed to be done, he still needed to step back and allow Nalangu to take her decision and then support her choice. As he closed his eyes, he said a little prayer for his daughter's peace of mind.

By mid-morning, Joy and the others were ready to leave. Joy, oblivious to everything, loaded up all the bee homes into the trailer. He tried to get a few moments alone with Nalangu, but she seemed distant this morning. He said his goodbyes to all.

Nalangu was speaking to Sironka and Joy watched them intently. He saw that by the end of the conversation, Sironka looked worried. He gently placed his hand on his daughter's head and walked back to the jeep. Nalangu waved a goodbye once the jeep started moving.

The whole ride back, Sironka was quiet.

14

PASSING ON

When Joy and the others reached their boma, Joy was greeted by the village children. They clamoured all over him in excitement. He made his way into Namelok's enkaji and saw her brewing tea. She gave him the widest smile possible and told him how much everyone had missed him.

As the day turned to night, both her younger children refused to leave his side. Lketinga, the youngest, fell asleep on his lap. Joy carried the kid to his bed and tucked him snuggly next to his older brother. This home felt more like family to Joy than what he had known about family. He then washed up and slipped into bed. It was so good to be back home.

Sironka came in much later than usual that night. Namelok could see that Sironka was restless and she asked him what was troubling him.

'Nalangu wants to get married to Koinet as soon as possible. She informed me of her decision today,' Sironka said, worry clear in his voice.

Namelok smiled and her eyes twinkled. She looked so happy with the news. 'That's wonderful. You should be happy that she is going to marry a good man,' she said.

'Yes, I am happy that my daughter has decided to get married to a man of her choice unlike so many other

Maasai girls. But I know that she has fallen in love with Joy and will not acknowledge it. Not to herself or anyone else. Joy loves her too, but he has not told her either. I could see it in their eyes today. But they are both trying to do the right thing,' shared Sironka.

'Does Joy know about Koinet or Nalangu's decision for an early marriage?' asked Namelok.

Sironka shook his head. 'No, he does not know anything about any of this. I realized that my daughter will not marry any person who can take her away from her family and country.'

Namelok was silent for some time and she shook her head in despair. 'How will we break the news to Joy? He just got over his drinking problem. I hope this does not push him over the brink again.'

Sironka was lost in thought for a while. 'Yes, there is a strong possibility that he may start to drink again. I also worry about him becoming addicted to Miraa. I see that some of the young warriors keep chewing on it these days.'

Namelok knew that Sironka's fears were not baseless. Some of the younger men were often seen lazing around under a tree, eyes glazed over, mumbling away to themselves. Alcoholism and drugs were quite rampant among the Maasais.

'If Joy decides to go down that path, we cannot stop him. This will truly be his test. I hope he gets through it, otherwise we'll go back to square one and have to start his healing all over again. I will not give up on him.' Sironka spoke in a determined voice. They both retired to bed, each lost in their own thoughts.

The next week, Joy was busy stringing up the bee homes up in the trees. They looked like beautiful little gift boxes as they were suspended high up in the sky. They had been painted a bright yellow with thin light blue stripes. The women of the tribe were excited. They sang and danced as every new bee home went up.

Once all the bee boxes were strung, Sironka called a meeting. Joy was asked to be a part of it. They all gathered under the grandfather tree. Sironka talked about how Joy had learnt to set up a vegetable patch at the missionary school and how important it was for them to start growing their own food and to incorporate fresh vegetables into their diet.

Many of the women and elders scoffed. 'We roam the forest. There is enough food for us there, and the cattle provide us with all that we need. Why do we need to grow our own food? We are the Maasai. Our ancestors were warriors and pastoralists, not farmers,' Lemauni, Sironka's younger brother, said.

Sironka nodded in agreement. 'I agree, brother. But if we become an eco-village, we will have to feed the tourists what they can eat. They will not eat raw meat or blood like us. Also, land is becoming scarce everywhere. We will need to find a space of our own, otherwise our children will be left with nothing. This learning is not for us, it is for them. We will need to change some of our ways and also find other ways to sustain ourselves. We need to make enough money to educate our children to be part of the urban world. A good education is an absolute necessity.'

A murmur went through the circle that had gathered around the tree. Joy could see that some shook their heads in agreement and some clicked their tongues in displeasure. An old lady, all wrinkled and bent over, walked to the centre of the circle and spoke in Maa.

Her voice was clear and strong. 'I have seen the old and the new. I have seen lush forests, and now I see drought all around us. I have seen the forest teeming with animals, and now I also see scarcity. I have seen that we could roam free, and I also see barbed wire walls keeping us away from our mother, the forest. Change, like death, is a constant. We will all need to respect it. I give my wholehearted support to Sironka, we need to strive for abundance in the future.'

The people were silent for a while. Then, one by one, all raised their hands in support of Sironka's idea.

Sironka requested Joy to help them set up the vegetable patch, and Joy agreed at once. It was also decided that all able hands of the tribe would help Joy in the task. Joy first drew up a blueprint. He was excited and started the project the same day.

He realized that he was learning something new every day. He liked creating new possibilities for the future of the tribe.

The village women came to help him once they were done with their housework. During breaks, he would look at a polaroid picture of Nalangu. He missed Nalangu very much and hoped he would meet her soon.

One day, Namelok came to work on the patch earlier than the rest of the women.

'You finished your housework early today, Namelok?' Joy asked her.

'I thought if I put in a few extra hours for a few days, we can get finished in time, before Nalangu's engagement. When that happens, everyone will be busy celebrating.'

Namelok felt sad about breaking the news to Joy like this, but she knew it had to be done as the day was fast approaching. From the corner of her eye, she could see that his hands slightly trembled. His face was ashen. She continued. 'She and Koinet will be engaged in a proper European ceremony as per the wishes of her biological mother, and then she will be married after a few months. The engagement ceremony will happen in a week. Nalangu arrives tomorrow to stay with us,' said Namelok.

She could see Joy's face crumbling now, and he turned away, pretending to sow some seeds. She wanted to reach out and console him, but knew that it was best to let him make peace with his feelings. She moved away to weed an unruly patch. After a while, Joy excused himself and walked away. Namelok said a little prayer for him.

Later, she told her husband that she had done what he had requested. As she told him that, she could not stop her tears any longer. It had been difficult breaking Joy's heart. He was a good man.

Sironka consoled her. 'Namelok, I think it's best if I shift out of your enkaji with Joy. We will live in one of the new ones that you have built for the tourists. He needs space to come to peace and must find a way to deal with the emotions that are going to surface.'

Namelok agreed to the new living arrangement. That night, Joy decided to spend time with Olamayian and his other warrior friends. When he returned, Namelok was waiting and was secretly relieved to see that he was not drunk.

The next day, Sironka informed Joy about their new living quarters and saw that Joy seemed relieved by the news.

As Joy worked on the vegetable patches, he saw Nalangu arrive in the ranger's jeep. She looked radiant; her beauty always took his breath away. They caught each other's eye and nodded a greeting. Joy gave her a welcoming smile, but he could feel the invisible wall growing between them. It made him sad because he knew he had lost her forever. He wanted to go as far away as possible from her as he was nervous that he would not be able to hide his love for her. He was sure that his sadness would be apparent to people and he would embarrass her, the family and himself.

That night, he ate his meal early and went off to his new enkaji. He lay in his bed, full of muddled emotions. He touched the shell strung around his neck and called out to Ollie silently. He closed his eyes and remembered their time together and the thought calmed him down. That night, Joy dreamt that Ollie and he were swimming. They played and sat together on the beach. When he woke up, an odd sense of peace enveloped him.

As the days rolled by, Joy kept himself as busy as possible. He stayed far away from Nalangu and the engagement preparations.

Finally, the big day dawned. Koinet and his family arrived early in the morning and were given the enkaji next to Joy's. Koinet was a handsome young man, extremely well-spoken, well-dressed and he clearly loved Nalangu. Joy knew in his heart that this was the best thing for Nalangu. With a husband like Koinet, she would live a good life. He truly wanted her to be happy and have the best. He tried to keep up a happy front, but many times during the day, he had to go away to calm himself.

Father Frances arrived and finally, the ceremony started. Joy watched Nalangu. She looked resplendent in her Maasai outfit. Her shuka, the traditional robe, was bright red in colour. Jewellery made of colourful beads adorned her hands as bracelets and ankles. What really got his attention was the thick collar made of colourful beads that sat prettily on her slender neck. He noticed that even her sandals were decorated. When she put the ring on Koinet's finger, he noticed that she looked tense and uptight. Koinet, on the other hand, was grinning ear to ear. When she saw Sironka, her eyes filled with tears. Sironka nodded. He came forward and placed his hand on her head and whispered something in her ear. That visibly calmed her down.

That evening, the villagers were all dressed in their finest attire. It was a riot of colours. The women wrapped themselves in bright kangas, their heads were wrapped in kitenges, a thicker fabric. All the Maasai men dressed in the same way: they wore their red robes, braided their hair and expressed their individuality in the way that they draped their cloaks and the patterns with which they painted their bodies and faces.

Everyone was in high spirits. A cow was slaughtered and a feast was cooked. The warriors danced the jumping dance, called Adumu. As always, Olamayain jumped the highest. They sang, danced and the elders drank a fermented drink called mead. As the evening proceeded, the party became louder and feistier. Joy excused himself and walked back to his enkaji. He was emotionally drained. However, he was unaware that Olamayian had noticed how hurt and sad his friend was.

Joy had a restless night. The next morning, he woke up very early. He had barely slept. He started to attend to the vegetable patch while everyone was still asleep. He worked through the morning without bothering to eat. At mid-afternoon, the children were playing and everyone was busy with a normal day of work. Earlier, he had seen

Namelok leave the boma to pick up some firewood. As he worked at the patch, he heard a blood-curdling scream from the cattle enclosure.

He ran towards it and when he got there, the sight that met his eyes drained all the blood from his face. Nalangu was trying to stop a water buffalo from charging at the already injured Lketinga, her half-brother. But the beast had hooked his horns into the child's body. It tossed him up in the air. Joy instantly picked up a large stone and threw it at the water buffalo. It hit the beast on the head. Dazed, the buffalo ran into the bush.

Joy rushed to Lketinga. The child was bleeding profusely. He was still breathing, but every breath was shallower and more feeble than the last.

Joy picked up the child and ran with him to the courtyard. By now, some elders and women had noticed what had happened and came forward. Joy tore the child's shirt and the sight that met his eyes made him almost look away. He saw one big, gaping hole in his chest where the horn had got stuck. He took off the shirt and placed it on Lketinga's wound and asked for someone to get some water.

There was a sudden hush in the crowd. People parted and let Sironka walk to his child. He gently sat down next to his son, took his hand and slowly started to hum and sing a lullaby. It was a song that Namelok often sang to the children. Joy saw the little boy's eyes fill with tears. His lower lip trembled. He tried to say something to his father, but all that escaped his lips was a hoarse, inaudible whisper.

His father placed his fingertip on his son's lips, wiped the boy's tears and smiled gently at him. He moved Joy's shirt aside to see the wound and Joy heard him suck in his breath. But he looked up and talked to his son reassuringly, in a voice that calmed the boy. Sironka asked Joy to find Namelok and bring her back to the boma. But Joy was too shocked to move. Two young boys heard and ran to fetch Olamayian and Namleok. By the time the water arrived, the young boy had breathed his last breath. His eyes had now glazed over.

Joy was reliving the same pain, despair and confusion that he had experienced when his son had died. His breath became visibly shallow; he started to sob and mumble incoherently. He started to rub Lketinga's small hands and feet, frantically trying to revive the little boy, asking all standing around him to help or do something. But he could feel that all the life had drained out of his small body. Sironka placed his hand over his son's eyes and shut them and then he gently stroked Joy's back.

'Joy, his soul has left his body and he won't be coming back.' Joy looked up, and for the first time, he saw tears streaking down Sironka's face. Sironka gently picked up his son's body, held him close and walked towards Namelok's enkaji. Joy followed him and then helped him settle Lketinga down on the floor of the hut.

'Joy, can I get a few moments alone with my son? I need to say my final goodbye to him,' Sironka said. Joy could see it was taking Sironka all of his strength and resolve to not break down.

Soon, the tribe started to congregate outside the enkaji. They did not enter till Sironka had come out and given them permission to enter.

Joy was worried for Namelok. He remembered how broken his wife had been when their son had died. Everything had ended for both of them that day. He wondered if Lketinga's death would destroy Sironka's family like his had fallen apart after his son's death.

He vividly remembered the day his son died.

That day had started like most other days, with them bickering and fighting over some stupid thing. She was busy feeding their son at the breakfast table. He entered the room and could not find something. He had needed it urgently. When he asked her about it, she was very abrupt and rude to him. That set the ball rolling. He lost his temper.

He felt that she was lazy and incompetent. She did not bother to keep her side of the bargain in this relationship of theirs. He did his part by bringing in the money, why was she unable to do her part? Most of the time, the house was a mess, toys were strewn around, and unwashed dishes piled in the sink. She was always tired and found small excuses to sulk and pick a fight with him.

She screamed back at him. Soon they were in the midst of a full-blown verbal spat. They were busy hurling abuses at each other and had failed to realize that their child had choked on the last morsel of food he had been fed. When Joy did notice, he did everything to revive his son. He kept begging god to save his son and he promised that, in return, he would do anything. But the baby had turned blue in the face and had stopped breathing.

Their son had died silently while they were busy fighting.

Suddenly all those memories started to surface. He felt the same, old bodily sensations he had felt the day his son had died. His legs started to tremble, his mouth went dry, his stomach started to cramp, and tears rolled down his cheeks. He wondered if he was crying for his son or

Lketinga. He felt broken, sore and worthless. He could not save his son, nor could he save his little friend, Lketinga.

His hands, caked in Lketinga's dried blood, were trembling. His nails were dirty. He tried wiping his hands on his shorts but they too were covered in blood. Someone offered him a wet cloth to wipe himself. When he looked up, he saw it was Nalangu. Her face was streaked with tears. She reached out and held his hand, as if she were drawing strength from them.

'I wish it was me, not Lketinga. I know god is punishing me. I could have saved him, but it all happened so fast. I got scared,' said Nalangu, sorrowfully.

Joy could see her trembling like a leaf. He wanted to hug her, but instead, he gave her hand a reassuring squeeze. He looked up and saw the worried look on Koinet's face. Her fiancé was waiting to console her, so before Joy embarrassed her and made a fool of himself, he got up to go back into his enkaji.

At some point, he heard someone wail and knew it was Namelok. He knew the pain that she was in. When his son had passed, he had been so angry with everything—including his wife. He had been oblivious to her grief. He was curled around his own hurt and he often blamed her for not paying attention. Now, after so many years, sitting in the middle of an African jungle, he realized that she knew their son before he had. She had carried him in her womb. The child had heard her voice, her heart beat first. Her grief must have been greater. She had once even called herself a murderer, and he had done nothing to reassure her. In fact, he had isolated himself from her. He held his head in his hands, and his heart filled with regret and despair. Now, as he realized how insensitive he had been, he understood that she had been right in leaving him. She deserved better.

Joy went to check on Namelok after a few hours. As he entered Namelok's enkaji, he could see that Sironka had wrapped the little boy in one of his red robes. He was told that the funeral would take place the next day, early in the morning—it was already late now. Namelok lay next to the lifeless body of her son, stroking his face, gently whispering something to him as tears ran down her cheeks. It was heartbreaking to see her like this.

He could no longer bear to sit in Namelok's enkaji. He felt as if he was going to burst with all that pain. He sat under a tree for a few hours in a daze. Day turned to night. The air was still, even the breeze knew that Lketinga had gone away. Joy knew that Lketinga's death had changed something deep within him. He had not fully dealt with the grief of his son's death. Around 7 p.m., Olamayian walked up to Joy alongside Legishon and his younger brother.

'Joy, can you feed and look after them for tonight? I think they will feel more comfortable being with you. Joy, I want you to know that water buffaloes are worse than lions. They are known to be quite bad tempered. You did your best to save him,' said Olamayian.

'Olamayian, I would do anything to save my family. But I could not save Lketinga,' said Joy sorrowfully.

The young Maasai patted Joy's back. 'I know, Joy,' he said.

When Olamayian left, Joy could clearly see that the young boys were in shock. He got them to change and eat. He then made their beds next to his own. He tucked them under his mosquito net and told them a story, and soon enough, the boys were fast asleep. Sironka came in, late at night, looking completely drained. He sat down on the bed and hung his head in despair.

Sironka wiped the tears that escaped his eyes and said in a gruff voice, 'We Maasai, believe that once a person dies, their journey has come to an end and all his sins are transferred to the ones he leaves behind. But I have been shown something very different in my visions. I know that my son is now a part of the energy that is around us, so he will always be close to me. But it still hurts because I am human.'

He paused and drew in a sobbing breath. 'The thing is, Joy, we humans often say that we can't help the way we feel, that we don't choose our emotions but actually, we humans are the only species on earth who can choose their emotions and feelings. I choose to be vulnerable now, so hold space for me and don't get scared and run away if I become emotional. Because even the wise one can cry. In holding space for another who is grieving, lies a lot of learning.'

Joy nodded. 'I sometimes do not understand what you say, Sironka, but I know you are a wise man. Today, I hurt like I have lost one of my own. I will hold space for you, like you have done for me innumerable times.'

Sironka leaned across and patted Joy's head affectionately. 'I know, my son. You are a part of my family. I also know that you are hurting not only because you lost Lketinga, but also because you have experienced loss yourself. Death is the most perfect beginning that the creator has created. It is at this point in life that we are again given a chance to restructure and realign our lives and to evolve spiritually. Strength also means allowing things to fall apart, and having the courage to step back and watch in stillness,' Sironka said.

'But Sironka, what I have come to realize is that I don't fear dying as much as I fear seeing a loved one die.' Tears were streaming down Joy's face by now.

Sironka spoke in a calm voice. 'Joy, death is very powerful. With every death, there is so much learning accessible to a soul. Doorways open up. Instead of living on the surface, we are forced to go deeper within ourselves. It brings about change, and change is uncomfortable and inevitable. We have to ask ourselves: what has this situation taught me? What opportunities has it brought my way? There is more learning for us in death than in our day-to-day lives. Still, we fear death and run from it. In some odd way, I have come to understand that the gift of death and dying is wisdom and transformation.'

He wiped a tear that escaped his eye. 'We humans try to numb ourselves to the loss. We do not welcome the pain that endings bring forth. We are jubilant about new beginnings and births, but we forget to celebrate death. We brush it aside. But endings need to be embraced. We have to give ourselves time. This process cannot be hurried. Know that each one heals in different ways and needs more or less time accordingly.'

'Sironka, I would like to tell you something. I have not spoken about it before. My little son choked to death on a morsel of food. My wife was feeding him, and I chose that moment to fight with her. At first, I blamed my wife, but it was me all along. I feel like a murderer.' Joy suddenly broke into sobs as he spoke.

Sironka reached out and held Joy's hands. 'You should know, Joy, that death is always a choice of the soul, not an accident waiting to happen. Don't burden yourself with guilt. You and your wife did exactly what you were supposed to do that day. Your son's life was going to end that day. It had already been decided by all three of you before you all incarnated into this lifetime. We all are playing our part in a play we have written. My son was to die today.

'We make our life the way we want it to be so that we can learn our lessons. Like I have told you earlier, we chose the main characters, the events, the outcome and even how we will die. It was how it was to be. Accept it and learn from it. Don't allow it to break you, and it will make you stronger.

'I know how you must have hurt. I may be the wise man of the tribe, but I am a father too and it is as difficult for me now as it was for you then. Wisdom does not lessen the pain. I don't want to stop my tears because I know I have to grieve completely. I must do this to be able to laugh at some point in my life again. I know that this pain will pass, but tonight, I feel the pain and I will be with it.'

'My mother often told me that I should not be ashamed to cry and grieve. But like the rest of the world, I also saw it as a weakness,' Joy confessed.

Sironka shook his head. 'That is not an awakened world. Death pushes us to either become an island or to bond with others. I guess you became an island.'

Joy nodded in agreement. 'Sironka, people say that even after a loved one dies, they are with us. But I want to touch my son, hear his laughter, carry him on my shoulder. I know that will never again be possible. I will never see him and feel him again and that is the truth,' Joy said.

'I know what you mean, Joy. The living don't see the dead. But the dead can see the living and I know they worry when you are sad. So do them a favour, raise your frequency. Dying is as essential as living because that's when we all go back to our source. We go back home. In reality, we continue living. But we are without a body, in a place that is so much more peaceful, joyous and filled with light,' Sironka said, with a faraway look in his eyes. 'Learn to be happy for them, move away from your selfish wants and desires of wanting them next to you.'

He then got up, walked across to sit on the ground and rested his back against a wall. 'Mother Earth is always more grounding. I need her energy now.'

'Sironka, why don't you rest? We can talk later,' Joy suggested.

'I feel that it's best to have this conversation now. I do not want Lketinga's death to go to waste. Maybe this was one of the major reasons you were brought to me. Lketinga came into our lives for a short span of time and now he has left. But I know we all had a good life together with him. It is so essential for us to live each moment with each other; we need to create everlasting memories. But instead, we fight over small things. Many of us are so busy doing something that defines us in the external world that we forget about the people who love us and who help define our inner world,' Sironka said.

Joy could see that in a few hours it would be morning. He asked Sironka if he wanted some tea and Sironka nodded. Joy lit the fire and started brewing a cup of milk tea, the way Namelok made it.

'Joy, did you and your wife talk about your son after he passed on?' Sironka asked.

Joy looked up. 'We rarely spoke about anything after his death. Just the essentials so that we could continue to live with each other,' he said.

Sironka nodded. 'The universe has again presented you with an opportunity to heal this hurt with Lketinga's death. I want you to remember every little detail from the time you knew of your son's conception to the day he died. Do not miss anything. As per tradition, the Maasai don't mention the name of the person who has died. It is a bad omen. But in a vision, I was guided to move from tradition and forge a process that heals the grief and pain that comes along with death. It is for the ones that have been left behind. We humans need to create rituals to say our goodbyes. It helps the living to readjust and the spirit to know that we are working on healing ourselves. This brings peace. As a family, we will be doing this for Lketinga, and I would like to guide you through this process too.

'Grief needs to be felt to its fullest. We cannot forget, but we can take out the energy, the charge of that memory. You may not follow what I say, but I want you to be a part of the grieving ceremony. You will remember your son, you will remember your father, your mother, and you will also remember Lketinga. This is going to be a painful process, and promise me, you will not numb this pain from now on. There is a lot to learn now. Let's honour the death of our ancestors by working on ourselves. Do not stop the process of healing that has started in you,' Sironka urged.

Joy nodded, agreeing. They sat in silence for a while and then the two men retreated to their beds.

The next day, when Joy woke up, the sunlight was streaming in through the windows. The boys had left and so had Sironka. He got ready and walked out. He heard singing in the distance and he followed the sound till he came across a large crowd. Joy stood on the side, watching the way they bid farewell to their dead. Lketinga's body was placed under the shady, grandfather tree. He had been smeared with fresh oxen blood and fat. All the members of the tribe were given a chance to say their goodbyes. After that, a few able young men, along with Sironka, took the body into the forest to be kept in a spot where the scavengers of the forest would come to feast on him.

Once they all left with the body, Namelok slowly walked back to her enkaji. Joy spent the entire day in the vegetable patch, sowing and weeding. In the afternoon, Nalangu came across to bid him goodbye as she needed to get back to the mission. Koinet was to drop her off. He could see it in her eyes: she was heartbroken and still in shock. Joy was able to recognize the emotions associated with grief by now. He mumbled a farewell to her.

By dusk, Sironka had returned. It was dark and silent inside the hut. He saw Namelok in a corner, a bowl of untouched ugali next to her. Sironka made some tea and gently coaxed Namelok to drink it. Joy cooked a meal for them and Sironka managed to feed Namelok. From that day onwards, Joy saw Sironka taking charge. He tried to nurture his family and himself back to the living. Joy knew this was not how Maasai men were by nature.

Joy did his part to help the family. He taught the boys, cooked a meal once in a while, helped Legishon in collecting firewood. Olamayian dropped by more often, and the family huddled up around the fire but not much was said. They brought up random, funny memories and he would often catch Namelok smiling. She had started eating a little as time went by, but her eyes were sad and her spirit had broken.

Joy's days now started early. He checked on the beekeeping project. The vegetable patch had started to sprout, and the women of the tribe helped him often. After a week, he saw Namelok joining them. She was slowly getting back into a routine. One evening, over a cup of tea with the family, Sironka informed Joy that the grieving ceremony was to start the next day.

Sironka instructed Joy on how to be a part of the ceremony. 'Sit at a comfortable distance, and let your memories of the ones that have passed on surface. Good ones, bad ones. Live each memory as if it was happening right in front of you. Slowly, when it does not make you happy or sad anymore, give it a form, like that of a ball or a bird. And then release it up in the air.'

'The women of the tribe will help Namelok. They will talk to her about Lketinga's childhood, the food he liked to eat and funny incidents. She will cry and break down when the memories start to surface. I have taught her to release it. But you will need to do this by yourself. I will be around to help you if I feel that you are getting stuck. But you will do this for a few hours every day,' Sironka instructed.

Joy nodded. 'I will give it my best shot. I may have done something like this on the boat, but the pain has resurfaced again. I guess it never goes away.'

Sironka smiled and gently explained. 'I am sure you did not release it to the creator. Surrender the memory and complete healing will be yours.'

Joy hesitantly said, 'I feel more comfortable grieving alone.'

Sironka shook his head. 'Joy, remember what I told you about being an island. In the urban world, people very rarely hold sacred space for another to remember, to heal, to cry. Here, in our world, this is the way we live. In order to move on, we need to let go of our guilt, shame, hurt and often, we need others to help us. We should be surrounded by our community, our tribe. You may take a few days or you may take a few weeks, but you will do this religiously every day with us,' he explained.

Next day, by mid-afternoon, the women had started to gather under a tree. Namelok sat in the centre of the circle. They started to sing, and then, a woman would get up and talk about Lketinga. Then another woman would do the same. The first day, Namelok did not cry much and neither did Joy, who sat at a distance. It was difficult at first to dig through his memories. He was so used to brushing them away.

As the days went by, the memories came flooding in. There was no stopping them. Nor could he stop the tears, the laughter or the smiles. He remembered, he lived the memories, he cried and released them. After he had finished, he would just curl up and lie silently under the tree. Sironka kept an eye on him. Joy did this every day, religiously. After that, he would take a bath, hoping the water would wash off the sadness that had started to envelope him. This little ritual would make him feel slightly less teary eyed. He would then go back to his hut, cook or read some books that he had borrowed from Father Frances.

For the first few nights, he woke up with terrible nightmares. Sironka and the boys were no longer in the hut, so he would lie there alone, wondering if this process was actually good for his soul. But as the days turned to weeks, he felt lighter. He slept better, smiled a little more and one day, he just knew he could stop the process. The same memories still surfaced, but they did not hurt at all. The tears had stopped. Something felt fixed inside of him, and he was so excited that he wanted to share it with Sironka.

When he went to find Sironka, Namelok said that he had gone to walk about in the wild for a few days. When she saw the surprised look on Joy's face she said, 'This is his way of being and he needs to do this to centre himself. He stood by the whole family and now we need to give him space.'

Joy curiously asked, 'Are you okay with it?'

Namelok smiled. 'I may not like many of his ways, but when I decided to love him, I knew I would love both the good and the not-so-good in him.'

After a few days, Sironka walked back into the boma. Joy was happy. It was good to see the wise old man again.

15
UNITY

Over the next few weeks, the whole boma was undergoing major renovations. The excitement was now building. The eco-village project was actually coming together. They were aiming to win the best boma award at the Maasai Olympics. Sironka was not too fond of competitions, but he kept saying that he wanted to show the rest of the tribes a possibility for their future. Things were looking up. The research team had confirmed a three-month stay. Father Frances had received so many bookings that he had to refuse some of them.

Joy was busy helping Namelok build the cooking and dining huts. He was amazed by how good she was at the work. The process of creating seemed to have had a healing effect on her. Before her son's death, she had seemed like one of the happiest people that he had met. Seeing her sad made him sad. Now she would occasionally talk about Lketinga and cry a little. Joy too felt comfortable talking about his son without breaking down or feeling guilty.

One evening, Father Frances drove up in his old, beaten down jeep. He had come to help them through the last touches to the cooking and dining huts. He also put the finishing touches on the tourist huts. As Father Frances got off the jeep, Joy rushed forward and hugged him. That took Father Frances by surprise. These days,

Joy welcomed any company. This feeling of togetherness was new to him. Olamayian often teased him about how talkative and social he had become. But Joy was different. He felt happier, lighter and he wanted to be around people. He noticed that he had started to laugh more than usual. Joy walked to the back of the jeep to bring down Father Frances' luggage. But he stopped when he saw Nalangu sitting there.

Father Frances winked at him. 'I wanted to surprise Sironka and I thought it would be best to bring his precious daughter here for a while.'

Joy smiled and nodded a greeting to Nalangu. He felt so clumsy around her that he wanted to turn and walk away.

Father Frances was oblivious to the discomfort between Joy and Nalangu. He carried on chatting. 'Sironka insisted that I stay in these new eco huts. I felt that Nalangu would be the best person to help set up the kitchen. We can get the rooms fitted out in a few days with the help of the rangers. I heard some of the resorts are closing down and auctioning their stuff, so maybe, tomorrow we can drive across and pick up some essentials from there.'

Joy picked up Father Frances's bags and deposited them in the hut next to his enkaji. After a while, he saw Father Frances and Sironka, along with a few elders, sitting around under the grandfather tree. Plans were being made, a to-do list was drawn. Many hands were raised in agreement and disagreement. Joy cooked a meal and Nalangu helped him with it. They did not speak much as they cooked and avoided eye contact. But he still felt like he was healing just by being around her.

After dinner, they all sat outside around a bonfire and talked about the new pandemic that was raging through the world. Apparently, world economies had crashed, and several countries had taken a hit because of it. Entire nations had gone into lockdowns, and it seemed like the whole world had come to a grinding halt.

'Why would such a thing happen to the world?' asked Father Frances.

Sironka, who was sitting on his haunches and putting another log into the fire, cleared his throat to speak. 'I guess the new world is being ushered in. A new way of being could not come forth if we carried on like before. So everyone has had to stop and reset. Mother Earth is vibrating at a different frequency. I can feel her energy has changed, and it will keep changing. It is as if the whole of creation has been activated again. Many species will perish. Even among the humans, many bloodlines will come to an end and many new ones will emerge. We humans love to hold on to the old ways of life. But we have to understand that Mother Nature is the constant creation of new life. The old will need to perish to make way for the new. The earth will rumble, shake and shed, and I feel like the virus is her creation.'

Father Frances nodded. 'Being out here, in the middle of the forest, we remain untouched and hope we remain safe for good.'

'We will,' said Sironka.

Joy's mind drifted off to Galgibaga, and he hoped that everyone was safe and healthy. He loved being near the forest, but he also missed the ocean. Over the past few days, he had been missing Ollie so much. He had often caught himself rubbing the shell that he wore around his neck.

'Joy, I got you something. One of the exchange students from Europe donated a backpack with an outdoor survival kit, and a sleeping bag. I thought I would get it for you. I saw you carrying your belongings in a shuka last time, when you came visiting,' said Father Frances, handing him a backpack.

It was quite compact and had the correct amount of pockets to store all his stuff. Joy was like a little boy. He turned it around and was all smiles as he unclipped it and looked inside to see all the goodies packed in it. 'Thank you, Father. This is my first bag since I left the shores of India. I hope I get to use it soon.' Joy said, joyously.

Father Frances looked at Sironka and said, 'You will need to take the boy out so that he can use his gift.'

Sironka nodded and smiled. Soon the men retired to their respective sleeping quarters.

Days were spent fitting the enkajis with thin, white cotton curtains stitched by the women of the tribe. The rangers brought in mattresses, which had been salvaged from a resort that had closed down. The kitchen was also being equipped with some pots and pans, under the keen eye of Father Frances. Olamayian informed Joy that Koinet had many contacts in the ministry. They had helped their tribe financially to set up this eco-village. Soon, they would be coming to inspect the project.

Joy too realized that working on the project made him happy. He enjoyed the creative process.

Soon, the big day arrived. The inspectors came and loved every bit of their handiwork. After the inspectors left, there were many rounds of jubilations, songs and dances. Father Frances bid his goodbyes too. But Nalangu decided to stay back with the family.

Sironka then took Joy by surprise, asking him to join him for a walk in the forest.

'I feel like something amazing is going to happen in your life, Joy. Bring your backpack, we have to make use of it. It's just for a night, but please do bring your mosquito net. Namelok will make my life miserable if you get sick with malaria. You will need some drinking water and something to eat. And I have to teach you to sleep under the night sky,' Sironka said.

Joy excitedly packed up some essentials and met Sironka at the entrance of the boma. Then they both walked off into the night. They must have walked for an hour or two when they came across a small watering hole.

'This is the spot I want to show you. This is where the magic will take place,' Sironka said excitedly.

Joy looked at the watering hole but he saw nothing magical about the spot.

Sironka found a tree from where the watering hole was clearly visible.

'This is one of my favourite spots. I come here quite often. It has the spirit residing in it, so let's rest here for the night,' Sironka said happily.

'Spirit? Like ghosts?' Joy asked, scared.

Sironka put his hand on his forehead and shook his head in exasperation. 'Spirit, like god, the creator. We call him Enkai.'

Joy could see Sironka was silently laughing at him.

They sat under the tree, made a fire pit and then got a small fire going. Sironka started to roast a few sweet potatoes and other vegetables that he had carried with him. Joy rubbed himself down with the mosquito repellent.

'You are lucky, Joy, you have not contracted malaria.'

'You forget that I am an Indian. We are made of sturdy stuff. I am also extremely careful about what I eat or drink.

I keep applying mosquito repellent and Namelok has now taught me how to make it myself,' Joy said proudly.

While the vegetables cooked, Joy took out a calabash, uncorked it and poured out the yoghurt he had made. The two of them then put the roasted vegetables in their gourd bowls, topped it up with yoghurt and salt and had a hearty meal.

While Joy went to wash the bowls in the watering hole, Sironka was busy finding tall, thorny branches. He placed those around the tree to keep them safe from wild animals. He could see Joy was uncomfortable, but he knew that Joy needed a little of this discomfort. He needed to overcome his fear of the wild. Joy helped Sironka double-check and re-adjust the branches so that there were no gaps. They made their beds under the tree, and then Joy settled down under the mosquito net. A cool breeze was blowing, and there was a slight nip in the air by now.

'I am glad I have a sleeping bag. This is really good stuff. It's soft and adjusts to your body temperature,' Joy said happily.

Sironka scoffed. He said that he preferred his shuka over an artificial bag any day.

After a while, Sironka turned on his side and faced Joy. 'How do you feel after releasing all those birds into the air? I saw them flying past many times.' It took Joy a minute to realize that Sironka was talking about his healing process.

Joy smiled and said, 'I do feel lighter, for sure.'

But what Sironka said next stunned him.

'The dark clouds around you have lessened, but they tend to come back when you see Nalangu. You do love my daughter, don't you, Joy? Naserian told me and later on, I saw it in your eyes,' Sironka said.

Joy was visibly shaken. His little secret was out. He had tried so hard to hide it. So if they knew, may be Nalangu knew too.

'I am sorry, Sironka. I did not know that she was promised to another. My love for her is pure and simple,' Joy said, red in the face with embarrassment.

Sironka looked at Joy with eyes full of love. 'Why are you apologising, Joy? If you say your love is pure then it needs no explanation and comes with no conditions. Love taps you on the shoulder when you least expect it, and before you know it, you are deep in its grasp. When you love, you are experiencing what the creator has intended for us and wants us all to be...pure love! It is the most powerful emotion. Humanity needs to vibrate at love's frequency and feel more of it. Be grateful that you have experienced this emotion. My daughter is a beautiful woman. She is wise and gentle. She will always do what she feels is right for her family and tribe.'

'I feel that she is upset with me. Perhaps she has caught on to how I feel,' Joy said, suddenly worried.

'Every time a relationship breaks or does not materialize, you need to ask yourself what lessons you have learnt from it. Ensure that this experience makes you a better human being, and don't blame the other person. Just keep being grateful, even when your heart is breaking. Know that relationships are not just about being together, but about partings as well. Sometimes, they need to end when we have learnt our lessons. I am just so glad you fell in love with Nalangu. It is apparent that you are keen to live and create again.' Sironka paused. He knew that Joy would need a minute or so to understand what was being said.

'The path of love is not always strewn with flowers. You have dealt with it very well already. You kept your promise, and you have not gone back to your addiction, not even when you were going through a heartbreak. You should truly be proud of yourself, Joy. One of the toughest things to do in life is to stand by your word. That is the way to honour yourself. I remember you saying that you want create a better life for yourself. You are giving yourself a chance to do just that now,' said Sironka.

'I was tempted to start drinking to drown my sorrows, especially on the day she got engaged. But something in me knew that it was not the solution. As time goes by, I just know, deep within me, that I am strong,' Joy confessed. 'But I feel so confused when I see Nalangu. I don't know what to do most of the time. Should I turn away or stay? Should I tell her how I feel or just let it be?' Joy laughed. Then he shook his head and continued. 'What a mess this is! I don't want to be around her any more, but when I spend time with her, I feel so complete.'

Sironka laughed too. 'What you are going through seems worse than facing a lion. But be truthful to yourself and your feelings. When you are in a relationship, now or in the future, observe yourself. Understand what makes you tick. Can you take rejection? Forgive the other? Is your love conditional? For example, if you look after me, will I too look after you? Can you love a person with all their faults? Are you a good listener? Are you loyal? Are you truthful to the woman you love about your emotions and who you are? In this case, the woman you love is Nalangu and she deserves to hear you. Talk and let the words flow from your heart.'

'There is a trick I learnt from my ancestors. Slow your

breathing, close your eyes, and when you open them, allow the great creator to talk through you. And when you start to babble and mumble, slow your breath again and repeat the process. You will be surprised by how powerful your words will be,' Sironka said.

'Sironka, I don't know if I should even consider being with another person. I have been unfaithful to my wife—many times! I have hurt her enough. I am scared that I may mess up a good relationship even if I am blessed with one. Maybe I am not cut out for it.' Joy shrugged.

Sironka reached out and snuck his hand through the mosquito net and laid it on Joy's forearm. He reassuringly squeezed it. 'Don't doubt yourself so much. The union between a man and a woman is beautiful, and it is essential. Don't stop yourself from experiencing love again. If it has come calling again, let it in. Don't let the past bind you or the future scare you. Just be in the present. If it feels right in the moment, go with it. Allow this love for Nalangu to be consistent in you, let it live in you for eternity. Let it expand and emanate from your whole being. It will act as a guiding light in your future relationships. Instead of depleting you, it will empower you to create beautiful connections of the heart in the future. People will want to be around you. They will give and receive love—because that's all humans want, and have wanted from the beginning of time. Is it possible that this is why Nalangu has come into your life, to open you up again to this divine, powerful emotion and to teach you to let go without breaking down?' Sironka said.

Joy lay there, listening to Sironka's strong, clear voice. Slowly, the scrambled emotions and knots within him started to unravel and fall into place.

'I love her very much, and what saddens me is that I can't show her how much I love her,' he finally said.

'Joy, everyone who comes near you should be able to feel that love and that nurturing power. Don't keep it just for Nalangu.'

As Sironka spoke, Joy could sense something opening up within him.

'Can I confess something, Sironka? When I met Koinet, I was slightly jealous because he is better looking than me in a Maasai way, very well settled, and I guess I can't grudge her choice,' Joy said sheepishly.

Sironka laughed aloud. 'Stop talking about appearances and achievements. True love sees beyond all that. Sometimes, when the other makes a choice, we just have to respect it and move on. But unfortunately, we often feel stuck and start to find faults in ourselves. We shrink our being to a dot and become insignificant in our own eyes. We believe we are not good enough. Do you know why the great divine wants us, as humans, to experience love?' he asked.

Joy smirked. 'I guess he wants to entertain himself, because we end up making such fools of ourselves. He must have a good laugh.'

Sironka smiled. 'I agree, the divine has a great sense of humour. But when we fall in love with another person, we experience the purest emotion. This is the closest we get to the source; this is the energy the creator is made of. The world is made of loving and compassionate energies. It makes us feel strong, beautiful and happy. It makes the world beautiful. Love unlocks the abundance within us. When we love another, we learn to love ourselves too. I hope you can see the magic, Joy,' he said.

Sironka's words made Joy feel peaceful.

'Let's sleep now, Joy. Tomorrow morning, something magical awaits us,' said Sironka. And within minutes, Sironka was fast asleep.

Joy marvelled at Sironka's ability to sleep so well. Joy lay awake, thinking about how he had felt a lack of love, nourishment and unconditional acceptance in all his relationships. He had not asked Sironka how to be when in love, or how to feel abundance in his life.

Sironka had said something about breathing, which he did not understand yet. Sometimes, Sironka was easy to follow. Sometimes he was not. Joy slowly drifted off to sleep, remembering the sound of Nalangu's laugh, how her nose crinkled when she smiled. He thought of her happy eyes.

'Joy! Joy! Wake up, boy.' Sironka was shaking Joy awake.

Joy got up. 'Is everything okay? Are we in danger? Have the lions come to eat us?' Joy mumbled grumpily.

'Yes, the lions have arrived. Yes, we are in danger,' Sironka said, and Joy's sleep vanished from his eyes.

'We are in danger of missing the most beautiful sight. Come stand by me,' Sironka said, laughing now. He was standing near the thorn bushes that encircled them. It was quite early in the morning. The sun had still not risen, but the sky was faintly lit. Right there, in front of them at the watering hole, were the lions and their pride. Hippopotamuses slowly lowered themselves into the water, yawning and lazily chuffing and grunting. Elephants were happily swishing water over their large bodies, while their little ones looked comical as they kept tumbling in the water. The zebras, topis and gazelles quenched their thirst without a care, standing right next to the lions.

Sironka was happy as he could see the wonder in Joy's eyes.

'I know that you have seen these animals during the day at the game reserve with Olamayian and the rangers,' he said. 'But this sighting, early in the morning, is beautiful because both prey and predator come together, in peace, to drink water—the source of life. When I was a young boy, my father brought me here and he called it "the unity". As a man who has a few years left before I finally close my eyes, when I see this sight, I can still feel the energy of oneness. Every time I see it, I feel like a little boy again.'

'I have waited long to share this sight with you, but you were not ready! This sight always reaffirms my beliefs of the human race living in peace someday, coexisting without fighting each other. All that is needed is to connect to the source of all life. We will receive what we want. We will not have to fight and take it from the other. There is no difference between the lion, you or me.' There was a slight shakiness to Sironka's voice by now. Joy even saw a tear escaping Sironka's eyes as he continued to speak. 'Always remember this sight when someone hurts you or does not act appropriately. Just know that you are them too. Always come from a space of compassion. There is goodness at the core of everything. Sometimes, it's just lying buried.'

Joy nodded. He looked at the animals drinking water, side by side, in peace. None were scared of dying at this moment, because they all had faith in the other. Their fear was replaced with the knowledge that all was well. They both stood there, watching the animals silently. The sun started to warm the earth. Some animals started to walk back into the forest. Sironka turned around, rolled up his bed, dislodged the spear that he had stuck into the ground and waited for Joy to pack up. They carefully moved the branches aside and walked back to the boma in silence.

On the way, Sironka laid his hand on Joy's shoulder. 'You are doing good, Joy. Flow like a river, slow and steady, and you will see that you are in a good space.'

'Before we get busy, Sironka, I have some questions. How am I supposed to be love? I know you said to breathe, but I do not understand it,' Joy said.

'Joy, you just need to be joyous, just like your name. Start spending more time in nature, do things that make you happy, surround yourself with people who make you laugh. You will feel alive and peaceful, and then you will smile. Remember to slow your breath for a few moments, and you will notice that your thoughts will slow down too. And in those few moments, you will be love itself. Similarly, when you see Nalangu, slow your breath, shift your focus to something around you—a tree or the sky and observe it in detail. The shape, the colour, the smell and so on. Slowly, you will see how things change for you,' Sironka said with a laugh.

Joy stared at Sironka. He then smiled and shook his head. 'I wish life and love were as easy as you make it out to be! You amaze me sometimes. I am still trying to understand what the connection between breathing and love is. But you are a wise man and I will not question this wisdom. I will remember to smile today. Now, how do I feel abundant?' Joy asked.

'That's very simple. Just thank god for all that is in your life. Thank everyone for being who they are and what they have done for you,' Sironka explained calmly.

Joy looked puzzled. 'That's abundance?'

'You will understand in time, but start by doing this and the magic will unfold,' Sironka said.

Joy did not understand what Sironka meant. But he knew by now that understanding would dawn on him some day.

He went into his hut and slept for a few hours. After a good breakfast of ugali and some fruits, he emerged later in the day, ready to take on the world. And the first person he bumped into was Nalangu!

Like always, he decided to walk far away from her. When he reached the vegetable patch, he let out a deep sigh, and then another one. He realized he was slightly out of breath. Joy wondered if he had been holding his breath. Or was it because he had walked too fast? The old man was right. Love had something to do with breath. So during the day, whenever he saw Nalangu, he kept reminding himself to slow his breath and not run away from her.

The silence between them was deafening, but he did not allow that to scare him. He also noticed, for the first time, that Nalangu was quieter than usual and her eyes were sad. Or maybe, he had become more aware of his surroundings. But he did notice that just slowing his breath had helped him get through the day. By evening, he could find the courage to be around her for a little longer than usual.

The next few days, everyone was busy with last-minute details. They were preparing for the government inspectors who would come to inspect their boma. Joy did all the paperwork and expense sheets and taught Olamayian how to maintain them. The inspection went off without a hitch, and within a few days, they were given a go-ahead to operate and market themselves as an eco-village for tourists.

Nalangu was busy. She was training the ladies of the tribe to cook food that the Europeans and the rest of the world could eat. The new huts looked neat, clean and comfortable. Soon, they received their first few guests. The jeep arrived with them and the big trailer was full of their research equipment.

There were four of them. The group leader, a Canadian man called Allan, was tall, blond, blue-eyed and thin. After much song, dance and welcome speeches, the members of the tribe went back to their enkajis and the trailer was secured with plastic sheets for the night.

The next day was spent setting up the research equipment and radio systems in a tent next to the cooking hut. Days were spent out in the game reserve, tracking animals and photographing them. Afternoons were assigned for rest and snoozes, as it was way too hot to be outside. And by the evening, everyone was ready for a good time around the camp fire.

The whole research group had grown fond of Joy. They had realized that he was a resourceful person. He could understand them, get their work done and his managerial skills were excellent. One evening, Allan's team started talking about how they had signed up for the research project. Allan asked Joy about how he had come to the boma. Joy tried to avoid the conversation, but Allan was persistent. 'I come from a place called Goa, in India,' he said hesitantly.

'Yes, I know of Goa. I have been there with my friends. It is a very charming little place. The sea, the food, the music. The people there are very friendly,' Allan said.

'I hated the place when I was growing up. I thought Europe was the best place to create a life for me and my family. I worked in England for ten years,' Joy said.

'What work did you do?' asked Allan.

'I was an investment banker. I wore the suits and ties. I laced up my brogues every day when I went to work. I had thirty people who reported to me.' When he mentioned the firm he had worked for, Allan was surprised, since it was a reputed multinational.

Both Sironka and Olamayain were listening to their conversation. Sironka realized that he had never asked Joy what he did for a living before. But then, Joy rarely spoke about his past.

'What is an investment banker doing in the middle of the African bush?' Allan asked.

Joy smiled. 'I guess the tribe needed a handyman and I needed them too,' Joy said. They all laughed at that.

'Will you ever go back to India?' Allan asked.

'I don't know. I have never felt the urge to go back to my country since I arrived in Tanzania. Sometimes, I miss the house I grew up in and the sound of the sea. But right now, I am quite content with doing odd jobs and being a part of Sironka's family,' replied Joy.

'Do you think you will marry one of the beautiful Maasai women and live here?' Allan asked teasingly.

Joy looked away. He then looked down at his feet. 'I have not thought that far. I am a trained fisherman who became a banker, who then entered the hospitality business. Now I am the boma's handyman. I don't know any more what I want to do, but I am certain that I don't want to do what I was doing earlier,' Joy replied honestly.

Olamayian and Sironka noted Joy's vulnerability. Sironka cleared his throat and spoke. 'I know what Joy is feeling. Sometimes it's okay to not know everything. Keep asking and searching with a pure heart, the universe will answer you. When it's time, you will be shown the way.'

They all fell silent. Sironka could see that Joy was sad, and he was the first to retire for the night.

Joy had just settled down in his bed when he heard Sironka's voice.

'Joy, can we talk or are you tired tonight?' he asked.

Joy invited him into the enkaji and made tea for both of them.

'I felt worried after hearing you talk today. Is everything okay with you?' Sironka asked.

'All is fine, Sironka. Conversations like today make me slightly confused and sad. I really don't know what I am supposed to do with my life. Being with you has changed me. I am not the man that I was in India. I am happier than before, but in some moments, I question my purpose. I don't know why I am alive. Everyone knows where they belong, what they were meant to do in life. I am clueless now,' Joy confessed.

Sironka nodded. 'Joy, non-clarity is pushing you to seek out the truth. Be grateful. Don't worry, all will be clear in time. I didn't know you were so well qualified and held such an important post in the urban world,' Sironka said.

'What's the use of it now? I made a mess of my life. I have realized that knowledge does not make you a wise man,' Joy said in a nonchalant tone.

'I feel that it's time to initiate you into the circle of energy. That's why the ocean brought you here, to me, in the first place. It feels like the time is now,' Sironka said.

'Circle of energy? What will happen during and after the initiation?' Joy inquired.

Sironka shrugged and said, 'I really don't know what

will happen to you during the initiation. It is different for everyone, but very few are chosen to experience it. But I do know what will happen to you *after* the initiation. You will have complete clarity on all aspects of your life. This process requires some preparation. After this experience, you will not be the same man. So be prepared for some major changes in your life.

'All that has been happening to you is the universe's way of waking you from the deep sleep that you have been in. Sometimes, you need to be shaken, destroyed, stripped of all that you know and hold dear. Just like the caterpillar that undergoes metamorphosis inside the cocoon before it can become a butterfly. I am sure that there is something phenomenal that you need to do or achieve in life before you leave this world,' Sironka said gently.

'What happened when you were initiated?' Joy asked Sironka.

'When I was initiated into the circle of energy, I experienced so much knowing and bliss that I did not want to come back to the world of the living anymore. I had become a sort of a hermit. I could survive out in the wild and made do with very little. I lived with the wild animals, ate fruits and berries, laughed a lot, and learnt about the beauty and wholeness of being. I realized that trees and animals are very close to the source of energy. Just by observing them and observing the cycles of the moon, the clouds and the rains, I learnt so much about myself and the great power from which I am created.'

Sironka paused. He had a faraway look in his eyes.

'But divine intelligence had other plans for me. I was asked to go back because I needed to connect both these worlds for people who needed to know the way. The silence out there is alive. I hear the animals talking. I have conversations with my ancestors. I keep wondering when I can go back to living that way. But I am told to wait. It is not yet time,' Sironka said.

Sironka could see that Joy's curiosity had been piqued by this anecdote.

'How was it for you to come back to your family?' Joy asked.

'It was difficult for me to leave behind the beauty and peace and to get back to all my relationships. I just felt so happy when I was not anyone's husband, father or friend. When I came back, I maintained minimum interaction with the tribe and my family, because I felt I did not need all this. But then, I learnt compassion and patience when I was with the tribe. I became a family man again. I saw human frailty, resilience, anger and hatred. And then, I saw undying loyalty, love and hope. I guess that's what god sees in us humans too. Surrendering to my life purpose was tough, but I am so glad that I did it,' Sironka said.

'Sironka, you can do this. You are the laibon for your tribe, I am just a simple man from a fishing village in Goa,' Joy said.

'Joy, I am just a simple, old Maasai man, but I am what I am. You need to own your power. You are a divine spark! What you do in the end does not matter. You may choose to be an investment banker again or the handyman of the tribe. You may be a forest ranger or even do nothing at all.' Sironka looked into Joy's eyes as he spoke.

Joy listened, mesmerized.

'Real magic happens when you align yourself to the creator of this universe, surrender yourself to that energy completely and allow it to flow through you. It will start to awaken dormant abilities within you. It will also use your already present abilities to create something good for humanity. It will guide you, your actions, your words. You will change people's lives, bring healing where there is sadness, bring sunshine where there is darkness. Your soul has an agenda. It's best to go along with it without fighting or negotiating. The ride can be a crazy one, full of trials, pains and many moments of pure joy. But I assure you, it will all be worthwhile.'

'Do I have time to think over this? I feel like this is an important step in my life and I want to be absolutely sure about it,' Joy said, quite overwhelmed.

Sironka smiled, nodded and started to get ready to leave. Joy put a hand on his shoulder and squeezed it. 'Sironka, thank you for sharing your journey with me. Just being with you has made me learn.'

After Sironka left, Joy blew out the oil lamp. He made his way under the mosquito net and snuggled deep into his bed. He could see the moonlight streaming through the window. The room felt so snug and warm.

This was a good life, there was nothing wrong with it. But he felt the same old restless feeling again in the pit of his stomach. It scared him. He knew that whenever this feeling came on, his life took a major shift. He wondered what he would do if he went back to India. Was his house in shambles? Or maybe his wife had decided to stay in it with her new lover? They must all think he was dead. He thought about all the things he had learned from the Maasais in Tanzania—love for their land, love for their animals, conservation of natural reserves and habitats. If they could change their ways—from hunting the animals to conserving them—anyone could do the same.

He thought of Ollie and hoped that the turtle was safe. He remembered his time on the trawler and how the fishermen threw the injured turtles into the sea, knowing very well that the turtles would not make it out alive. If Ollie got stuck again in such nets, he would have no one to help him. Just the thought of this made his heart beat faster. He rubbed the shell that was strung around his neck.

How was he ever going to keep Ollie safe? How could he be so stupid as to let go of Ollie? How did he get so weak as to start drinking again?

He shook his head, trying to get rid of the fear and the self-loathing that had taken hold of him again.

That night, Joy tossed and turned in his bed. Early in the morning, he finally fell asleep and dreamt that he was walking on a beach. He saw Ollie at a distance and he could feel himself bursting with excitement and happiness. He ran to Ollie, sat on his knees and hugged him. But Ollie slowly made his way back into the ocean. Joy tried following him, but the waves kept pushing him back to the beach.

The next moment, he was sitting on the front porch of his house in Goa. His mother was stitching a button on to his old shirt. She looked up and smiled at him.

'Joy, I have kept your coffee on the dinner table with some bun maska,' she said.

She looked happy and healthy. She was humming like she always did. The radio was playing in the background. He entered the house. It was dark and damaged. Weeds were growing out of nooks and crannies, but the dinner table had a fresh table cloth and candles lit in a beautiful silver candleholder. There was a warm glow around the table. He saw a plate full of fresh buns and his coffee was steaming. He picked up a bun, and when he turned around, his mother was in the room, trying to pick a fallen chair. She looked up and smiled at him.

'Joy, please remember: nothing is broken and over till you say and feel it's over,' she said as she caressed his face and planted a kiss on his forehead.

He woke up. He could still feel his mother's hand on his cheek and the touch of her lips on his forehead. He lay there, in bed, confused. *What had the dream been all about?* He could hear the birds chirping and knew that it was soon going to be daylight. He got out of bed and started to get ready for the day.

The day went by, just like all the other days in the boma. In the evening, he got the chance to talk to Sironka and he told him about his dream.

'It is quite prophetic. It is a dream of hope and abundance. Have you thought about the initiation?' Sironka asked.

Joy nodded. He said that he was ready to go through it.

Sironka smiled. He said, 'We will need three days to complete the ceremony. The research team will be going away soon. They would be in Dar-es-Salaam for a few days to restock on supplies. That's the best time to initiate you. It needs to be done before the moonless night.'

'What am I supposed to do before I get initiated?' Joy asked.

'You will need to fast for a few days before the initiation,' said Sironka.

'I have never fasted...ever...in my life,' exclaimed Joy.

'Then mentally prepare yourself to be without food and water for a few days. Set your mind to it,' said Sironka.

'One last question. Has anyone ever died in such a ceremony?' Joy asked earnestly.

'Not till now, but you can be an exception,' said Sironka. When he saw the horrified look on Joy's face, he laughed loudly. 'Cheer up, boy! You should know, I stopped being serious with you a long time ago. If you die...' Sironka raised his eyebrows and shrugged.

Joy completed Sironka's sentence. 'Yeah! I know, it will be a good day to die.' Joy too laughed now.

16

INITIATION

The next week was hectic, to say the least. The research team had to cover new territory and needed to carry food every day. Nalangu and the other women woke up quite early to cook for them. Joy had started helping them every morning. He would get the fire started and milk the cows. By the time he came back, Nalangu would have started preparing a big pot of maize porridge. He helped her make lunch as well. It was so peaceful, working alongside each other.

Their work had a rhythm to it. It somehow soothed all the pain and made him feel calmer. It was funny that now, with him doing all the breathing and smiling, he sensed that Nalangu was more at ease around him. All he wanted now was for her to be happy. He had truly made peace with the situation between them.

The following week, Allan and his research team left for Dar-es-Salaam. That night, Sironka and Olamayian came to Joy's enkaji after dinner. He knew it was about the initiation ceremony.

Olamayian spoke to Joy. 'Are you sure about this, Joy? You don't have to feel obliged to do this just because my father has asked you to. This is not the only solution, but yes, this is the fastest way to find your answers. It may sound mysterious when he talks about it—as if a doorway to another dimension is going to open up and angels playing the harp will welcome you to drink from the cup of wisdom! It's nothing like that. Many of our practices and beliefs are laughed at by the urbane world. Some are barbaric and some, like this, can take a toll on the human body.'

Joy smiled. 'Olamayian, I agree with you. A few months ago, I would have run from the suggestion. But right now, deep inside me, I just know I have to do this. I feel lost again.'

'I want to inform you about how things will pan out for you, Joy. You will be given some awful smelling drinks to consume on an empty stomach and you will be sick. It's like a detoxing process that you will need to go through to receive the spirit. You see, my father talks about all the nice things in the ceremony, but you need to know the not-so-nice details too,' said Olamayian.

'Olamayian, you forget that I am good at swallowing things. I have swallowed the ocean thrice. Having been an alcoholic, I have thrown up quite a lot as well. Jokes aside, I feel like this process is necessary. I tried to kill myself once, and I don't want to go down that path again,' Joy said in a determined tone.

He saw that Sironka had not spoken a word. *That was unusual.*

'Sironka, I'll be okay. Please don't worry,' he said, pressing Sironka's shoulders reassuringly.

Sironka smiled and nodded. Then they parted. That night, Joy slept a deep, dreamless sleep.

Over the next two days, Joy ate very little. He was allowed to drink some nourishing soups. He was fasting to prepare his body for the initiation. It was not as tough as he had thought it would be. His body already felt lighter.

On the third day, Joy woke up and stayed in bed for a while, longer than his usual routine. He packed his backpack and then, he went across to the kitchen. The women were drinking tea. He could hear a lot of giggles and laughter.

Namelok saw him and said, 'I heard you are going out with Sironka and Olamayian on a walk. We are deciding the menu for a feast we will throw when you return. We always celebrate after a soul quest.'

Joy smiled. 'I just hope that the lions don't eat me,' he joked.

'They don't like the taste of Maasai meat. You are a brown Maasai now, they won't eat you either,' she said.

Nalangu was giggling, then, in a sober tone, she said, 'Joy, remember once you finish the ceremony, please drink the water that I have boiled and given to Olamayian.'

She spontaneously reached out and hugged him tightly. Joy was taken aback by her sudden show of affection. She backed off, blushing a dark shade of red.

Soon enough, a ranger came to pick them up and drove them to the edge of the game reserve. As they got off the jeep, Olamayian informed the ranger that they would meet him in two days, at noon, at the same spot. Then they picked up their camping equipment and walked into the game reserve.

They must have walked for a few hours. It was getting hotter as the day progressed. Joy was thirsty, but he noticed that Olamayian and Sironka did not reach for their calabash either, so he let it be too.

They came to a spot that looked like a clearing in the middle of the forest. There was a watering hole at some distance. 'So getting eaten by the lions is a strong possibility,' Joy thought to himself.

They walked towards a clump of bushes. Olamayian moved them aside to expose the mouth of a small cave. They had to bend down to enter it. It was dark and musty inside and it felt like no one had been there for a while. Joy saw signs of soot on the wall. Someone had drawn stick-like figures. There was one wall with an extended stretch of paintings on it.

Olamayian spoke softly. 'This is our ancestral cave. We have all come here to get insight, and we have all found answers to the most difficult problems here.'

They placed their backpacks and camping bundles against a wall. Then, Olamayian went outside and broke a few branches full of leaves. He bundled them together and used them to clean the cave. He got another such bundle ready and handed it over to Joy and asked him to dust the walls. Sironka came back with some dried branches. He broke and cut them with his knife while Joy sat in one corner of the cave, trying to arrange a makeshift bed. He also emptied the contents of his backpack as he watched the duo building a small fire pit.

Sironka took out his earthen pot and placed it over the fire pit. He added water and began to brew something that smelled awful. Joy looked at Olamayian and pulled a face in mock horror. 'Is that it?' he joked.

Olamayian smiled at Joy. 'It's our ancestral plant. It helps you through the quest. Everyone can't brew this concoction. The plant chooses those who can. My father is one of the few privileged ones. He can hear it talk, and it will listen to him and help you. I would not call it a drug, but yes, it is a vision inducer. We all believe that it can only be brewed in a sacred space, like this cave, accompanied with prayers and rituals that our ancestors have created for us. It can do more harm than good if taken unsupervised, and it cannot be used as a mood-enhancing drug.'

Joy nodded and Olamayian added, 'Besides this, we will feed you a soup made of herbs. The soup actually tastes quite good. Anyway, I'd better be off. I must collect some of the herbs in the forest before it gets too dark. Why don't you come with me?'

They walked into the forest and Olamayian started to hum a song as they walked. As they moved, something would catch Olamayian's eye and he would bend down to pluck a few leaves. Joy noticed that around some plants, he would stop humming. He would kneel down next to a plant or a tree, close his eyes, mumble something that sounded like a small prayer before he plucked the leaves and put them in his cloth bag. Once he had collected a bundle of differently coloured leaves, he turned to go back.

'Olamayian, why were you saying a prayer before you plucked some of the leaves?' asked Joy.

'I am asking the leaves for permission,' Olamayian said in a very matter-of-fact voice. 'It's best not to eat anything or drink water, Joy. After eating these, you will feel your stomach cramp and you will purge for a few hours. There is a small stream at the back of the cave where you can clean yourself,' Olamayian said.

By the time they arrived back to the cave, it was dark. Sironka had taken whatever he was brewing off the fire and it had been left to cool on the side. Olamayian washed the leaves, and then sat down on his haunches and started to make the soup, which he served Joy in an open calabash bowl. Joy slurped down the soup and ate all the leaves. Sironka and Olamayian ate some fruits, fermented milk and thick sticks of ugali packed in a small parcel made of leaves. They sat around the fire and talked about Olamayian's impending marriage. Joy felt very sleepy and crawled under his mosquito net and fell asleep.

Joy woke up in the middle of the night because of extreme pains in the stomach. Thank God, Olamayian had warned him! He walked towards the sound of water, behind the cave. He found a place behind a bush and passed an extremely watery stool. He covered it up with mud and dried leaves, and then walked back to the cave.

Olamayian was waiting for him. 'This will carry on for a while. I am here if you need me,' he said.

As the night proceeded, Joy went back and forth, between the cave and the stream, multiple times. By early morning, his legs were weak, his head felt light. As he lay down in his bed, his body started to shiver.

Joy's last thought was of his mother before he closed his eyes. He felt someone wiping his brow with a wet cloth. After some hours of restless sleep, he woke up. It was hot in the cave and he was sweating profusely. Sironka again fed him a small portion of the soup.

'Is this your concoction?' Joy mumbled.

'No Joy, I need you to clean the insides of your body. The actual concoction comes later in the night,' Sironka said.

By mid-afternoon, Joy started to feel extremely nauseous. This time, Olamayian helped him to the stream. He threw up yellow bile, and it felt like his stomach was sore. When they got back to the cave, Sironka had dusted and cleaned up Joy's bed. They both helped him back into it. Joy slept again. He dreamt of his son, his mother, his father and gradually, his mind went blank.

He slept for hours and woke up in the evening. He lay there in his bed, the warm glow of the fire making him feel safe. He heard a hyena laughing in the distance. He was too tired to be scared of the wild. He looked over at Olamayian who was sitting in one corner, sharpening his spear.

'Please I cannot take any more of that soup,' Joy pleaded.

'I also think you've had enough. We will start the ceremony once it gets dark. A part of it will take place here, and the other part will happen near the watering hole,' said Sironka.

'Is that why Olamayian is sharpening his spear?' Joy asked, his eyes large with fear.

Sironka smiled. 'You need to stop being so fearful of the wild, Joy. Know that you are safe with us.'

Joy rolled on to his side and realized that he did not have the energy to get up. 'Sironka, my brain has gone blank. I can't think coherently anymore. I am nervous,' Joy said in a very feeble voice.

'That's exactly how it must be. It's a good space to be. You will see your visions clearly. The worst is over, now for the fun.' Sironka then started to hum a song and it slowly lulled Joy back to sleep.

Olamayain woke Joy again. He asked him to change into a shuka and made him wear a few bracelets and neck pieces. 'These are symbolic, ancestral jewellery that our ancestors wore. You are a part of our family, so it is okay for you to wear it. You are not circumcised, and we have asked for permission from the spirit world. They agreed. This will keep you safe and protected while you journey.'

Sironka was chanting as he placed stones in an

elaborate circle around the fire pit. He then asked Joy to come over and sit next to him. Sironka seemed to be in a different world. His eyes had a faraway look. He shook his rattle, hummed, danced and sang. Olamayian joined him and this song carried on for a while. The sound of their voices, the smoke, the smell of burning herbs and his overall weakness made Joy feel drowsy again. Sironka sat down and handed Joy a bowl and told him to drink it up. Joy did so obediently.

'Now close your eyes, slow your breath down, like I have taught you,' said Sironka in a soft voice.

Joy slowed his breath and soon, he could feel something starting to swirl within him. There was a tingling warm sensation at the base of his spine. It slowly spread and moved upwards. It felt as if a small tornado was at the centre of his chest and he was being sucked into it. His ears started to buzz. He tried opening his eyes, but could not. He knew, by now, that he was swaying. He tried to sit upright but it seemed impossible. He felt the surge of electric energy pass through him and past him, then he felt something expand within him.

He could not think or focus on anything anymore. His eyes suddenly flew open and the first thing he saw was a pulsating, shimmering, sparkling body of light sitting near him. He instinctively knew that it was Sironka. The energy inside of him had become so powerful that he knew he had to get up and move. He tried to walk, but he staggered around like a drunk man.

He managed to walk outside into the cool night air. That felt good. But it still did not calm the energy that was surging through him and racking his body. He felt hands holding and guiding him. At some point, he felt someone swinging him off his feet and carrying him. Then he was put down. He saw water and knew that now he was at the edge of the watering hole. When he looked into the water body, the water looked different to him. It was shimmering and lit from within. He knelt down by the edge of the watering hole and felt as though the water was like a mirror. He first thought it reflected the stars in the sky, but soon, he realized that it was alive with a million, small, twinkling lights from within which emitted a light blue glow. The lights would dart around, creating shapes like flowers, horses and other images, some of which he could not place.

When he put his hand in the water, he saw that his hand too was glowing and shimmering with the same blue, sparkling light. At some point, he saw a very large, green ball emerging from the centre of the watering hole. It felt like a cloud, and it floated up and it took the shape of a turtle. When he looked into the eyes of the turtle, there was instant recognition. It was Ollie, a much larger version of him.

Joy reached out and stroked Ollie's head. 'You came to keep me safe. I knew you would never leave me,' Joy said in a relieved tone.

Ollie's eyes had a strange kind of light. It made him want to look deeper and he got sucked into them. He was in a tunnel and streaks of lights ran in straight lines along it. The tunnel was alive and breathing. It expanded and contracted as he moved through it. Its walls and layers were permeable, like fine coloured mist. The wind swished past his ears and ruffled his hair. It felt as if he was moving at a great speed. Suddenly, he found himself sitting on a boat in the middle of the ocean.

Ollie was on the boat with him. The turtle was speaking like animals do in animated movies.

'It's good to see you, Joy! I thought you would never find your way back to me. But the Great White did tell me to keep trying to connect to you. And today I had a feeling and I knew that we would connect.'

Hearing Ollie speak took Joy by surprise.

'Don't be surprised, Joy! In this world, we can talk and understand each other. We have a little catching up to do, but first I would like you to look into the water now,' Ollie said.

Joy obediently did what was asked of him. As he stared into the water, he saw images slowly floating up to tell him Ollie's story. He saw himself pushing the boat, then losing balance and then drowning. He saw Ollie following him and asking the dolphins to save him. He saw the whole journey unfold like a movie. He saw the Great White swaddling him in weeds, sucking him into his mouth and keeping him safe in his stomach as the storm raged. He saw himself being spit out on the beach.

He saw Sironka waiting for him, and the sea and the sky talking to Sironka.

Joy looked at Ollie. 'Sironka always knew I was going to come to him?' he asked.

Ollie nodded. 'Yes, he knew! I am glad you've seen what happened. You know now that we were destined to be in each other's lives. I first met you when you were a young boy. We played on the beach together for many days,' Ollie said.

That's when Joy remembered Ollie as a little turtle that he had found on the beach. He fondly thought of the times they had spent together.

'I had a dream, Joy. I had to find you, which I did, and now we meet in the spirit world. I am your animal protector, and I promise to be with you always. I will guide you and look after you.'

Joy was overwhelmed. Ollie loved him so much. 'Will I see you physically, in the real world, again?' Joy asked.

Ollie laughed. 'Joy, sorry to burst your bubble, but this is the real world. The world you and I live in is the dream. Someday, if it is to be, we will surely meet. Otherwise, you can always talk to me in this world. But till then, honour my kind. I need your help. The times are not kind to us. There is a big change on its way for the planet and all those who live in it. We all have to change, reinvent, readapt and relearn—including the human race. And you will have to be a part of this movement,' Ollie said.

Joy was silent for a while. 'How can I help?' he asked.

'Just surrender to the energy that created this world and it will guide your next move. But for now, my friend, we both need to do one last thing. We need to merge into each other, become one. You will imbibe all my qualities. You need these on your journey as a human soul. You need to look into my eyes again, and just allow yourself to flow,' Ollie said in a calm, reassuring voice.

Joy did what Ollie asked him to. Slowly, he could feel his hands turning into flippers. He felt a large shell on his back. He could feel his tongue and throat thickening.

'It's okay, Joy, this is only for a while and with practice, you will become better at merging with me whenever you need my strength. You now need to look to your right,' Ollie instructed.

When Joy looked, he saw a large elephant with a tusk. There was a white glow surrounding the elephant. He could hear Ollie telling him that this was Sironka. Joy smiled and he now knew why Sironka was so good with elephant stories. He looked to his left and saw a large lion whose body also glowed in the moonlight. His mane was lit and bits of it would spark, break away and fly up into the night sky. Joy knew that it was Olamayian.

'Now, Joy, you need to look up, towards the heavens. It's time to surrender,' Ollie guided him in a gentle, calm voice.

When Joy looked up into the night sky, he saw a shooting star. It slowly started to move towards him. The star came closer to him and stopped right in front of him. It glowed brightly. He kept staring at the star, not knowing for how long but at some point, he felt immense peace descending over him. It slowly merged into him. That's when he blanked out and collapsed into a heap.

Sironka and Olamayian, who were standing on either side of Joy, picked him up. Olamayian slung him over his shoulders and carried him back to the ancestral cave. Joy's eyes were wide open, but he was far away, lost in a dream world.

Olamayian gently lay him down on his bed. 'Is he going to be okay, father?' he asked.

'Yes, he will. The universe and the ancestors are talking to him. Let's clean him up for the night and let him lie in peace,' said Sironka.

They took Joy to the stream at the back of the cave. There they bathed and clothed him, with great care like they would for a little child. Thereafter, they carried him back. Joy closed his eyes and fell into a deep sleep.

When the sun rose high up in the sky, Joy stirred. Olamayian came to him, 'You okay, brother?' he asked.

Joy smiled a blissful, lazy smile. 'I guess I did not die after all,' he said, and breathed in deeply.

'I feel so good and clean from inside. Peaceful, no pain, very light. I know what Sironka meant. This energy can be addictive,' Joy said.

Sironka entered the cave and smiled down at Joy.

'Welcome back. You did good, my son. I was so worried and kept wondering if I was doing the right thing by putting you through this experience,' Sironka said with a hint of relief in his voice.

Joy held Sironka's hand. He brought it to his lips and said, 'Thank you. I can't thank you enough for this. I will not lie, I did feel that I would die at some point, but I knew you would not let any harm come to me.'

Sironka lovingly stroked Joy's head. 'I would have stormed all the three worlds to keep you safe, but you went through it like a dream. Now it's time to go back to our boma. Do you feel like you have the strength to walk back?'

Joy slowly got up and realized he was quite steady on his feet.

'Joy, you should know that over the next few days, you will have many visitors from the other side. They will come to talk to you or just be around you. Don't be scared, talk to them,' Sironka said.

Joy nodded, 'Before the initiation, this information would have spooked me out, but now I guess I understand the other side a little bit more.' He then looked at himself and saw that he was dressed like a Maasai. He laughed. 'The women call me the brown Maasai, so now I am one,' he said.

Olamayian walked towards him and took off the arm bands and amulets that he had put on Joy. He asked him if he wanted to change his clothes as well.

Joy smiled, 'Actually, I feel quite comfortable in this. I wonder why I did not ever try to wear the red robes before. It's quite airy—all the way up to my legs. It is keeping me quite cool.'

They started their long trek back to their pick-up point.

Olamayian uncorked a calabash. 'You better drink some water. My sister insisted I carry it for you. Take small sips,' he said.

Joy took the first few sips and the drink truly felt like sweet nectar.

The jeep was waiting for them at the edge of the game reserve. They got in and slowly made their way back to their boma.

Once they reached home, Joy got off the jeep and walked back to his enkaji. He did feel different, much lighter and expansive. He realized that all his five senses were extremely heightened. He could hear every leaf rustling and every bird chirping. Everything around him—the colours of the leaves, the earth and the sky—was more vivid. Even the stones were vibrating with life.

The cool interiors of the enkaji calmed him. He stacked his bag in a corner and lay down. He could feel a buzzing sensation around him. He was aware of his every breath and it calmed him down. Slowly, he drifted off to sleep.

After a while, he felt a pair of hands on his shoulders and a faint voice coming through. Someone was shaking him and calling out his name to wake him up. Joy opened his eyes and saw Nalangu, looking very concerned, leaning over him. When he opened his eyes, she stood up.

'Are you okay? My father asked me to let you know that it's best if you can wash yourself and eat something and then rest. If you need some company, walk over to Namelok's enkaji.'

'I have the urge to eat something sweet,' Joy said.

'I can get you some honey cakes. Namelok is making them for the feast,' said Nalangu.

'When is the feast? I am so excited about the food. It is really weird because I am not usually concerned with food,' Joy observed.

Nalangu smiled. 'The soul quest brings out the urge to live life to the fullest, my father often says that.'

She stopped at the doorway and asked him if he would like a soup.

Joy shook his head. 'No way! I am scared of drinking any more soups after the last few I have had,' he said in an adamant voice.

Nalangu laughed.

Once she had left, he unpacked his bag, washed himself, and by the time he returned to the enkaji, some food and cake was kept for him near his bed. He ate and slept for hours. He dreamt of his father. He slipped into a lucid sleep and at some point, he felt that he was not alone in his hut, just as Sironka had warned him. But the thought did not scare him. This new world felt comfortable. It was as if he belonged there.

He spent the next two days in his enkaji and ventured out only to answer nature's call and clean up for the day. At regular intervals, some food was kept in his hut by Legishon, and he ate with pure delight. Everything smelled and tasted better than usual.

One morning, he woke up early and knew that he was ready to step out of his enkaji. He had slept enough. He took his gardening tools and started to weed and prune the vegetable patch. It had been looked after well. By early evening, he saw Sironka sitting in his favourite spot under the tree.

Joy walked up to him.

'Come sit with me, Joy. You look relaxed and happy. Did you have any more insights?' Sironka asked.

Joy nodded. 'Yes, many insights. Like you said, I had many visitors from the other side. I could hear a lot of whispering and music. At first, it confused me but later I felt very calm and happy.'

'We believe that the ancestors come to visit a person after he undergoes a quest,' Sironka said.

'Most of the time, I slept. But sometimes, I could see my life play out like a movie in front of me. I was in a dream-like state, half awake and half asleep. I realized why something had happened and what part I had played in it. My head is still full of what I saw. I have partially understood, but it will take me time to sort through all the images. But it's a good start, taking responsibility for my own life. One of the biggest breakthroughs was learning why I chose my parents,' Joy said with a big smile.

Sironka teased him. 'You are beginning to sound a little like me,' he said.

Joy laughed, 'I will need a few more years to be so cuckoo. A mad man, like you. I am only an understudy. But it would be an absolute honour to be even a little of you.'

Both men laughed loudly.

'My wife Lena often used the word cuckoo. I have heard someone using the word after a long time. Did you know that she took pains to teach me how to speak English? I can't thank her enough for it.' Sironka looked up at Joy and winked.

'I am glad you are on the way to cuckoo-land. You have to start somewhere, and it takes courage to think and be different. But now let's get back to the insight you had about your parents,' he coaxed.

'Well, interestingly, I chose them because I had to take on their fears, their limiting beliefs and emotional blocks. Then I needed to break the pattern, work through them, be the change so that the next generation does not have to deal with the same issues that I did,' Joy said.

He could see the surprise on Sironka's face. 'That is very interesting, Joy. I never thought of it that way. This is ancestral medicine! You are blessed to have access to this insight,' Sironka exclaimed.

'I need to be the change for my family tree. I can't blame them for how I turned out. To begin with, this all was my choice, exactly like you said. I am my father and I am my mother too; they live in me. I speak and it is likely that I unconsciously think like them as well. Instead of being ashamed of who my parents are, I am now quite proud of the fact that I am the son of a fisherman who had a few faults. It's not about forgiving him. You spoke of it at the mission but I did not understand it then. I guess the initiation helped me understand all that you have been teaching me.' Joy took a deep breath. 'Who am I to judge or punish anyone? I have such strong opinions. I wasted so much time doing exactly that. Instead, I needed to show my father and all the people in my life that I loved them,' Joy said.

Sironka nodded. 'One's parents and one's home are energy points, like the watering holes we saw in the forest. Both, the relationships and the place nourish us. Sometimes, we don't get that because we choose not to.

And that's where community, a tribe of like-minded people, becomes so important when we are growing up.'

Joy listened intently and said, 'I spoke to my father at length. I made peace with him and I made peace with my son as well. Sironka, I now know your spirit animal is an elephant. I also saw that you knew I was coming to be with you.'

Sironka smiled. 'I waited for you and sent Olamayian to bring you back when the sea brought you to the beach at Paje, but you were not ready then. I guess you still had not hit rock bottom. You needed to kill the old Joy—every last bit of you had to be broken for you to transform and reinvent yourself.'

Joy shook his head in disbelief. 'How did I ever think that suicide was the solution? Now I know that only when you attach too much importance to the external world that you lose connection with yourself and think of suicide.'

They were both silent for some time.

'Oh, I also met Ollie. We are now friends forever. He and I have great conversations now,' said Joy.

'That's good, Joy! Remember the first rule of having a spirit animal is to honour him always. You must keep connecting with him as much as possible, ask him to clear your confusions, listen to his guidance, and follow through with your actions. Now he will be your guide and will teach you to always be connected to the source.' Sironka patted Joy on his back.

Namelok brought tea for both of them and after a short chat, she left them alone again.

'Now is the best time to start your next quest,' Sironka said.

Joy had a look of horror on his face. 'Sironka, please!

I do not want to drink another soup or shit my guts out anymore. I thought this was it,' Joy pleaded.

Sironka laughed. 'No, nothing so drastic this time, Joy. You just need to go deeper, spend more time and remember the saddest memories in your life and heal them.'

Joy thought for a while. 'My son dying while I was busy fighting with my wife, losing Ollie because of my addiction, not being supported or acknowledged by my father, seeing my mother being beaten by my father and being helpless to do anything about it because I was so young, the feeling of not belonging anywhere and not having any friends, and also...finding out my wife was having an affair,' Joy recalled.

Sironka then said, 'You need to hold on to these thoughts for a while. Now, can you recall the happiest moment in your life?'

Joy thought for a while.

'They are fewer and more difficult to come up with. My son's birth, seeing Ollie emerging out of the water to meet me, Sunny throwing a surprise birthday party for me, hearing the radio and drinking coffee in my family home, eating my favourite meals cooked by my mother, being out on the sea with my father, swimming in the ocean with Ollie,' Joy said.

'Yes, these sound like very happy memories. That's good! All the good memories and bad memories are powerful moments in your life. All these things have happened for a reason, so dwell on them. Don't brush them aside. Just to help you, I can talk of a few incidents in your life,' Sironka said, putting down his tea.

'The birth of your child points towards creativity

and new life. Eating the food your mother cooked says something about nurturing. The abuse you witnessed says something about standing up for those who cannot speak or defend themselves. Your wife loving another likely says something about a lack of abundance. Sunny throwing a birthday party has to do with creating special moments for other people. The memory of home points towards the need to feel grounded and rooted. Being rejected by people is a feeling of separation.

'As you spend time with yourself, think about these moments. Slowly, a pattern will start to emerge. The dots will be connected. You will know what it is you want to do or stand for in life, and how you can use your talents to help and serve humanity. All souls are born to help and serve humanity, but when we are born, we forget the bigger picture and start living lives that are completely centred on doing, creating and hoarding for ourselves. Wars are fought because we love power, land and money.

'Anyway, I am at peace now. I know you are empowered with the spirit. In time, you will figure it out. You are now your best teacher. You have the keys in your hand, so unlock the door to abundance,' Sironka said.

'After all this talk, I am feeling hungry again, Sironka.' Joy rubbed his belly and they both laughed out loud.

'Good! Good! Welcome back to the living. Feed your senses, they are all finally functioning,' Sironka said, and offered Joy a chocolate that the research team had gifted.

17
HOME

Allan and the research party came back to the boma. That night, the women cooked a special dinner to celebrate Joy's quest and to welcome their guests back. They made Joy's favourite food and tried their hand at some of the Indian food that he had taught them to cook. He was pleasantly surprised by it. They had actually done a very good job at it. There was much laughter, singing and dancing, and Joy participated in all the activities instead of just watching. This time around, he felt like one of them. He could jump like the Maasai, but not as high as Olamayian.

Joy spent the next few days with the research team in the game reserve. After his initiation, Joy realized that the game reserve had a different energy and feel to it. He could feel life pulsating all around him. He soon realized that he loved being near nature. There was no way that he could go back to living in a city anymore! He needed to hear the call of wild animals or the ocean.

He had fond memories of Paje. He remembered the time he lived in England—it was a beautiful, green country, but the African forest and Galgibaga had a charm of their own.

He also started to notice the passion with which Allan worked. He was a lot like Olamayian in the way he tried to save and protect the animals. Their dedication to the cause was inspiring and he soon realized that he too needed to do something that he loved and was passionate about.

What really mattered now was creating a sense of family for others and himself, a place to belong. He wanted to protect those who were unable to speak up for themselves. He wanted to show the way forward for people who were lost, just as Sironka had done for him. He really wanted to leave the world in a better place for the future generations. He was very sure he was not going to make any more compromises in life.

Joy often thought of Goa these days. He missed the smell of salt in the air. He missed swimming in the ocean. He missed the small village market. He was soon sure that he was homesick, even though he did not know if he had a home left in Goa. The feeling would come back to plague him every day. He even dreamed of walking on the white sands of Galgibaga beach, swimming with Ollie, being on a boat and watching his house from the ocean.

He knew he needed to talk to Sironka to make sense of his feelings. One evening, he walked across to Namelok's enkaji. Sironka was sitting under the tree and was in deep conversation with a few government officials about some permissions required by the research and conservation team. Joy waited patiently till the officials had left.

Sironka then saw Joy and asked him to sit down. 'So when are you planning on travelling back to India?' Sironka asked.

Joy was taken aback. 'How did you know? I was thinking of that possibility. I just wanted to talk to you before I made up my mind,' said Joy.

'I always knew, Joy. I saw your journey back to India

when I initiated you at the watering hole. My heart has been heavy with the thought of parting, but I know that the time has come to move on to the next phase of your life. This does not mean an end for us, but I know you need to go back to India. It's the next chapter in your life, a fresh start, a brand new picture to paint,' Sironka said in a calm and steady voice.

By now, Sironka could see the distress in Joy's eyes. 'Don't be sad, my son! Your destiny awaits you in India. If you live in Tanzania, you will survive. But that's not the aim of your life. Survival is an instinct, one that animals are given so as to be alive in the wild. Humans go much beyond that, which is what makes us an evolved species. You need to transform yourself. The old Joy has died on the night of your initiation. Death means transformation, it means new life. So Joy, it's time to create just like the creator,' Sironka said with a smile on his face.

Joy nodded. 'This feeling has been there for a few days, but I guess your words have given me some clarity.'

'Joy, the universe is now pushing you forward, ever since you surrendered to it. A snake that does not shed its skin will die. Always know that there are three constants in life—change, experience and death. Make friends with them,' Sironka said with a twinkle in his eye.

'Sironka, how will I live without you? I may just get lost again. I am a little nervous—what if I go back to being an alcoholic some day?' Joy asked.

Sironka put back his head and laughed till the tears rolled down his cheeks. 'Stop talking like a child! I know you are afraid to move, but movement means growth and growth leads to learning. Joy, deep down, you know that you will not get lost again because you have connected to the one who has created us all. The source will guide you and keep you safe. Yes, there will be days where you will fluctuate between confusion and clarity. I too experience that. There is a wise voice inside you, listen to it. The idea is to be in the space of clarity more often and you already know how that space feels. I have taught you to let go of your thoughts and slow your mind.

'Living a conscious life is not rocket science. Just expand beyond your limiting beliefs, blocks and fears. It's very simple. You need to move inside of yourself instead of out. So breathe, slow down, let go of your thoughts and smile, Joy. A new life awaits you,' Sironka said.

They hugged each other and sat in silent communion for a long time.

Then, Sironka picked up a small pebble. He held it between his palms, closed his eyes, breathed into it and then gently placed it into Joy's hand and wrapped both his palms around it. 'This stone has the energy of this land, the people, the animals and me. Keep it with you and when you feel powerless or fearful, remember us. Our spirits will come forward and surround you. We will fill you with our strength.'

Joy held it tightly as tears rolled down his cheek. He knew the time had come to part.

Over the next few days, Sironka informed everyone that Joy had decided to go back to India. It sent ripples through the tribe. Many tried to convince him to stay. Namelok even offered to buy him his own cattle and find him a good, pretty girl who would bear him healthy children. Joy was absolutely touched with the outpouring of love. He now knew how wonderful it was to be part of a whole community.

It was different from his life back in Goa. He had been

ridiculed, laughed at and had never really felt a part of the village community. Now he knew it wasn't because of them, it was him. He had felt and believed that he was separate, so people around him had distanced themselves and that had fed his beliefs.

Once Joy was completely sure that he was going back to India, he realized the first thing he needed to do was get a passport. When he mentioned it to Allan, he was more than happy to help Joy. He immediately made a few phone calls and got his contacts in Dar-es-Salaam to get Joy an appointment at the Indian High Commission. It was decided that it was best for Joy to take a flight instead of going by sea. Father Frances checked the details and they managed to find a direct flight to India that flew out every alternate day. Rates for the flight ticket were checked and Joy calculated that he had sufficient money to travel back to India.

While Joy was arranging his travel back to India, Allan and his team arranged a farewell party to thank Joy for all that he had done for them. The night before he left, they all gathered around a camp fire. The research team helped cook the dinner. Father Frances was invited to be a part of the evening and he brought some bottles of wine, which were polished off in no time by the elders. Speeches were made, the women sang songs of friends parting and safe travels. They all danced with gay abandonment and with every hour, Joy's heart grew heavier because he knew that the time to say his goodbyes was coming closer.

Olamayian was watching Joy and knew that his friend was sad. He walked across and sat next to Joy and held his hand. 'Joy, we have a choice now. We can be sad or we can celebrate. We all choose to celebrate the start of your new life in India. I know you are sad. I can feel it. We all know that births and unions are moments to be celebrated, but it's also important to celebrate partings and death. We celebrate because we are so grateful for the time that we got to spend with you. Always know that this is your home too. If it's to be, we all will meet again someday, but till then, let's sing songs of the ocean bringing you to us. Please come and dance and sing with us,' he said encouragingly.

Joy got up reluctantly. 'You know that I am not a good dancer. I have two left feet,' he muttered.

Olamayian laughed and had a mischievous glint in his eyes, 'We are good jumpers though, so jump with us. Let the song vibrate through your body. I assure you, if you jump all the sadness will move to your feet and Mother Earth will take it into her belly. Give her your sad energy. She will use it to grow more trees and thrive.'

Joy joined the circle of dancers. He danced, he laughed, he hummed and he felt like a young boy again. Soon, the heaviness in his heart disappeared. He laughed at Legishon's stupid antics as he and his friends tried their best to mimic Joy's way of talking and laughing. He smiled at Namelok's long speech on how Joy was a shining example to all the young Maasai men; they too could try to be useful around the house, support the women of the tribe instead of pruning themselves like birds and cats.

When Sironka was asked to say a few words, he got up slowly, walked up to Joy and placed his hand on his head. He smiled, and in a low whisper, he said, 'My son, Joy, my heart knows the truth that life never ends, so I know we are not parting. I will always remember you like I see you now—happy, smiling and at peace.'

He pointed to the centre of Joy's chest. 'Always know

that we, our boma, the family, will always live here within you. I bless you with abundance in life and may it be present in the lives you touch.'

He bent down and kissed the top of Joy's head, patted his cheek and walked away to sit with the other elders.

Every moment since his initiation, Joy had been responding with an outpouring of acceptance, love and support, which he knew was a gift from the universe for surrendering to it. He knew he was blessed.

The party ended and they all slowly walked backed to their huts. Joy too got up to his hut.

Sironka called out to Joy to join him. As Joy sat down next to him, Sironka said, 'Joy, before you go, I need to share something. Know that the vibrations of the earth are changing and you may feel it for a while. Soon, everything around us—and all that we are made of—will change and be of a higher divine frequency. Collectively, humanity and the animal kingdom, need to improve and be ready for this new era that will dawn. Now every human will be super human, an upgraded version of themselves.'

'We are all on our way to becoming wiser than we were before and will all play an important role in creating change. There will be changes in the way we perceive life, the way we live, love and create and like always, the animal kingdom has known about this much before the humans. The universe is choosing to awaken many to their grandest potential—just like Ollie was chosen, like you are chosen—so as to herald this change. You need to go back to awaken more people by sharing your incredible journey,' Sironka said.

Joy nodded, again knowing that time would teach him to understand how he could be instrumental in this respect.

The next day, Joy packed his backpack and was in the process of folding his much-used and worn-out mosquito net, when Nalangu entered his enkaji.

'Can I talk to you before you leave?' she asked hesitantly.

Joy realized that she looked a little distressed. Her eyes were moist with unshed tears. 'Something is upsetting you, Nalangu, what is it?' Joy was concerned.

'I guess I should have spoken to you earlier, but now it's time for you to leave.' She smiled through her tears. 'I learnt a very valuable lesson over the past few days and wanted to talk to you about it,' she said.

She sat on the bench near the window. The sunlight streamed through and her hair looked like molten amber in the light. Just looking at her, sitting there, warmed Joy's heart. She was a beautiful woman, inside out.

Nalangu wiped her tears. 'What I realized is that we often keep everything that needs to be said or done for the last moment. I kept finding excuses to not talk to you. I don't want you to leave without letting you know how I have been feeling. I have not been myself since my father told me that you love me. I felt guilty and angry. It felt like I had cheated on Koinet. I was not angry with you for falling in love with me, but I have realized that I was angry at myself for being so weak, for not keeping my distance and drawing the line. It took me some time to acknowledge that I love you as well. I am not ashamed or guilty anymore for being in love with you. I withdrew because of my confusion and what I missed out on was our friendship,' she sobbed.

Joy came and sat down across her on the bench. He reached out and wiped her tears. 'Don't be angry or sad, Nalangu. My heart breaks to see you cry. You have always treated me with kindness and respect, and I am so happy that we both felt love for each other. Like your father has often said to all, it is the purest and most powerful emotion. I never understood it before, not until you made me realize its power. I know we will carry this love in our hearts always, even after we part. It needs to strengthen us, not make us weak. And about you choosing to be with Koinet, I respect your decision. He is a good man and I know he will make you happy. You will be a good wife to him. This is how it was to be for us, like your father says.'

She looked up at him, smiled and thanked him. 'I will miss you very much, Joy,' she said.

'I will miss you too,' Joy said as he leaned forward, held her head and kissed her on the forehead. 'Don't be sad, Nalangu, ever. You are brave for having the courage to tell me how you feel. I now realize I was more of a coward than you. I would have left without talking to you. I guess I did not tell you the truth because I feared losing our friendship, but we very nearly ended up messing that up as well. You are beautiful, kind, honest and wonderful. Just know that always.'

Nalangu smiled. 'No, you are not a coward. You are just a decent man.' She reached into her shirt pocket and pulled out a small wooden piece and she handed it to him. 'I polished it smooth and I put a small hole on one side. You can string it up and wear it around your neck. It's a piece of wood from my father's favourite tree in the mission,' she said.

Joy rubbed it between his fingers. It felt cool and smooth to his touch. He thanked her. He saw tears gathering again in Nalangu's eyes. She was biting down on her lower lip to stop it from trembling.

'Thank you, Joy, for loving me and also for letting go of me,' she said. While he was wiping her tears, she caught his hand and pressed it against her cheek and sobbed. 'Just know that I will always love you without any expectations, but I choose to be with Koinet and my family. I love my country, its traditions, the forest and in this present moment, this is my reality,' she said, clarity tingeing in her voice.

Joy nodded and wiped his own tears. She reached out and hugged him. They stood, embracing each other for quite a while and suddenly, she moved away and left. He stood there, all alone. He could still feel her warm body on his. For a while, he did not know what he was feeling. However, gradually Joy could feel relief spreading through his body. He felt lighter to have told her how much he loved her. Truth was liberating, in some odd way.

He packed the last of his belongings. Then he looked around at the enkaji one last time—the mud floor, walls of sticks and ash, the small windows. This was home too and he would always remember it fondly. He made his way out into the sunshine.

The whole tribe had gathered to say their goodbyes. Father Frances handed him a small slip of paper with the address of the mission and his e-mail on it, reminding him to drop him a line once he reached back home safely.

Joy hugged the children and thanked Namelok for all that she had done for him. Nalangu was nowhere to be seen.

Olamayian gave Joy a long hug. 'Look after yourself, brother. I will be too far away to fish you out of the ocean now.'

Joy smiled.

He saw Sironka standing at the back of the crowd. He walked to him. 'Sironka, I don't know what to say.'

Sironka smiled. 'Don't say anything, Joy. We don't need words between us. This is not the end. I will not deny that I feel a little lost and sad in my heart, but this too will pass. Have a safe journey back home to India and make all of us proud by being and doing exactly what you want to do. Remember, you will inspire people by just being who you were meant to be. Always remember the way you love is the way you will live your life.'

Joy gave Sironka's hand a final squeeze and walked back to the jeep. The ranger who was going to drive him to the train station asked him if he was ready to go and Joy nodded. The ranger started the jeep. Slowly, they made their way out of the boma. Joy watched the tribe disappearing in the rearview mirror till they became a speck in the distance.

Joy reached Dar-es-Salaam quite late at night and managed to find a small hotel near the Indian High Commission. Allan had fixed an appointment for the next day. He had a very restless night. He got up at the slightest sound—a car honk, a guest speaking in the other room. What really disturbed him was the sound of the television. He had become extremely sensitive to sounds, and to make matters worse, he woke up feeling disoriented. He still had two whole hours before his appointment. He took a long bath and headed downstairs for some breakfast.

A buffet had been served in the hotel café overlooking a small garden. Some guests were sitting around the café, eating, discussing their schedules. He picked a spot outside, in the garden. He tried to read a newspaper. So many of the headlines made no sense to him. He soon realized the extent of the pandemic. World economies were now slowly limping back to life, he read. When he looked at the date on the newspaper, it suddenly struck him that a year had passed since he had left the shores of Goa.

His body had adjusted to living in the heat without so much as a fan. The air-conditioned environment of the hotel made his body ache, ever so slightly. He soon realized that he had stepped back into a different world. He knew how things worked in it but he did not feel like he was a part of it. Being with Sironka, he had realized separateness was not the solution. He needed to relearn, adapt and adjust as soon as possible.

After breakfast, he walked across to the Indian High Commission. The lady at the gate asked for his name and found it on her list. She told him he was early and would need to wait. She then escorted him to a lounge. Joy sat there and waited.

Soon, a short, portly, middle-aged Indian man walked out of a room.

'Mr Joy? My name is Anuj Sharma. Please follow me,' he said.

Joy followed him into a plush office.

'Allan was insistent that I needed to meet you and hear your story. I was to decide only then if I should send you home or back to him,' he smiled.

Joy smiled. 'Sure, I can tell you my story,' he said.

Joy started to narrate his story. He could see Mr Sharma's expressions changing. He was mildly curious at first, and soon he was completely engrossed in the story. Watching his reactions, Joy was reminded of the night he had heard Sironka telling the story about the origin of the elephant. Once he finished narrating the story to Mr Sharma, there was silence in the room.

Mr Sharma got up and walked towards the window. With his eyes fixed outside, he said, 'Joy, I don't know what to make of it! Some of it sounds like a fairy tale, some like a movie script. You seem to have done the impossible. Crossing the ocean in a small boat, guided by a turtle, living with the Maasais as an active member of a tribe, living in this country without identification for over a year—all of this is far-fetched. But something tells me that this is not just a story. And Allan has confirmed it… So please come back tomorrow morning, I'll issue a passport for you.'

Then he picked up the phone, spoke to someone on the other end, and a woman walked in.

'Joy, please follow Jane. She will do the necessary paperwork to get your passport ready,' he added.

Joy got up and reached out to shake Mr Sharma's hand. 'Thank you for trusting me,' he said.

The next day, Joy picked up his passport early in the noon and by late evening, he was waiting in the airport lounge to board his flight. There was a small stall for food and he chose to buy some ugali with a little curry. As he ate the food, his heart grew heavy. He was on his own again. This chapter of his life finished here.

He reached up and rubbed the shell and the wooden piece Nalangu had given him. He slowed his breath and could feel himself calming down. He knew he was going to be okay. Sironka, Ollie, Nalangu, his father, his son and his mother all lived in him and around him. He was not alone anymore. And like Sironka always said, something old had to die for something new to come alive. The circle of life had finally come alive for him.

In a while, the gates opened and every one was called to board the flight. As it took off, he saw the twinkling lights of Dar-es-Salaam slowly fading. He felt the flight easing as it picked up height. He felt sleepy. As he closed his eyes, Joy knew that the next stop in his journey of life would be India.

The storyteller got up and stretched. 'Let's take a break! Any questions?'

A young man sitting in the aisle raised his hand. 'Do we have to go through hardship to gain wisdom and heal? Can't the journey be an easier one? Joy and Ollie had to cover two continents. Joy almost died twice. Why couldn't Joy just heal in Goa itself?'

The storyteller smiled, scratched his beard, and then said, 'I love this question because I too had the same queries. But I guess that sometimes, it is essential to journey. We need to move out of our comfort zone. That shakes us up, makes us face uncomfortable truths about ourselves and empowers us for the destination we have chosen. And very often, the destination we have chosen is a mystery. Joy physically journeyed across miles so that he could learn to journey at will from his head to his heart. Also, it was his soul's choice to meet up with Ollie and Sironka.'

After a pause, the young man asked again. 'The other part of the puzzle is why so many hardships and pain? Can't there be a happier way to heal?'

The storyteller laughed out loud. 'Like I said, we humans love to suffer. When we suffer, it feels like a battle worth fighting, and then the win is sweeter. But know that we need and choose these challenges to heal our wounds and to heal others. In turn, we heal the world.'

With that they all dispersed for a short break.

18

THE ARRIVAL

As Joy's plane touched down in Mumbai, the air hostess rattled off a list of do's and don'ts. They were all asked to wear a protective face mask, face shield and gloves before they disembarked. As he made his way through immigration and picked his bags up at the luggage belt, he was surprised to see computer screens everywhere; he heard a very robotic voice telling them what to do, how to behave and where to go. The airport looked sterile, like a hospital, and it felt as if he was in a science fiction movie.

The world had truly gone through a major change while he had been away. Maybe it was good that he had missed a major part of the pandemic because this way of living felt sad. He looked at the time. He had a few hours before he would have to catch a bus to Goa. He made his way out of the airport and was hit with a blast of air. The air smelt like India. A little bit of spice, a little bit of salt, fish, mud and incense. He smiled, thinking how some things never change. He had finally made it back. It was unbelievable.

Then he caught a taxi to the bus station.

There were very few people on the bus. The sights and smells of India tugged at his heart strings. He watched the markets, the tall apartment buildings and the clusters of slums whiz by. As they made their way out of Mumbai and left behind the bright city lights, he started to settle back into his seat. His mind kept wandering back to Africa. He wondered what Sironka was doing at this moment—probably sitting under his favourite tree, chatting with another elder. He missed Sironka's wrinkled old face. He hoped that someone had weeded the vegetable patches over the past few days. He thought of Nalangu. He missed them all so much.

He must have dozed off. The next thing he felt was a big jerk. He woke up with a start. The bus had come to a halt. The driver got up from his seat, stretched and looked back. In a very loud voice, he announced that this was only a twenty-minute-long pit stop. He was not surprised that he had slept so well. After all, it had been a tiring journey and he had not reached his destination yet.

After an hour or so, they reached Panjim bus station and found out that a bus was leaving for Galgibaga within an hour. He realized he was hungry when he saw a whole lot of freshly baked buns piled up at the tea stall. He bought a cup of tea laced with spices and a few maska buns. He dipped the bun into his tea out of habit and took his first bite. He could not stop smiling. This was pure heaven!

The bus to Galgibaga was announced, and as he made his way to the back of the bus, he felt relief washing over him. This was the final leg of the journey. After a couple of hours and numerous stops, the bus meandered into his village. When it stopped near the village temple, he got off, slung his backpack over his shoulder and made his way to his house.

Nothing much had changed in Galgibaga, except that

people were wearing protective face masks. None of them gave him a second look. He just looked like a regular backpacker.

He took a shortcut to his house. The foliage was dense and overgrown. He pushed his way through it and emerged at the rear of the house. As he walked around the house, he saw changes. The paint had peeled off, the walls were covered with moss and wild creepers, part of the roof had caved in, the front door had a big lock on it and the windows were all sealed with planks of wood. Clearly, they had all thought that he was not alive anymore and the house was left to slowly crumble into oblivion. He stood there for a while, taking in the sights and sounds that surrounded his home. If he had to make this his home again, he needed to roll up his sleeves and get down to repairs.

He wondered if Maria had keys to the house. But then, on second thought, he did not need a key. As a young boy, he used a secret entrance, a door concealed in the loft. He sometimes used it to leave or enter the house, evading his father. He walked around to the side of the house. The mulberry tree still stood there. He climbed up the trunk of the tree and got on to the roof. He slowly made his way across the tiled roof. He reached a small, concealed door. He used all his might and managed to slide the door open and peeped into the house.

The air was still and musty. Light filtered into parts of the loft where the tiles had been dislodged. He carefully made his way into the house, crossed the loft, the floor boards creaking under his feet. The stairway that led into the main house was still strong and sturdy. The furniture in the living room was covered with blue plastic sheets. He tried to switch on the lights, but they refused to brighten the rooms. The power supply had been cut. He walked through each room and saw that pigeons had made nests in nooks and corners. He made his way to the storeroom at the back of the house to look for the tool box. He instinctively knew where the drill machines and saws were kept, and he picked up the bag of tools and then walked back to the loft, across the roof, and this time, he effortlessly swung himself down the tree.

He walked to the front of the house. He immediately started sawing off the locks. Once that was done, he started to unhook the planks from the windows. That was tough work. He finally managed to open all the windows and let in some fresh air. By late afternoon, the house felt less damp and musty. He had decided to find a way to connect the electric wires of the house to the main power lines. It was illegal to do such a thing, but he needed electricity. It was really hot and sticky. He promised himself he would go to the power station and pay up pending bills the next day.

He carefully climbed up the electricity pole, connected some wires and as he walked back home, he saw a warm glow of light emanating from some of the rooms. He then cleaned his room, oiled and dusted the fan and made his bed under it. He strung up his most prized possession—his mosquito net—above the bed. He smiled at the memory of how Namelok had ensured that he carried it with him.

It was early evening soon.

He needed to go buy some groceries before it got too late. He hurriedly dusted himself and took off in the direction of the local market. He bought some drinking water and rations at the local grocery shop. On the way back home, he found a small food cart at the corner of the church and decided to get some food packed.

Once home, he settled down on the front porch and munched on the food. The sound of the waves and the slight breeze calmed his overactive mind. He remembered his mother and what she had told him in his dreams about not trying to mend what is not broken. He instinctively knew what he wanted to do with the house.

He looked up and saw that the sky was lit with stars. He thought of what Sironka had told him about his ancestors being up there, looking down at him, taking care of him. The thought filled him with a feeling of strength. He knew that he was protected, supported and loved. He did not feel alone anymore. He knew it was okay to be by himself. He then took a long bath, slipped into bed and within no time, he was fast asleep.

The next day, he woke up early and made his way to his hideaway on the beach. He took off his t-shirt and walked into the ocean for a long swim. It felt good to be back in the water again, but he missed Ollie. He came back home, set up a make-shift kitchen under a tree and built a fire pit, just like he had seen Sironka do. He rustled up some eggs, and when he was done with breakfast, he set out to work on the tasks he had set for himself that day. His first stop was the barber shop. He got his beard trimmed and cut his long hair.

The next stop was the bank. The gentleman at the reception desk looked up when Joy entered the small bank. Joy sat down and told him who he was and handed over his passbook to get his account looked into. The man looked at the name. Then he looked at Joy. He asked Joy to pull down his mask.

The man suddenly took off his glasses and jumped up,

smiling at Joy. 'You are alive! Oh my god! You are alive!'

'Yes, I am alive,' said Joy, and then he saw that it was his schoolmate, Bhaskaran. They both hugged.

'Everyone in the village was convinced that you had committed suicide or had an accident. What happened to you? Where did you disappear?' asked Bhaskaran.

Joy told Bhaskaran a shorter version of the story, filling in some details of his journey across to the east coast of Africa and back. Bhaskaran heard him patiently, but Joy could see that he was still struggling with the facts.

'The news of your return is going to create a big stir in our sleepy, old village,' Bhaskaran said.

'I don't mind being the new entertainment for Galgibaga. The best part is that nobody has recognized me yet,' Joy said, laughing.

Bhaskaran walked around the table to stand next to Joy. He put his hands on his shoulder and said, 'Joy, I presume that you have not spoken to anyone yet. I want you to know that your wife is now married to a chap called Anthony.'

He had just confirmed what Joy had already guessed. Joy realized that the news had not evoked anger, jealousy or sadness in him. He smiled and nodded. 'Thank you for letting me know, Bhaskaran. I was wondering where I could find her and it could have gotten awkward. Anyway, I just dropped by to get my account reactivated. I want to withdraw some money,' Joy said.

Bhaskaran checked Joy's account details and Joy was surprised to hear his account balance. He had received a large settlement sum from his previous company and was financially in a sweet spot. That brought a smile to Joy's face. He silently thanked the universe.

Joy withdrew some money, thanked Bhaskaran and then headed out to buy himself a new mobile phone. In Tanzania, he had never felt the need to connect with anyone but now this was a necessary evil in India. He needed to get his life back on track. After that, he stood in line for hours and paid the electricity and water bills. He finally got back home quite late in the evening. He switched on the lights and the house looked depressing and gloomy. He wanted to create a nurturing space for himself as soon as possible. This needed to change.

Over the next two months, Joy worked on getting his life in order. All his ancestral land investments were secured, his bank accounts and savings were organized. He realized that he was a different man now. He was more alert and focused; he had loads of energy; and he was listening to his instincts and functioning with complete clarity. He had made tremendous progress on the house with the help of a local team. He had kept the old Portuguese structure intact but worked on making it more comfortable. The new roof had cost him a bomb, but it was worth every rupee. He took pains redesigning the kitchen, equipping it with modern amenities. He kept the old coal stove intact, which gave the kitchen a cosy, rustic feel. It was turning out to be a project of love.

The news of his arrival had spread through the village and when he passed them by, the villagers would stop to look at him. Some old friends of his father's would stop him to chat and were pleasantly surprised by how much he had changed. He never had many friends, only acquaintances. But the villagers soon realized that this was not the same Joy who had disappeared from the village one stormy night. Gone was the sulky, drunk recluse and in his place was a cheerful, friendly and fitter man.

While the team worked their magic under his supervision, he tried his hand at building a vegetable garden in the backyard. He would make frequent trips to Panjim for farming supplies. On one of these trips, he saw Maria getting out of a car, carrying a baby in her arms. He stood rooted at the spot; his heart beat increased. But he remembered what Sironka had taught him. He took slow, deep breaths. As his nerves calmed down, he took a good look at her. She looked happy and that, oddly, made him feel happy for her as well.

She saw Joy and stopped in her tracks. Her face turned white with shock. He instinctively felt that this was not the time to meet and talk, so he turned and walked away. Joy knew, deep in his heart, that she would come seeking him one day. She needed closure as much as he did.

The day came sooner than he had expected—a week after they had seen each other. It was a cool, breezy day. He had made himself a well-deserved, strong cup of coffee after working most of the morning with the plumbers. He sat on a cane swing under a tree in the front yard. He had successfully managed to clean up the space with the help of Bhaskaran's wife, who was a professional landscape designer. Bhaskaran and Joy would now meet often and they spent time together. He had also reconnected with his old schoolmates and had become the official chef for all their get-togethers.

Joy knew that people loved to eat the food he cooked. He made it a weekly event for all his friends who would come over to his place with their families. He had crafted a nice long, wooden table with log benches around it. He placed it under a canopy of trees. On a whim, he bought a few lanterns and strung them over the table and it surprisingly brought a dreamy feel to the corner. This table had become the focal point of his personal and social life. He worked on it, ate all his meals there, and entertained his friends and their families here as well. The children would run around the garden, the women talked and giggled and when he saw this, he counted his blessings. Not even in his wildest dreams had he ever imagined that in the end, this was how things were supposed to turn out for him.

As he nursed the warm coffee cup in his hands, he closed his eyes, heard the birds chirping and then, he heard someone calling his name. He knew that voice. It was Maria. He opened his eyes and saw her standing a few feet away.

Joy was the first to smile. He unhurriedly got up, walked to her, reached out gently and hugged her.

'Maria! It is so good to see you,' he said.

Her eyes teared up. 'You are alive!' she sobbed.

Joy released her and took a few steps back and smiled at her. 'I now hear that line so often that I feel it's like a constant reminder from the universe to be alive,' he said.

He got her to sit down and fetched her a cup of coffee.

'I saw a baby in your arms the other day. I am so happy for you and Anthony,' he said.

'That's my daughter. She is two months old,' she smiled. 'I am so sorry Joy, we all thought you had drowned. The storm was so fierce that night. I waited for a few months before accepting Anthony's proposal.'

He patted her forearm reassuringly. 'Yes, the sea was rough that night, but I guess someone up there wanted me alive and wanted you to be with Anthony. Just know that I am so happy for you. I think this was how it was supposed to be.'

Maria looked relieved. 'I had been feeling so terrible since I saw you.'

'And you look happier, Maria, since the time I last saw you. How is Anthony?' Joy enquired.

Maria smiled. 'He is good.' She looked down shyly. 'He really loves me.'

Joy laughed and had a twinkle in his eye. 'I am so glad it's different and better than the relationship we had. You deserve the best. We both really messed up.'

'When I told Anthony that I had seen you, he suggested that I should meet and talk things through with you,' Maria said.

'Maria, when I was in Africa, I often wished that I would have a chance to talk to you about our son's death. We both just shut down and buried our feelings after it happened. I guess it was so hard on both of us. I was not the nicest man back then, and you still put up with me,' Joy said.

'Joy, neither was I the easiest person to live with after our son died. I felt lost. I was angry at the world, and at god. I felt as if it was a form of punishment and wondered how a loving god could do something like this. I looked at other people's children and could not understand why these children were still alive and our son had died. I felt like I was responsible for his death, like I had killed him. We both broke, and broken people are dangerous people because they don't realize that they unconsciously leave a trail of destruction around them.' Maria's eyes were full of tears again.

This was the first time they were talking about their son without blaming each other. Joy's eyes misted over as well.

'I hope you understand, Maria, that it's not anyone's

fault. A friend taught me to be kind to myself, and I would like to tell you the same thing. We can never get over his death, but we can learn to survive it. Stop beating yourself up about what happened. We can't change it. The same wise old man also told me that death is not an ending, it's a continuation. Our son is somewhere up there, looking down at us and smiling. So let's give him more reasons to smile. We were both blessed to know a beautiful, simple soul, even if it was for a short time. I have learnt to count my blessings. His death crushed me, but the man I have become now would not exist if he had not experienced death. Our son has gone, but we both are still alive and I have the chance to tell you how sorry I am for hurting you and not being there for you.' Joy looked into her eyes as he spoke.

Maria could see that he genuinely meant everything that he was saying. She smiled through her tears. 'How have you become so sensible, Joy? You sound and look like a different man.'

Joy laughed. 'I had a lot of help in the last one year. I finally found myself.'

A sad look crossed Maria's face. 'You know Joy, you stopped being present in the relationship, or for me. We just stopped talking or touching each other way before our son died. I stopped being your girl, and you stopped wanting me. I knew you were being unfaithful to me. I wanted to confront you, but I soon realized it was useless. There was nothing left to talk about anymore. Our marriage, the trust and faith I had in you, it had vanished. I decided to compromise but it was the most depleting experience. Only now do I understand how nourishing a wholesome relationship can be.'

Joy listened to her quietly and then said, 'I want you to know that there was nothing wrong with you. I should have known then that I was emotionally defunct. There was so much more to life, but I never saw its beauty. I was always short of time. I was running away from everything that spelt happiness. I was lost all the time. It was the insufficiency and lack of passion in me that was reflected outward. I did not love myself and because of that, I was incapable of loving you. I can't take away the sad memories but just know that it was my state of mind, a lack of abundance and well-being in me that spilt all over in all aspects of my life, including the relationship. And I think we both had to learn some lessons together, which we have. Now, even though it's time to go our separate ways, we can part as friends.'

They were both silent.

She took a deep breath. 'Thank you for allowing me to talk, Joy. I feel better having gotten this off my chest. But I will need a little more time to get it all out. So maybe we will meet again some other day. For now, this is good. '

'Okay, till then let me entertain you with a story, it's called *Finding Joy*.' Maria laughed at the twist of words.

And after two more cups of coffee and some slices of cake, he finished telling her his story.

'It sounds like a Disney movie, but I know you are speaking the truth. I must warn you that no one around here is going to believe many parts of this story of yours,' she laughed.

Joy nodded. 'Most of the time, I just follow my intuition and I pick and choose how much to divulge and to whom. I realize that many of us have stopped believing in the magic of the universe. I was a non-believer and now look at me, I see magic everywhere. Look at the magic unfolding right in front of us! I never thought I could sit across a table and talk and laugh with you again.'

'Yes, this is magic!' said Maria. Her eyes twinkling like the young girl he had once known. 'So what are your plans for the future?' she asked.

'I want to get the house sorted first. My finances are in order. So, I have the freedom now to figure out what I want to do rather than rushing into something that I am not passionate about. I have been busy all these years, been doing things I never enjoyed because I thought that's what all of us have to do to live a good life. Now, for me, living with conscious awareness is a wonderful experience. I feel that I am a powerful creator of life. I have the ability to manifest the life I want, like I have a blank canvass and I can paint a new world for myself. I feel very empowered now,' Joy shared.

'So, is the shack still part of your future plans?' Maria asked.

'No, I don't feel like restarting the shack. I want to create something that will help the people of Galgibaga. I also want to give back to the ocean. She has given me the gift of life three times, and has been my teacher and friend. When I was on that boat, alongside Ollie, I swam deep into the ocean and have seen how beautiful the world underwater is. I saw a world that is also being polluted by us. I had promised myself that I would do something about the situation. So yes, I am full of ideas. But it still needs to take shape.' Joy was happy that he could share these thoughts with Maria now.

'I feel so happy when I hear you talk like this, Joy. You have clarity and I guess, slowly the rest will fall into place,' Maria said.

They talked for a little while longer and Joy asked her if she wanted to see the changes he was making in the house. She agreed. Maria loved every bit of what she saw. She caressed the old pieces of furniture. 'This is so beautiful, Joy. You kept the old and created the new around it. This looks perfect, like a picture from one of those interior magazines. I would have never thought this house could look so beautiful and serene. This new space looks like the new Joy who is grounded, peaceful and happy.'

Joy smiled. 'Thank you, Maria! I never thought I would hear you say this about me.'

'By the way, Joy, have you found someone special in your life again?' Maria enquired.

Joy looked down and pondered over how much he should share. But, if he had decided to take Maria as a friend, he needed to be honest with her. 'Yes, I did meet someone special in Tanzania, but I guess it was not meant to be. She is now engaged to a wonderful man. Her name is Nalangu,' he said.

'I am sorry about that, Joy,' Maria said.

'Please don't be! I guess both Nalangu and I learnt what we needed to learn during the short span that we knew each other. I have learnt that partings can be filled with nobility and kindness instead of hatred and anger. All relationships are not about staying together. I have learnt that when the time comes, I must go through it with unconditional love and awareness. Right now, I am in a happy space, so don't worry. When the time is right, someone will waltz into my life,' Joy said, laughing.

Maria smiled. 'Joy, just know that I am there for you as a friend. I promise to always stand by you.'

Joy took Maria's hand and brought it to his cheek

in an affectionate gesture. 'We have both had a major breakthrough today. I am very proud of both of us—from being friends to sweethearts and lovers to spouses to worst enemies. And today, we stand in front of each other, as friends again. If there is anything I can do for you and Anthony, I would be glad to,' Joy said sincerely.

He walked her to the main road and they hugged. He stood there till the car disappeared and then, he slowly walked back home. That evening, he wrote a long mail to Sironka. He knew that Father Frances would read it out to him. He needed to let him know that he was doing okay back in India. He wrote about Maria's visit and thanked Sironka for helping him create a better, newer version of himself. He was like an upgraded computer now, he was getting better every day, and he was able to find joy in the smallest of things. He had actually started to love, respect and understand himself better. He now knew he deserved good things.

The next day, Joy made his way to the shack. He walked around and saw that the roof had caved in at the kitchen area. He pushed open the front door with some effort. Light was filtering in through the windows, and the place felt like it was part of a forgotten story. Layers of dust had settled all over the place, moss and patches of damp fungus were growing on all the furnishings.

He walked around making a mental note of all that he could salvage. He made a few calls as he wanted to address this part of his past as soon as possible. While he made his way past the back of the church, he crossed the spot where he had chanced upon Maria in Anthony's arms. He paused for a second, then shook his head, smiled and walked ahead. What a long way the two of them had come!

19

MASTER PLAN

As he walked down from the shack and moved towards the beach, he noticed that a new make-shift straw hut had been erected. He was curious. No one was allowed to construct anything near the beach. How had the green brigade of the village allowed it? Suddenly, he got worried. He hoped nothing had happened to the old men.

He walked closer to the hut and saw boards hanging on the outer walls. It all looked slightly official, and when he read the notice boards, he realized the forest department had set up a twenty-four-hour watch station to keep the turtles safe. This brought a smile to his face. He walked into the hut. Sitting on a long bench were two men in ranger uniforms, busy eating their lunches.

They looked up. 'What can we do for you, sir?' one of them asked.

'I am happy to see that some action has been taken to keep the turtles and marine life safe,' Joy said.

One of them got up and started to wrap up his empty meal box and walked outside to wash his hands. Joy was invited to sit with them and the ranger patiently explained how the number of visiting turtles had drastically dropped last year. On one day, hundreds of turtles had washed ashore dead and bloated; many of them were females full of eggs.

'I guess they were entangled in the fishing trawler nets,' Joy remembered the night when Ollie nearly died.

'These trawlers illegally fish at night with LED torches and the fish are attracted to the light. They rush towards it. The nets are already laid and they get caught,' said the ranger.

'Is it not against the law to fish during the great turtle migration and especially during breeding season?' Joy asked.

'Yes, it is,' said one of the rangers, 'but the fishing mafia don't care.'

'We now have a twenty-four-hour patrolling beat on the beach and in the sea. We catch some, others escape. They are back again soon. I think a lot of money changes hands for these illegal fishing activities to continue,' said the other ranger, looking very dejected.

'Is the local NGO headed by Chandrakant Satoskar and his friends still active?' asked Joy.

'Oh yes, they are quite active! They were instrumental in getting the forest department to help the turtles. But sometimes, it feels like a losing battle,' said the ranger.

Joy enquired about the turtle numbers and was told that very few had come this year compared to the last. He realized then that he had missed two seasons.

'Are you from Galgibaga or another village, sir?' the first ranger asked.

'I am originally from Galgibaga but have been away for a while,' said Joy. He then shook hands with the rangers and told them not to lose heart and keep doing the good work.

As Joy walked back home, he wondered what would happen if Ollie ever decided to come back to this beach.

He shuddered at the thought of Ollie dying on the way. The last time he was there to help him and set him free. The waters around Galgibaga had become unsafe and he needed to do something soon.

As the days went by, the idea that had been floating around his head started to take shape. He had found a mission. He wanted to find or create a safe environment in and around Galgibaga for the turtles to breed and live. And of course, for Ollie to return to him. He also knew he could not do this alone. He needed to do his ground work first.

He started to strike up conversations with the fruit seller, with youngsters at the grocery shop, even the bread man who came on his cycle every morning and the fishmonger and his group of friends. He wanted to know their views on why the turtles had slowly stopped coming to Galgibaga and if the decline in numbers worried them. What were their dreams for their little sleepy village? What dreams did they have for themselves? He received mixed reactions and some interesting insights. These propelled him to further research on what was happening in the rest of the world. Perhaps a solution could be found for Galgibaga and the turtles.

The youngsters really did not care about the turtle numbers declining or Galgibaga being infested by tourists. They wondered why the elders and NGOs were stopping their little village from growing into a major tourist hub—it had all the ingredients for it. They felt that the narrow mindset of the elders was preventing the village economy from growing. There could be more jobs for everyone if hotels and shacks opened up.

Some of the villagers felt that it was futile trying to save some strips of land, even if it apparently had some unique and rare flora and fauna, names of which they could not even pronounce. Experience had taught them that, one day, when they least expected it, the government would find a way to cut it all down and build ugly factories there, just like they had built the highway. They also had their own apprehensions about saving a two-kilometre stretch of the beach for turtles. The turtles were not in danger on the beach alone. The whole migration route was under threat.

The tea stall vendor under the bridge had a perspective that made him sit back and think. The vendor believed that the tonnes of sunscreen cream that tourists used on the beach was contaminating the sea. The world was coming to Goa and poisoning the seas and polluting the environment.

Others feared that the sea gods were upset with Galgibaga and the declining turtle numbers were a sign of god's wrath; soon the other good fish would start to disappear too. They were a fishing village and this was a really bad omen for the fishermen.

Some of the village residents really did not care, they just wanted to leave if they got a better chance, like Joy himself had done. There were only a handful of people who wanted to preserve the old way of living.

After spending hours on the internet, collating all information he had gathered, Joy had a plan in place. He felt that he could turn the situation around for the people of the village and the turtles both. He printed out his plans, made a folder and went to meet the activist, Chandrakant Satoskar. He found out where the old man lived. The man who was once the bane of his life was now his only hope!

He crossed the river, parked his cycle against a tree

on the side of the road and walked towards the house. He knocked on the front door. A lady came to the door dressed in a cotton kaftan, her salt and pepper hair was plaited.

'Yes, what can I do for you?' Her voice was soft and gentle.

'I wanted to meet Mr Satoskar. My name is Joy,' he said, introducing himself to the woman.

'My husband has gone for a meeting to the temple. He will be back in a while. You can go and meet him there, if it is an urgent matter. Or you can wait here in the verandah, if that is alright with you,' she said.

Joy agreed to wait and settled on one of the plastic chairs. He noticed that there was a peaceful air surrounding the house. He just sat there, in the meditative space. The lady came out with a tray of small eats and a cup of tea.

'I hope you drink tea. I made some for myself and brought a cup for you,' she said.

'I would love a cup of tea, thank you,' Joy said.

They both sat on the verandah and sipped their tea in silence.

'How do you know Chandrakant ?' she asked him.

Joy smiled as he recalled their encounters.

'Before my accident, I had a shack near the beach. He and his friends were usually very upset with me, so I am not someone he will look forward to meeting,' he said.

She suddenly took a little more interest in him. She leaned forward and asked, 'Oh! Are you the man who drowned in the storm? The villagers call you the ghost who walks again!'

Joy laughed. Soon, they both heard the gate latch being lifted and Chandrakant walked in. He looked the same except for his hair, which was all the more grey. He was not a very tall man, but he had an air of quiet authority and wisdom. His beady eyes brimmed with intelligence. Joy remembered him as someone who did not mince words and would say what he believed was right.

He looked at Joy curiously but did not recognize him.

Joy folded his hand to greet him. 'My name is Joy. I owned the shack at the beach. I bought it from the German man. We have not had pleasant encounters before.'

Chandrakant smiled and nodded. 'Yes, I remember you. The whole village is talking about your reappearance. You had given me a few sleepless nights with your grand plans of turning our village into another Agonda. Are you here to tell me that you are reopening your shack?' asked Chandrakant.

Joy smiled, 'No, I don't plan on opening the shack again. I have come back to you with some plans but they are not about turning Galgibaga into a place like Agonda, but into something more holistic.'

Chandrakant sat down and drank a glass of water. 'I am getting older and it's getting tougher to fight hair-brained ideas, but I will not give up. I will continue to oppose anything that will harm this village, so I am warning you. I may shoot down the idea if I don't like it,' he said immediately.

Joy nodded. They both sat down in the verandah.

'So, rumour has it that you went to Africa and lived with some tribe for a year?' Chandrakant asked.

Joy smiled. His story was reaching others like a game of Chinese whispers.

'Yes, you got that right. But before that I was lost at sea on Anthony Braganza's boat for a few months.

I managed to survive because a wild sea turtle helped me all the way,' Joy said.

Chandrakant looked at him. Surprise and disbelief were written all over his face. 'A sea turtle?' he asked.

'Yes, an Olive Ridley male turtle. I call him Ollie. He came all the way with me from Galgibaga to the east coast of Africa,' Joy said.

Chandrakant looked puzzled. 'That's not the regular route for the Olive Ridley turtles. And that's a very large distance for this breed of turtle to cross,' he said.

'I guess he did it for me,' Joy replied.

'Has he come back with you?' Chandrakant enquired.

Joy shook his head. 'No, we lost touch while I was in a small sea side town called Paje. But I know he is alive and waiting to meet someday. And that's why I have come to you for help.'

Chandrakant looked at Joy with renewed interest. 'You have changed. I can't put a finger on it but something is different about you,' he said.

Joy nodded. 'I guess the ocean, Ollie and the simple, indigenous Maasai tribe taught me how to be a human again.'

'I am quite interested in hearing your plans for Galgibaga, but I must confess, I am more interested in hearing about your journey,' said Chandrakant.

'I better warn you, Mr Satoskar. Some parts of the story will sound a little fake but I would like to tell all the facts because I feel you need to know what has changed, motivated and moved me to seek you out,' said Joy.

He started to narrate his story. The old man patiently heard him. There were times he would lean forward, his eyes filled with wonder and anticipation. And at times,

Chandrakant would have a faraway look in his eyes. But throughout, Joy knew he had the old man's attention and he was enjoying the narration. They took a small break for lunch. Late in the afternoon, when Joy finished telling his story, both the men sat in silence for a while.

Chandrakant looked at Joy and smiled at him. 'This is quite a story, my boy. Don't think that I don't believe you, because I know in my heart that you are speaking the truth. That's something I have learnt with age. When you hear something for the first time, we need to trust our first reaction to it, which often tells us to believe or not to believe. All I can say, Joy, is be proud of your truth, stand by it and fight for it. You have returned with a different energy. I can feel it myself. The first time I met you, you were a rude, obnoxious, condescending man, but today I see a very humble man sitting in front of me.'

Chandrakant got up gingerly. 'I think we better call it a day. I missed my afternoon nap. I need to lie down for a while. So if you can excuse me, I will hear your plans some other day,' he said, trying to stifle a yawn.

Joy stood up and said. 'I should be the one apologizing. I came unannounced and you still entertained me. That was very kind of you. I also want to apologize for being rude to you when we first met.'

Joy then bent down to touch the old man's feet.

Chandrakant was touched by the gesture and he fondly touched Joy's head as a gesture of blessing.

Joy stood up and held out a folder full of work. 'I want to leave this folder with you. I feel like there is a possibility to recreate a bright future for Galgibaga. Having lived with the Maasai I learnt a lot about myself, about family, about community and about how to protect what matters to us and our future generations. I have also talked to a lot of locals here and have come up with some plans, all of which I have put down into this folder. I request you to find time to go through it and we can catch up some time later,' Joy said.

They exchanged mobile numbers and Chandrakant told Joy that he would get in touch after studying the file. They shook hands and Joy leisurely made his way back home.

That night, he felt like celebrating. He had taken his first step towards doing something he believed in. He made pasta with dollops of butter, garlic and fresh herbs that he had plucked from his garden. He sat down on his favourite table outside, switched on the lanterns, connected his phone to the small speaker that he had bought recently and played some soft music. At some distance, he saw the fireflies lighting up a bush. He realized he quite enjoyed this alone time.

He was now doing many things that made him happy. He had started to read books and he loved running in the rain. He had done up a part of the house as an office-cum-library and he spent a large part of his day there, researching, trying to build his network for the projects he wanted to start. Some days, he felt like dancing and he did not stop himself. He had invested in a good oven and enjoyed baking bread. To feed his masculine interests, he had joined an online carpentry class and he would spend a few hours on polishing and knocking bits and pieces of wood together.

He finished his meal and he sat there. It was peaceful. The slow hum of the waves was hypnotic. He thought about his time in India and smiled proudly that there had been no urge to drink alcohol. He checked his inbox to see if Father Frances had written back, but there was no reply. Joy decided that he was not waiting and wrote another mail to Sironka to tell him about his new ideas.

A whole month passed by. Chandrakant had not reached out but Joy was sure that his ideas and plans would be of interest to the old man. He could see the old man had a very young and vibrant spirit.

He had finally received a mail from Father Frances who informed him about Olamayian's impending marriage and about how Sironka had gone off for a twenty-day-walk after Joy had left. Namelok felt that Joy held a special place in Sironka's heart and he missed him. The bee project had really taken off and so had the bottled aloe vera gel project. The women of the tribe were producing and selling large quantities of it. Joy read the mail several times and wondered if he would ever meet his family in Tanzania again. They were the last thought he had before he fell asleep that night.

Early in the evening the next day, he heard his dogs barking. Two strays had adopted him and the house a while ago.

He got up from his study table and came to the front door. He saw Chandrakant and a few men walking towards the house. He got out to greet them.

'It's so good to see you, sir. I would have come to you if you had called me,' Joy said as he welcomed them into the house.

The old man smiled. 'We read your file, debated over it and I must confess, some of your ideas were quite interesting. I thought it was best to drop by. My friends here wanted to meet you because they could not believe that you are a transformed man now,' said the old man.

Joy threw back his head and laughed out loud. 'I hope I don't disappoint you,' he said to them.

Chandrakant smiled and patted him on the back. When Joy led them into the living room, all the men were visibly impressed. Joy then got them all some fresh lemonade to drink while they chatted.

Chandrakant cleared his throat and said, 'This is Angelo, he helps in the operations of the NGO, and this is Forsu, he looks into licensing, alliances and sponsorships. I look into all the legal matters and petitions. We think that you need to work with us for a while to see what we are doing and understand the challenges we face. Then we can bring the whole village together to help us create a future for the village that you envision.'

Joy nodded and asked when he could start. Chandrakant smiled at Joy's enthusiasm and said that he could begin the next day.

Joy spent the next few months working tirelessly with Chandrakant and the other members of the NGO. Joy realized how selflessly Chandrakant and his team had tried to save Galgibaga from becoming like any other overcrowded beach in Goa, where environmental laws were flouted shamelessly by the shack owners' association. Many in the town were waiting to find a loophole to start the urbanization of Galgibaga. He too had aspired to do that at one point.

The conservation teams, along with the National Green Tribunal, had managed to stop golf resorts and hotels from being built near their beach. Even though land had been purchased by top investors from Delhi, cases were fought and a stay order had been granted. Many of the villagers were not happy. But this small group of individuals fought hard battles, internally and externally, and they tried, in their own little way, to preserve what they felt needed to be saved.

Many youngsters who were a part of Chandrakant's NGO were losing hope until Chandrakant introduced Joy to the group. Now they talked about ways to infuse new thoughts, ideas and possibilities into their conservation efforts. Joy started attending village meetings and people saw him take on an active role. He now participated in community events and get-togethers. For six months, he fully immersed himself in the village life of Galgibaga and he was slowly being acknowledged by the villagers as one of them.

Some evenings, however, he sat alone, watching the waves on the beach. He wondered how his life had turned around, from being the village outcast to now being an essential member of the village. It dawned on him that his life now was a reflection of his current state of mind. He felt peaceful and happy, abundant in every aspect of his life, and he felt that Galgibaga was his village and its people were his tribe. He would do all that was needed to keep it safe and protected. What had changed was his perception.

One evening, when the team had gathered for their bi-monthly meeting, Chandrakant mentioned the plans that Joy had drawn up. He felt that it was time that they all brainstormed these plans. He was quite certain that in the next village meeting, which was a few weeks away, they could go ahead and present it to the village council and the villagers.

The days that followed were filled with endless meetings and tea sessions in Joy's garden around the wooden table. Plans were drawn up, some ideas were rubbished, some were applauded and soon, the blueprint for the future emerged. All the ideas were put down into a presentation. The plan was even broken down into phases. It was decided that Chandrakant, being the most respected in the village, should be the spokesperson for the group.

The day arrived. It was an auspicious day since the Bhairav temple construction had been completed and a village feast had been organized. After the first prayers were offered, all of them assembled under a make-shift shelter. Small speeches of appreciation were made by the village council, and then, the stage was handed over to Chandrakant. Joy could see why the old man had been worried and why he had wanted the plans to be set into motion as soon as possible. He looked small and frail, and even though his eyes twinkled with every new thought during meetings at Joy's house, even though he laughed the loudest at jokes, carrying a hint of a childlike glee, Chandrakant was getting on in age and Joy could see that he wanted to create a foundation for later generations.

Chandrakant cleared his throat and started his speech, reminiscing about his years of fighting various battles to conserve the old ways, to keep Galgibaga safe from the outside world. In the very next breath, he said something that took everyone by surprise. He said it was time to let the world into Galgibaga.

'They need to see how rich we are in our heritage, our culture, customs, the food we eat, why we fight tooth and nail to preserve certain patches of forest land and strips of beaches and not allow any construction to take place there. There is something special about the soil of our village. Galgibaga has a beautiful, simple, pure spirit and I want the world to experience it because it is healing. I lived in Mumbai for many years, but when I decided to leave the hustle and bustle of city life and come back here, my friends in Mumbai would ask me what I would do in a sleepy, old village. I said I would milk cows and that's what I actually did for a while. I milked cows,' Chandrakant said. People responded with smiles.

'I came to love this village of mine, may be a little too much and so I have caused a lot of heartache for some. The world needs to know and understand that there is a magic to this little village of ours—from the air we breathe, to the river that flows through our village, to the sand that lines our beaches. The turtles can vouch for that, as they have often chosen our beach to lay their eggs. Now their numbers are decreasing and that has been worrying me and many of us in this gathering. The flora and fauna that has always grown in our forests for hundreds of years is special and even ecologists come to study it. Many from the outside world want to cut it all down and build hotels here. They show up with government muscle power...' A murmur went through the crowd as they exchanged names of builders who had aspired to build the hotels.

'When I look at the way the world has changed around us, it scares me. I have fought verbal and legal battles with all those who have tried to change my little world. Many in the village have been upset with the way I function, so please forgive me, but I really meant no harm. I am guilty of trying my best to conserve the old ways, but I also see that many of the youth want to leave the village because they see no future here. It makes me sad. I feel that now is the time to make changes. I have also come to realize that I am not getting any younger, but my mind and spirit is still that of a young boy.'

A murmur rose through the crowd again and this time, it was the youngsters talking that the old man had changed.

'I had been thinking how to keep the movement going, and then one day, Joy came visiting with a file tucked under his arm and a story that made me think that maybe he was the answer to my worries. So now, here I am, standing in front of you all, with a dream for our little village. We have all been planning this for a while and we would like to present it to you all today,' he said with so much sincerity and hope shining through his eyes that, by now, the villagers were really curious to know more.

Joy had the presentation ready, but Chandrakant reached out and handed him the mike. Joy was surprised. He had thought that Chandrakant was going to do all the talking. But the old man insisted that Joy should do the honours, as this was his plan. Joy looked at the sea of faces before him. He remembered the night that Sironka had told his tribe the story of how the elephant came to being. Now it was his turn to weave some magic. He noticed a few faces that he knew, and it eased his nervousness.

'This is unexpected. I thought Mr Satoskar was going to do the hard work, and I would flip the slides for him.'

Everyone laughed. Joy knew he had broken the ice.

'So the village thought that I had drowned and died! I crossed the ocean on a boat that belonged to Anthony.' He waved at Anthony. 'I'll see how I can make up for that one day, Anthony.'

'The magical part is that the ocean helped me survive. A sea turtle kept me alive! When I swam and dived into the ocean, I saw the damage that we have done to the ocean and its creatures. I sailed on a trawler for a few weeks and learnt how we, humans, have complete disregard for the life and the gifts of the ocean. Then one day, I reached the east coast of Africa. I lived there for a while with a tribe that is thought to be backward and barbaric, but they actually are closer to being highly evolved humans, fully in sync with the elements of nature and themselves. They taught me why it is important to be a part of a community, they taught me about the essence of family in our lives, of being a friend. They taught me how to move with the ever-changing world around us, and that's what I would like to propose to you today.'

The villagers were listening to Joy with rapt attention.

'It is essential that we create an eco-system that will allow us to move ahead with the times, but on our own terms. Mr Satoskar has done the ground work for all of us and has kept the sharks away, but we can't just sit and do nothing about the gem that we have in our hands. He has mentioned how we have a wonderful village that the world needs to see. But they will only visit us and keep visiting us, again and again, if there is something unique about us. We should ensure that we are not turning our village into another tourist spot where people come to swim, eat, have late night rave parties riddled with drugs and sex.'

Joy could see that the youngsters looked doubtful again.

He continued. 'Goa's landscape is changing and people want something new. Rather than the regular, tourist fanfare, they need to experience something different and meaningful. We need to make them feel like they are a part of the village life. People want to believe in something that gives them hope that tomorrow will be better than today. They want to believe that they can contribute to something that will change the world. They want something that's not too complicated to understand. The people from cities want to go back to basic living, away from too much technology and machines—the normal trappings of the urban world. They want to experience a life that will include clean food, clean air, and peace.' Joy paused to have a sip of water.

'They also want to be a part of a community, a family. They want a sanctuary to heal in, and not be harassed with large bills or all the other touristy woes. So I feel, let's open our hearts, our homes and our village to the world. Let's create an eco-village instead of making our village a drug peddler's haven. I feel like this is an option we all can look at. I have worked on a smaller project in Tanzania that was very basic. This, I know, will be on a much larger scale but we all need to be a part of this project. Let's modify some of our homes or let's build some eco-huts at strategic points throughout the village—ones with a good view and where people from across the world can come and stay. Instead of having the seasonal business that Goa is known for, let's work towards creating a model where we can host guests throughout the year.'

Joy stopped when someone put up their hand and asked how they could do all this.

Joy started the presentation. And with each slide, he showed them different examples of eco-tourism efforts across the world. He came to a slide where he took Bali as an example. He spoke about the villagers in Bali building small eco-friendly huts using materials that were a part of their terrain, near paddy fields. The next slides were about how tourists themselves were enrolled in working on the farm lands with the villagers and he told them stories about how he too had learnt how to milk a cow in Africa, or build a vegetable patch and how happy it made him feel to have learnt a new skill.

By now, he could see he had a grip on his audience. They were laughing at all the right moments. He talked about a village resort in Sri Lanka that had one large community kitchen for the village guests, where the villagers cooked and the menu changed every day.

'We will get tourists who will live with us and eat in our village kitchen. If we do it right and market it well on the internet, others from across Goa will come to our village to eat our food as well. I remember, as a young boy, that the whole village talked about Mrs Rodrigues making the best fish fry. When I was in England myself, what I missed most was the food of my village and my mother's hands. So, let's introduce the world to our family recipes. The produce should be grown in our fields and the fish we serve should be fresh from the ocean, or what we catch on a daily basis. Let's teach people who come to live with us how to fish, how to bake our local breads—and we can charge them a fee for that!'

The baker stood up and clapped at the prospect.

Joy continued laying out the plan. 'I propose for us not to have small shops that sell the same stuff, because sometimes, competition breeds division. A wise man, back in Africa, told me that competition creates winners and losers. Let's change that in our village. We all should have a common goal. If one of us wins, all should win. We all should always do what is good for all at all times. If one shop does well and the other selling the same goods does not, it will create insufficiency in that shopkeeper's family. What we produce in our fields and what we fish should be sold to the villagers at a reasonable price so that everyone can have sufficient food for their families. Whatever is surplus can be collectively sold outside our village in an organized way. Let us all start following the old ways of fishing. I remember my father and his friends followed the seasons, they honoured the sea, they never fished too much or wasted the rest.'

Someone in the audience put up their hand. Joy walked across to him and gave him the mike.

'So what you propose Joy, is one bakery, one grocery store, one vegetable shop, one shoe shop, one big fish shop?'

Joy nodded in affirmation.

Someone across the room also raised their hand. 'You know, this is going to be tough. Some of us are landowners, some are fishermen, some are farmers who work for the landowners.'

Joy nodded. 'Yes, I agree. Maybe it's time to change the age-old systems. We all need to rethink how we can create a future free of feudalism and caste systems. Let's create a new way of life that can inspire others. Let's be the change. Let's mould our youth to become aware progressive thinkers and they too will value being a part of this village. They should always know that wherever they may go in the world, they have a home and a community to return to, where they can heal, rest, laugh and be loved and accepted.'

'I would like to start the movement by offering to turn my shack into a community centre, a place where the youth of our village can hang out, spend time, play games. When I was in Africa, I learnt to tell stories and I would really like to bring this tradition into our lives. I want us to tell them stories about the kings and queens of

India. I want to tell them stories of the sea and so much more. I want it to be a place where we can inspire and counsel our young people.'

Joy could see that momentum and excitement was building up in the group.

Someone else, in the front row, had put their hand up.

'I always wanted to run an ice cream parlour. But where will I get money to do this?'

That's when Chandrakant came to the rescue. 'A few like-minded people can get together and form a group. They can pool in their resources,' he said.

Joy could see heads nodding. He could see that Chandrakant was smiling while he flipped the slides for Joy. He was thoroughly enjoying the meeting. He had not expected that the villagers would take to their plan so eagerly.

Bhaskaran raised his hand, and while winking at Joy, he said, 'You may just be responsible for the village bank losing its manager. I am tempted to start a grocery store. Joy, you mentioned that we can make money in the non-tourist seasons. How is that possible?'

Joy went to the slide about an artists' village. 'We can think about taking in resident writers and artists who will stay for a longer time. They don't bother about it being tourist season or not. We can open up our homes as homestays, but we will need to modify our homes slightly. People need a comfortable stay and we can invite a few experts on interiors to help us.'

Chandrakant raised his hand, and his eyes twinkled with delight as he took the mike from Joy's hand. 'Otherwise, Joy can help us. He has done up his house very well, quite impressively for a man who once was the village drunk.'

Everyone laughed and Joy joined in.

Someone else stood up and said, 'With the pandemic, people are not travelling. Have you seen how bad the tourist season has been this year?' The others nodded in agreement.

Joy nodded too. 'Yes, but the situation will soon change. We may have lesser foreign tourists, but Indian tourists will come. Since Goa is largely pandemic-free, many tourists have started visiting. And also, an eco-village is not built overnight. Sironka, my teacher in Africa, took a few years and so will we. As we go along, we will learn, make mistakes, have disagreements. But if we all can come together with the common goal of creating a hope, a possibility, I know the universe will help us. People from across the world will come to make our dreams a possibility. So this is the first cut of our ideas. Do you have any more questions?' Joy asked.

Joy saw Anthony put up his hand. He could see Maria getting slightly uncomfortable. He walked across to him, smiled and handed him the mike.

'I would like to start by congratulating Mr Satoskar, Joy and their team for actually coming up with a great idea. This is the first time that I have felt hopeful for our village and Joy, it's okay that you crashed my boat! I am with you on this project, please count me in,' said Anthony.

The villagers clapped and Joy smiled and gave Anthony a brief hug. That was the only nudge the villagers needed and soon, everyone gave a thumbs up to the project. That's how, from that day on, Galgibaga became a home away from home to many, including the turtles.

20

FOUR YEARS LATER

It was early in the evening. Joy had just finished a storytelling session in the community centre. It was houseful, as usual. The audience were a mixed group of grown-ups, children and teens. Today he had told them the story of the lion that one day decided to cross the waters, from the shores of Dar-es-Salaam, and came to live in Zanzibar. He lived as the only lion, all alone, and was called the lion of Zanzibar. He was ruthlessly hunted by a slave trader who wanted his head as a trophy to be hung up in his house. He saw how the kids loved the character of the monkey who made friends with the lion. They mimicked the sound it made and cheered when he made an appearance in the story. Joy knew that this story would always be remembered fondly by all. Today was the third day of the turtle festival, an occasion that they all had been organizing for two years now.

It was turtle season. The great migration of turtles from the west coast of Sri Lanka had started, and they had slowly made their way across to Goa. He, along with Chandrakant and the many other sea conservation teams, had been trying, for years, to ensure that the turtle corridor would become a safe route for these turtles to travel. It had finally paid off. It was a constant fight with the fishery department, the government and the fishing mafia to ensure that the seas were safe, especially during the breeding season. But they had all jointly stood their ground and won.

For Joy, it was so moving to see how this little village in Goa was standing up for what they believed was right. They stood up for the sea, they stood up for the turtles and the future of their village. They left no stone unturned to ensure that the turtles came back to Galgibaga. And one day, the miracle happened, their efforts paid off. The turtles came back in full force and so did the people who came to their village to see the creatures.

The villagers decided to celebrate a turtle festival to commemorate the return of the turtles. They all believed that since the turtles had come back, their village had started to prosper. Galgibaga had become a major destination for nature enthusiasts. Many people came, some with their children, some alone and they stayed with the villagers to watch the turtles give birth and also to watch the magic appear from the sand as the hatchlings instinctively made their way back into the water. Throughout the tour, they kept a safe distance from the turtles. Other people also came to stay for long periods of time to heal.

Joy took a walk down the main market and he saw the gaiety with which the villagers had decorated the village. Fairy lights, streamers and buntings adorned the streets. The flea market was in full swing a slight distance from the beach.

Many of the locals from other villages and foreign tourists had come to sell their wares. He smiled at the sight. It warmed his heart. He knew it was not him who had come up with the idea. He could see the hand of god in everything now.

He remembered that Sironka always said that the creator creates miracles when you surrender all, and that's what had happened in Galgibaga. When the ball had started rolling, everything started to fit in like a jigsaw puzzle. Slowly, the word had spread, and people from across the world had come to help them create a future smart village.

Like every year, Joy waited for Ollie to emerge from the water. It was almost four years now and Ollie had not come back to Galgibaga. After waiting for a while, Joy slowly made his way back home. He rustled up a small meal for himself and sat outside on the verandah. He thought about his life and how it had changed so much. He could hear the music from the flea market in the distance; in a while it was going to become calm and quiet. They followed strict hours of opening and closing the festival so as to not trouble the wildlife, sea creatures and the villagers.

He got ready for bed and like always, he rubbed the shell that Ollie brought and the wooden piece that Nalangu had given him. He never ever took it off. They were a constant reminder of his life's purpose and the people who had helped him become the man he was today. After that, he closed his eyes and like every day, he felt grateful for all the good and bad things that had happened on that day, like Sironka had taught him. He knew that even the not-so-good was a blessing in disguise. He made it a point to talk to Ollie every day and hoped that he would dream of him. The dreams were a rare occurrence, but he would hold on to Olamayian's words of advice and not give up hope. May be some day they would meet, in this life time or another, but he knew Ollie was next to him in spirit. With that thought in his mind, Joy fell asleep.

It must have been middle of the night when Joy woke up. He felt an odd sense of restlessness. He got up and drank a glass of water, then walked to the window. He saw the moon in her full glory draping Mother Earth with her light. Everything glistened and gleamed. He was not sleepy anymore, so he made himself a cup of tea and walked out to the garden. He sat on the swing for a while. When he looked at the watch, it was 3.30 a.m. It was another day or two before the eggs would hatch, but the rangers were keeping a strict watch.

He decided to walk down the beach before he went back to sleep. As he made his way down from the house to the beach, he whistled to his dogs. They lifted their heads but they were way too sleepy to follow him. He made his way across the beach by himself and reached the nests. The guards were awake and one of the forest rangers came to chat. After exchanging a few pleasantries, on a whim, he walked towards his hideaway and sat on a rock that was jutting out and watched the sea. The swishing of the waves and the salt in the air brought back so many memories of his time on the boat. He did not know how time went by, and when he looked at his watch it was already 5 a.m. In three hours, the village organizing committee would have their first meeting for the day and he had to be a part of it.

He got up, dusted himself and started to walk back home when suddenly, a feeling in him made him stop. He turned around. Just at that moment, he saw a turtle emerging from the sea. He smiled. It was such a good sign. Galgibaga was getting luckier by the day. The turtles had come back in full force. Another nest was going to be dug. As he stood there and watched, the turtle slowly made its way out of the water and he felt something tugging at his heart strings. This reminded him of his time with Ollie in Zanzibar. The early morning light shone on the turtle's shell, and the turtle stopped and turned its head towards Joy. That's when recognition set in for both.

Joy, for a moment, felt as if he was dreaming. He could not believe what he saw, but from the shape of the turtle's head and the way the turtle moved, he knew that it was Ollie. He ran towards the turtle and sank down onto the sand. He reverently reached out and touched Ollie's head. He had often day-dreamed of this moment.

Ollie inched closer to Joy and snuggled up to him. Joy could not hold back the tears and took Ollie into his arms. Time stood still for both man and turtle. They both had dreamed of each other often, but nothing had prepared them for the love and peace they felt in their hearts upon being back together.

21

THE REVEAL

'So, I hope you all have enjoyed the not-so-short story,' the storyteller said as he ended.

What started as clapping from the front row soon became a roaring applause from the audience. He stood with folded hands. It took a few more minutes for the applause to fade.

'Thank you, thank you, so much. You have all been a wonderful audience,' he said. 'Just one more thing before we leave. A wise old man once told me that like the ocean chose Ollie as a wise one, there are humans who have been chosen to awaken. So hear this story knowing that you all are the chosen ones from the moment you chose to be a part of this evening.'

'Also remember that our purpose in life is to evolve into beings of divine light who will contribute to the well-being of the planet and also to uplift people to be the most magnificent version of themselves. Allow your wounds and scars to become a part of your transformative tool kit. Experiences and events that seem to crush us and bury us beneath a mountain of despair are, in fact, gateways to our greatness. We can use them to heal the world around us and align ourselves and others to the purpose of life,' he said.

'Now I would like to bid you all farewell.' He then gathered his bag and tied back his hair.

A very tall, elegant woman made her way to the stage.

She had the organizer badge pinned on to her shirt. She cleared her throat, and in a very gentle, soft voice announced that they were welcome to make a small donation to the village storytelling foundation. The fund would help expand the library built for the village children, and if they wished to make a donation, they could ask for her, Nalangu.

The name caught everyone's attention.

Someone in the audience spoke up. 'So if you are Nalangu, there must be a Joy too somewhere around. All this time, I thought that they were just fictitious characters in the story.'

She smiled shyly. 'This story is as real as it gets and yes, there is a Joy too.'

A number of voices chorused. 'Where is he?'

She threw back her head and her amber corkscrew curls bounced around in glee as she laughed. 'Well, he was the one telling you this story,' she giggled.

By now, Joy was half way down the stage. An elderly lady caught Joy's hand as he was walking past her and told him to go back on the stage. 'We are not going to let you go that easy, not after Nalangu dropped that bomb on us,' she smiled.

'So you are Joy?' asked a young man in the front row once Joy took his position.

'Yes, I am Joy and Nalangu is my wife,' he said.

'And where is Ollie?' asked a man from the back row.

Joy smiled. 'Ollie is well and he is around. He comes over during every arribada to visit me and Nalangu.'

Someone else in the audience raised their hand. 'I am going to ask the question that I bet all in the room want to know the answer to. Nalangu, why did you decide to come back to Joy?'

Nalangu smiled. She looked shyly across the room and said something that made Joy smile, and the rest of the audience teary-eyed.

'I made myself believe that the responsible thing to do was to stick by my promise to Koinet and stay in my country, but I knew what made me happy was being with Joy. It took me some time to trust my own deeper knowing and to align all of my choices and actions with my intention for love. You Indians, believe in many lifetimes but we, Maasais, believe we only have one. I do not want to live with choices that make me sad. I want to experience mad, crazy, unadulterated, passionate love. My father, Sironka, always said that it takes courage to do what is truly right for ourselves and the day we do it, a great love is born within us for ourselves. We understand it's time to make choices that will align us to the universe. This will unleash the energies of pure magic, synchronicity, well-being and happiness. I wanted to be with the love of my life and now every day I wake up excited and happy that I have made dedicated efforts to ensure my own happiness. I have shown up for my dreams and my potential. So me coming to India to be with Joy was not just about loving Joy but about me loving myself too.'

Joy smiled and saw how Nalangu had the audience enthralled.

He slowly made his way down the rocky path to his safe spot. The moon had risen and a cool breeze was blowing. Soon he saw a form emerge from the water and make its way to him. Ollie settled down next to Joy. It was a beautiful night as it was meant to be.

GLOSSARY

Arribada	A Spanish word meaning arrival by the sea. Every year, at the same place and time, thousands of female Olive Ridley sea turtles come ashore to nest and lay their eggs on the beach.
Boma	A group of enkajis (huts) enclosed in a fence.
Empikas	The group of Maasai men who were in charge of planning and executing the lion hunt.
Enkai	The powerful one, the Maasai god, creator of all.
Enkaji	The hut that is built by the Maasai woman for her family.
Kionet	The tall one.
Laibon	The most important person according to the Maasai religion. The high priest or the shaman. Their position is not political, but they wield influence as a healer and practitioner of medicine.
Leboo	The person born in the bush or outside the homestead.
Legishon	The polite one.
Maa	The language spoken by the Maasai.
Maasai	An ethnic group of people or a tribe inhabiting northern, central and southern Kenya as well as northern Tanzania.
Mingati	The fast one.

Nalangu	The one that has come from another tribe.
Namelok	Hope.
Naserian	The one born during peaceful times.
Olamayian	The blessed one.
Shuka	The fabric used by the Maasai to wrap themselves.
Sironka	The pure and clean one.

ACKNOWLEDGEMENTS

Around 11 years ago, there was a point in my life when my world changed overnight with the passing away of my father. Till then, I was a creative artist in the fashion circuit, but with his death I had to leave that life behind and join my family's business. I had to fight every day to survive in an alien world and work very hard to not end up as a disappointment to my family. Crunching numbers, selling products, and being answerable to over 800 people was overwhelming and it filled me with fear every moment, every day. To top it off, I was a single mother—both to my mother and my son. I had to prove myself in every aspect and I kept pushing myself harder and harder but the sheer pressure of keeping things together led to a meltdown. My body was the first to give in, followed by my mind. Nothing made sense anymore. In retrospect, I had not been able to process the pain and grief of losing my father and felt clueless and undeserving.

Then, finally, one day I closed my eyes and asked for help. Help from *above*. That's when shamanism and alternate medicine came into my life. As I started getting better, I began adopting a strong spiritual practice, and started learning about energy healing. Soon, I could feel a complete surrender to the universal scheme of things. When that happens, your intuition sharpens and you surrender to unlearning, thus breaking away from the beliefs that keep you chained to your old and confined ways of functioning. I realized that nothing in life is coincidental.

I had been a very private person and was happy living in the shadows. But as I grew spiritually, I started understanding that you can also get lost in the same shadows, if you don't have anyone to guide you. Let this book and my experiences become your guide. I know that every word I have written has been guided by a greater force that has created everything in this universe; and when *it* wants to bring about a change, *it* gets not one but a number of people to start communicating so everyone else can hear. In shamanism, teachers and ancestors teach through stories. It is considered to be the best way to teach, and I was introduced to this method of learning by Paul Hinsberger, my first teacher. He used to say that we need to tell stories to the world in a way that our listeners and readers are used to, but I have also come to realize that the creator has a quirky sense of humour—*it* chooses the most unlikely of candidates to do so.

Deciding to write this book, and then having it published for everyone to read, has been a great challenge in itself. I have no literary pedigree, but I had a story that was deeply rooted in my heart and was inspired by *it*. The journey of writing this book was often filled with moments of self-doubt and self-evaluation.

I would like to acknowledge a few people who stood by me and cheered me on, and without whose support this book would have never seen the light of day. These are people who kept me focused on the path of writing and not giving up.

My mother, Dr Blossom Kochhar, was the first to hear this story. I am immensely grateful to her for everything—I

Acknowledgements

am what I am today because of her. She has constantly infused me with deep learnings. Relationships are like mirrors, and my relationship with my mother has helped both of us learn and grow with what we reflect in one another.

I owe a lot to Sangeeta Jain, my family, my friend. She initiated me in my spiritual quest. Never one to mince her words, she has always shown me the mirror, and her kindness and generosity inspire me to stand up for myself and strive to become the person I am destined to be. I thank her for helping me with this book, patiently and tirelessly, and for giving it a structure that allowed the story to emerge.

Vivek Mansukhani, my friend for more than 25 years, whom I can't thank enough for his constant belief in the story I needed to tell, and for ensuring I found a publisher. He has also been a constant source of encouragement, pushing me to keep meeting deadlines.

I would also like to thank Dibakar Ghosh, my editor and publisher, for taking a chance and believing in the larger picture that the universe has in store for us, and the world. In his own wonderful way, he makes the world a better place by ensuring that the universal voice is heard.

I extend my deepest gratitude to my son, Aryman Sapru, my first true love. I have always respected his honesty and authenticity. He has taught me so much about life and love. I have based one of the main characters in this book on him even though he has not yet read the book.

I would also like to thank Vikram Singh for helping me with the book cover. His ideas gave direction to Gopal Krishnan and Rajdeep Ghosal, who helped in designing the cover. Rajdeep is an immensely talented artist who visualized and created the book cover after just one narration of the story.

But I would also like to talk about a man whom I came across in Galgibaga while conducting research for the book. Kishore Painginkar, president of the Poinguinkarancho Ekvott association, and his associate Domingo Caitahno X. Barretto, have been fighting selflessly to ensure that the Galgibaga beach continues to be a safe haven for turtles to nest on. They have taken on powerful people and have prevented many of them from building resorts and destroying the beach, thus creating a turtle corridor. I met a simple man still fighting to preserve something greed wants to destroy. He is so proud of his heritage and the little village he belongs to, and I heard all about his dream and what he wants for the future generations and the sea. I now know that meeting him was no coincidence. I can't thank him enough for taking out the time and talking to me, and giving me an insight into his world.

This book cannot end without thanking the rest of my family, my sister Beverly, Tanvi, Uncle Steven, my ancestors who have passed on, and all the people whom I have helped heal.

www.ingramcontent.com/pod-product-compliance
Lightning Source LLC
Chambersburg PA
CBHW031325230426
43670CB00006B/241